Euripides and the Politics of Form

Euripides and the Politics of Form

Victoria Wohl

PRINCETON UNIVERSITY PRESS

PRINCETON AND OXFORD

Requests for permission to reproduce material from this work
should be sent to Permissions, Princeton University Press
Published by PrincetonUniversity Press, 41 William Street,
Princeton, New Jersey 08540
In the United Kingdom: PrincetonUniversity Press, 6 Oxford Street,
Woodstock, Oxfordshire OX20 1TW

press.princeton.edu

Jacket art: Luigi Russolo, (1885–1947), *The Revolt*, 1911 (oil on
canvas), Haags Gemeentemuseum, The Hague, Netherlands /
Bridgeman Images

Library of Congress Cataloging-in-Publication Data

Wohl, Victoria, 1966– author.
  Euripides and the politics of form / Victoria Wohl.
     pages cm—(Martin classical lectures)
  ISBN 978-0-691-16650-6 (alk. paper)
  1. Euripides—Criticism and interpretation. I. Title. II. Series:
  Martin classical lectures.
  PA3978.W64 2015
  882′.01–dc23   2014036247

British Library Cataloging-in-Publication Data is available

This book has been composed in Baskerville 10 Pro

Printed on acid-free paper. ∞

Printed in the United States of America

10 9 8 7 6 5 4 3 2 1

For MG

CONTENTS

Let me begin by explaining my title. First, Euripides. This is not really a book about Euripides. It doesn't treat all his plays or offer a synthetic analysis of their characteristic features; nor does it provide exhaustive readings of the plays it does treat. I do aim to shed light on Euripidean drama, to better understand what it is doing and how. But the book's raison d'être, and my defense for adding to the enormous bibliography on the author, lies in the second half of the title. Euripides is offered as an illustration—not the only possible one, though not, of course, chosen completely at random—of an argument about the relation between politics and literary form.

My definition of politics is both narrow and broad. It encompasses, on the one hand, the formal institutions and political practices, the class relations and power struggles, the communal decisions and actions of the fifth-century Athenian democracy; and on the other hand, the ideological beliefs (collective and individual), the attitudes and attachments, the "structures of feeling" (in Raymond Williams's phrase) that subtend the institutional structures of the polis. Drama operates more directly within the latter, the psychic and affective domain of ideology, but in doing so (as I hope to show) it can intervene actively in the former. Thus, while my title is meant as an allusion to Fredric Jameson's "ideology of form," and a recognition of my methodological debt to his work, I chose the term "politics" in order to highlight the dimension of the polis and to insist upon the possibility of drama's real and material impact on the collective life of its citizens.[1]

By "form" I mean nothing particularly esoteric. Following Aristotle, I take the defining formal feature of drama to be its plot structure, the *muthos*. If tragedy is, as Aristotle defines it, a *mimēsis* of a *praxis*, an imitation of an action, the emplotment of that action is "dramatic substance . . . in its formal dimension."[2] The structure of the plot—its internal organization and the ligatures between its parts, its tempo and trajectory, recognitions and reversals, its "beginning, middle, and end"—will therefore be a central object of my analysis. But so, too, will be the many formal resources tragedy developed for elaborating its *mimēsis* and exploring the *praxis*: speeches and dialogue, monody and choral song, characterization, poetic language, visual spectacle. This list obviously draws on Aristotle's *Poetics*. The categories of his analysis are extremely useful even where they are incomplete or idiosyncratic, and I have found them good to think with, even at the risk of reproducing some of the philosopher's blind spots.[3]

One blind spot was deliberate. I have little to say about what the plays have to say, the specific content of their stated thought (*dianoia*). Concepts, themes, the ideas expressed by the characters and chorus are among the resources the playwright had at his disposal and will figure as such in the pages that follow. But my primary aim is not to trace political ideas or themes in Euripides' plays but to examine the political thought implicit within their dramatic structures. In focusing on form, I do not disregard content—I don't even know what it would mean to do so—nor seek to draw an artificial line between things that are, it goes without saying, inseparable and mutually defining. Form/content is a convenient heuristic antithesis—and I will discuss it in more general terms in the conclusion—but ultimately I wish to move beyond this opposition by showing that in Euripides (aesthetic) form is itself a type of (political) content.

The focus of this study, then, is the form of the dramatic action and the formal techniques the playwright deploys to develop it. One could analyze the political meaning of any given formal element in itself—the elitism of Euripides' virgin sacrifices, for instance, or the democratic assumptions behind his verbal debates—but my interest is in how these different elements combine to create meaning within a single drama. The book is accordingly organized not by formal feature but by play, with each play offered as an exemplification of particular issues or dynamics. Chapter 1 shows how ideological attachments are generated out of the suspense between narrative means and ends in *Ion*. Chapter 2 asks about the ethics of (lyric and structural) beauty and the politics of pathos in *Hecuba* and *Trojan Women*. Chapter 3 focuses on the "realism" of *Electra* and its utopian potential. In chapter 4, I read *Suppliants*, a so-called political tragedy, as a meditation on the possibilities and limitations of tragedy as politics. Finally, chapter 5 analyzes the relation between tragedy and its historical moment, focusing in particular on

Orestes. There is much else that could have been included: the narrative and political aporiai of *Iphigeneia at Aulis*, the imperial politics of familial recognition in *Iphigeneia among the Taurians*, the divided self and divided plot of *Heracles*, the formal chaos of political autonomy in *Heracleidai*. But, as I said, the point of the book is not to present a complete analysis of Euripidean drama but to offer a way of reading the politics of Euripidean form, and I hope that the five chapters below will provide a sufficient illustration of this approach and indication of its broader applicability.

It says something important about form, and perhaps also something about Euripides, that it has not always been easy to identify the most salient formal features—in some cases not even the basic formal structure—of any given play. Is it unified or fragmented? Bipartite or tripartite? Are its protagonists sympathetic or not? Where is its *peripeteia*? Does it even have one? Scholars disagree on virtually every point for every play, and I myself have spent more time than I had anticipated trying to decide, for instance, whether a particular scene is pathetic or bathetic. This is to say that aesthetic form is not an objective phenomenon with a fixed and discernible ontology but a matter of interpretation, the product of formalist analysis as well as its raw material.[4] If politics is built upon "a structure of feeling," aesthetics is "a feeling of structure," and form is something we sense in the course of watching or reading a play.

Perhaps "feeling," too, deserves some explication. This book proposes that the relation between aesthetic and political forms is mediated by affect. That tragedies generate affect in abundance should be obvious to anyone who has ever watched one. It was obvious to Aristotle, who identified tragedy's specific pleasure as the arousal of pity and fear. Pity and fear will be found in the pages that follow; but so, too, will many other emotions, including joy, hope, desire, anxiety, bewilderment, and discontent. My goal is not to track any particular affect—to add to the burgeoning scholarship on tragic pity, for instance—but to analyze the affective structure of each play as a whole. Any given emotion—pity, fear, etc.—is thus merely a species of the larger genus, and one, moreover, that does not necessarily function in the same way from one play to another. Desire, for example, will recur throughout the discussion, but the desire for a happy reunion that impels the plot of *Ion* is very different from the sadistic passion aroused by the sacrifice scene in *Hecuba* or the longing for revenge that structures *Electra* or *Orestes*. Desire and other affects are differently constellated within each play; they work on us differently, with different political consequences.

But who is this "us"? All scholars of ancient drama have to contend with the immeasurable and literally unmeasurable gap between their own personal experience watching—or more often reading—a play, and the experience of the original audience. That "original audience" is, of course, a heuristic fiction, and one that poses a double theoretical difficulty. The first is synchronic. The audience of Euripides' plays was primarily Athenian citizens.[5] But given that the Athenians rarely agreed about anything, it seems doubtful they were of one mind in their response to tragedy, either with their fellow viewers or (if tragic ambiguity produces ambivalence) even within themselves. The second difficulty is diachronic. Recent work on the reception of tragedy has made us aware how much our modern interpretations are shaped by the specific critical traditions we inherit, and how hard—if not impossible—it is to think our way back into the mind of an ancient viewer. I don't pretend to know how a fifth-century Athenian reacted to Euripides' plays. The best I can do is work from my own reactions, applying the cultural filters I know about (and there are no doubt many more that I don't know about) to try to imagine his response. There are various more or less awkward rhetorical fixes to try to conceal the theoretical difficulties inherent in this sort of project, but it seems more honest to stick to the first-person plural—to speak of "our" experience of a play or the way a scene affects "us"—in full recognition of the inevitable gulf (synchronic and diachronic) the pronoun conceals and the imaginative projection required to leap it.

The chapters that follow propose a way of reading tragedy politically. The plays I analyze do not, I think, put forward a specific political content: as dramas, that is not really their job. Instead, they shape political sensibilities, create political attachments, structure political feelings. They provide their audience with a framework for both understanding and experiencing their political present. Why "political"? Because fifth-century Athenians were "political animals" in general and were watching these plays as a collective body, on an occasion that was itself (among other things) political.[6] That is not to say that the plays spoke only and always to their spectators as democratic citizens: as we will see, the relation between the civic and the human is far from straightforward, and negotiating the potential tension between the two identities is part of the work of drama. But if the *politēs* never stopped being a human being, the reverse, I think, is also true, at least in the context of the City Dionysia; and whatever else the plays are doing—providing pleasure, teaching general moral lessons, exploring universal questions—they are also always thinking about politics and doing so, I argue, precisely in and through their aesthetic form.

By exploring the relation between Euripides' aesthetic form and the political forms of democratic Athens, I hope to shed light on each and, especially, on the way each shapes and is shaped by the other. To some, the balance will seem weighted too much toward the aesthetic. I have little to say about concrete Athenian politics, the specific debates and votes in the Assembly, the particular laws passed or decisions carried out. The reader will not learn whether Euripides was a radical democrat or a conservative, or where he came down on the crucial issues of his day. For others, the emphasis will fall too much on the political; they will complain that an aesthetics that locates the ultimate realization of literary form in political sentiment is not, strictly speaking, aesthetics. Objections from each camp come, perhaps inevitably, with the attempt to bridge the divide between them. This book was born from my own frustration with that methodological divide, the false choice between reading tragedy poetically and reading it politically. If, as I hope to show, dramatic form is itself a kind of political content, then that dichotomy no longer makes sense: to read the plays poetically is necessarily to read them politically.

Acknowledgments

Given that it deals with a performative genre, it seems appropriate that this project evolved in performance. It originated in four Martin Classical Lectures delivered in February 2011. I am grateful to my hosts and audiences at Oberlin College, and especially Thomas Van Nortwick and Kirk Ormand, for the opportunity to present my ideas at an early stage and for their warm hospitality. These initial efforts took final shape during a productive and enjoyable term at the Institute of Classical Studies in London, where a version of chapter 3 was presented as the T.B.L. Webster Lecture in November 2013. Between the two, many parts of the book were presented to many audiences, all of whom have helped to improve it with their (variously) sympathetic or skeptical questions and engaged discussion. Among these I am happy to acknowledge in particular the students in my Autumn 2010 Euripides seminar at the University of Toronto and the members of the annual Ancient Greek History and Political Theory Colloquium.

I have also talked informally about the project with many friends and colleagues. I have benefited especially from conversations with Jim Porter (about formalism), Chris Warley (about Adorno), Deidre Lynch (about affect), Miriam Leonard (about Williams), and Steve Waters (about the secret life of plays). Miriam Leonard also kindly shared her forthcoming work with me, as did Johanna Hanink. Kate Gilhuly, Alex Purves, and Nancy Worman all read chapters, and I am grateful to them for their generous and perceptive comments. Finally, Erik Gunderson read the manuscript both in whole and in part and talked through every idea in it. I am thankful for his patience through its many *peripeteiai* and for the astute feedback that helped clarify its *anagnōriseis*. Although I hope the book will be easy to read, it wasn't particularly easy to write, and he knows that better than anyone.

The project was supported financially by a research grant from the Social Sciences and Humanities Research Council of Canada and by the T.B.L. Webster Fellowship at the Institute of Classical Studies. Valuable research assistance was provided in the early stages by Lee Sawchuk and Marie-Pierre Krück and in the final stage by Marion Durand. My thanks as well to Rob Tempio at Princeton University Press and to the Press's two anonymous referees.

I've found it a pleasure to return to the study of tragedy, which was the topic of my dissertation at the University of California, Berkeley. Berkeley was and is a wonderful place to work on tragedy. I regret that while there I did not get the chance to study with Donald Mastronarde, to whose masterful book on Euripides I refer readers who want a more comprehensive view of the author. I was, however, tremendously fortunate to work with Mark Griffith. He taught me so much about tragedy and its politics, and his continuing support has meant the world to me. This book is dedicated to him, with gratitude.

Euripides and the Politics of Form

The Politics of Form

This book sets out to prove a very simple proposition: that in Euripidean tragedy, dramatic form is a kind of political content. The project is motivated by two separate but intersecting problems. The first is the problem of Euripidean tragedy. There are eighteen extant tragedies confidently attributed to Euripides and many of them are, for lack of a better word, odd. With their disjointed, action-packed plots, comic touches, and frequent happy endings, they seem to stretch the generic boundaries of tragedy as we usually think of it. These plays were performed in Athens at the annual tragic festival of the City Dionysia, and in this defining sense they clearly counted as "tragedies"; but they lack the unity of plot and coherence of theme, the consistent seriousness of tone, the mythic grandeur that we find in Sophocles and Aeschylus and that we associate with the genre of tragedy.

Here, for example, is the plot of Euripides' *Heracleidai* (*The Children of Heracles*). Following the death of Heracles, the eponymous children have been driven out of Argos by Heracles' lifelong enemy Eurystheus. Along with their aged protector Iolaus, they have wandered throughout Greece looking for refuge. The play opens with them in supplication at the altar of Zeus at Marathon, outside Athens. Eurystheus's herald comes on and tries to seize the children, but Demophon, the king of Athens, agrees to protect them, even at the risk of war with Eurystheus. The first episode ends with grateful praise of Athenian virtue. So far so good. But then Demophon learns of a prophecy that in order to win this war and save his city, he must sacrifice a well-born virgin to Persephone. Where is he to find such a virgin? All seems to be lost. Just then, a daughter of Heracles appears onstage—unnamed and unannounced— and offers herself for sacrifice. She delivers a noble speech, is praised lavishly for her act, and then killed. But after her death neither she nor her sacrifice is mentioned again. Instead, in the third episode a messenger reports that Heracles' oldest son, Hylus, has come with his army to join the Athenians in the children's defense. The decrepit Iolaus is eager to join the battle; he arms himself with weapons he can barely lift and hobbles off to war. In the next scene a herald reports the Athenians' victory and describes a miracle on the battlefield: old Iolaus was magically rejuvenated and, with the help of the deified Heracles, captured Eurystheus. This miracle, like the daughter's sacrifice, is marveled at, then never mentioned again. At this point the play seems essentially over: the children of Heracles are safe and the tyrannical Eurystheus defeated. But the final scene brings a sudden shift of direction when Eurystheus, up to this point the play's arch villain, delivers a sympathetic speech, explaining that his hostility toward Heracles was the gods' will, not his own. King Demophon decrees that the captive should be spared; but Alcmene, Heracles' mother, demands his blood, and the play ends with the chorus leading Eurystheus away to be killed, in violation of their own king's decree and the laws of their city.

This bare summary should provide some sense of the crazy structure of the play, with its fragmented plot of supplication and revenge, its multitude of weak and inconsistent characters, its wild shifts in tone from the high drama of Alcmene's laments to the comic scene of Iolaus's arming. Miracles occur and are promptly forgotten. The mood swings from despair to triumph to anxiety. The children are lost, then saved, then lost, then saved. In the final moments, the sympathies established throughout the play are suddenly reversed, as Eurystheus is rehabilitated and Alcmene calls for a lawless vengeance that the chorus seem prepared to execute, despite the play's earlier praise for democracy and its rule of law. Compare this to the plot of Aeschylus's *Oresteia*, where one act of violence calls forth another in an adamantine chain of crime and revenge spanning generations; or Sophocles' *Oedipus Tyrannus*, where Oedipus's fate works itself out, piece by piece, with a taut and inexorable necessity. In Euripides' play, by contrast, instead of actions following one another according to a logic of cause and effect, one gets the sense that anything could happen at any time.

What are we to make of a play like this? (And all Euripides' plays are, to a greater or lesser extent, like this.) The difficulty is not so much with the play's content: one can identify a certain thematic coherence around issues of gender, for instance, or read the play as an ambivalent reflection on Athens's imperial obligations.[1] The difficulty is rather at the level of dramatic form. Tragedy presents ideas through the imitation of an action, Aristotle's famous *mimēsis* of a *praxis*, but why is the action in Euripides' tragedies so fragmented and chaotic? Scholars have tried to explain away these plays' oddities by calling some "melodramas," others "romances" or "tragicomedies." But since these were not established genres in the fifth century, this response merely labels their peculiarities without explaining them.[2] Others have seen them as simply inept: Nietzsche isn't the only reader to accuse Euripides of having killed tragedy, and one often detects strains of special pleading or even self-loathing within Euripides scholarship. Obviously, a play like *Heracleidai* operates according to different aesthetic principles from Aristotle's creed of unity, consistency, and probability. Euripides' is rather an aesthetic of "*dissonance, disparity, rift, peripeteia.*"[3] But to note this, as many readers have, is again merely to describe Euripidean form without attempting to solve it—"solve," because in these plays dramatic form presents itself as a puzzle, or better yet, as a riddle that may or may not actually have an answer.

The second problem that motivates my project is one that has exercised critics of tragedy from Aristophanes on: that is, the relation between the play and its contemporary world, the political world of democratic Athens. Tragic dramas were, almost without exception, set in the mythic past, not in the fifth-century polis, and almost never allude overtly to their contemporary moment. As an institution, though, tragedy was deeply embedded in its political and social context, for the City Dionysia was a civic as well as a religious and theatrical event. Tragedy was produced by wealthy citizens and judged by a citizen jury; its choruses were composed of citizens, as was the bulk of its audience. The plays were preceded by a series of rituals that showcased Athens's might and magnificence, including the awarding of crowns to civic benefactors, the presentation of tribute by Athens's imperial subjects, libations offered by the victorious generals, and a parade of war orphans who had been raised by the state. Simon Goldhill has argued that the tragedies themselves should be read in and against this context of civic self-presentation. He shows how the tragic texts, with their insistent problematization of collective norms and values, "question, examine and often subvert" the idealized self-image conveyed by the festival, exposing the rifts and tensions within Athens's civic ideology.[4] In Goldhill's reading, the plays were not only socially relevant, but profoundly political, contributing to the discourse of the democratic polis. It is easy to see how this approach might work for a play like *Hera-*

cleidai, in which Athens braves war to protect the suppliants, only to get caught up in the lawless passion of revenge. The play's ambiguous patriotism both complements and complicates the civic ideology of the City Dionysia.

This historicizing approach to the plays has dominated tragedy scholarship for the past twenty-five years, and it has been extremely illuminating. Turning away from the solipsistic aestheticizing of prior formalist criticism, it has aimed to situate the plays within their historical moment, showing how they reflect and reflect on contemporary political life and thought in democratic Athens.[5] But as New Historicism has hardened into an orthodoxy, both in the field of classics and beyond, many have started to worry that in mining the texts for ideological content, it has cast aside important questions of literary form, giving scant attention to the formal structure and poetic language that differentiate a tragedy from, say, a tribute list. New Historicism proposed that social context could render the literary text fully lucid, but instead the text has become translucent. It has been transformed from the Keatsian urn of New Criticism, self-sufficient in its eternal beauty, into an ornate but ultimately vacuous container of an ideology that itself is thereby reified as its determinate content.[6]

In response there has been a call across the humanities for a return to formalism.[7] But the question now is how to stage such a return without losing the gains of historicism: how to study the aesthetic qualities of these literary texts without forgetting that they were the product of a specific historical moment with its own specific political concerns; or alternatively, how to speak about a text's politics without losing sight of its formal aesthetic qualities. The challenge is not just to keep these two sets of issues—the aesthetic and the political—in focus simultaneously, but to theorize their interconnection within the text itself, to identify the ideological work being done in and *by* tragedy's aesthetic form. What is needed, in short, is an immanent critique, in the sense proposed by Theodor Adorno.[8] Through its formal elaboration, Adorno argues, art seeks to establish its autonomy from the social, but by that very gesture it incorporates the social within itself. Thus "the unsolved antagonisms of reality return in artworks as immanent problems of form."[9] In the course of spontaneously pursuing their own internal formal logic, works of art register reality and crystallize ideology: they provide imaginary resolutions to real social contradictions, give formal expression to ideas that went unexpressed or were inexpressible in their society, expose and even expand the limits of possibility of their contemporary context, a context that they can thus properly be said to create. An immanent critique moots the historicist-formalist debate by seeing the work of art as most thoroughly historical where it seems most purely formal, and displaces questions about the conscious intention (the "political message") of the author, whose aesthetic choices, whether he intends so or not, inevitably enact ideological assumptions and entail ideological commitments.[10]

From this perspective, the formal peculiarities of Euripidean drama—the vertiginous twists and turns, the constant irony and shifts of tone, the unexpected appearance of gods—can be seen not just as artistic experimentation for its own sake or, worse, as dramatic incompetence that presaged the death of tragedy, but instead as a specific way of articulating meaning, including political meaning. The structure of these plays is not just a vehicle for political expression, but is itself a kind of political expression, an immanent engagement with the dilemmas and contradictions of life in the democratic polis.

This politics of form is not, of course, unique to Euripides. Jean-Pierre Vernant famously argued that tragedy as a whole encodes the tensions of its historical moment not only in the ambiguities of its language but in its very structure: the genre's defining alternation between individual heroic protagonists speaking in the contemporary dialect of fifth-century Athens and a collective chorus singing archaic lyrics stages a chiastic dialectic between a heroic, mythic past and a democratic, civic present that characterized the "mental world" of fifth-century Athens.[11] Vernant shows us that tragedy does not have to try to be political: regardless of whether a particular play aims to present a political message or seeks to deliver a political lesson, the genre is inherently—immanently—political.[12] This is true of works like Sophocles' *Oedipus Tyrannus* or Aeschylus's *Oresteia* no less than of Euripides' *Heracleidai*: structural unity and thematic coherence have a politics of their own. To that extent Euripides offers merely a specific instance of a general phenomenon, but a particularly good one, because his self-conscious formal experimentation and ostentatious formal innovation call attention to form itself. They force us to notice form and demand that we think about it.

Audiences since antiquity have risen to this challenge. Euripides was famous (or infamous) already in his own time for his formal novelty. In the underworld poetry competition of Aristophanes' *Frogs*, he is alternately damned and praised for his daring transformations of the tragic genre: his simplification of tragic diction, his introduction of quotidian

subjects and characters, his new melodies and meters. This formal originality was more than simply an aesthetic matter. Accused by his antagonist, the (politically and aesthetically) conservative Aeschylus, of
degrading tragedy by filling the stage with all manner of miscreants—
cripples, beggars, women in love—the spectral Euripides responds that
by giving a voice to everyone his plays teach the audience "to think,
see, understand, twist things around, to scheme, to suspect wrongs, to
consider things from all angles" (957–58; cf. 971–79). His tragedy, he
boasts, is not just technically innovative but democratic (*dēmokratikon*,
952), and it is the latter by virtue of being the former.

As Aristophanes' infernal poetry contest demonstrates, Euripides'
contemporaries were attuned to the political implications of aesthetic
form in general, and of his aesthetic form in particular. It was widely
agreed, for instance, that different musical harmonies and rhythms had
specific and identifiable effects on the moral character of the audience:
the Lydian mode was soft and effeminizing, the Dorian induced manliness and restraint, and so on. Accordingly, *mousikē* (music, poetry,
dance) was the object of intense ethical and educational concern.[13] In
the late fifth century, much of this concern centered on the so-called
New Music, an avant-garde musical movement for which Euripides was
often presented as the poster boy. For its critics the formal innovations
of this movement—its greater melodic flexibility, metrical heterogeneity, and syntactical freedom—were not only symptoms of the license
and chaos of the radical democracy, but in fact their cause: Plato attributes Athens's degeneracy to the mixing of musical genres, one of the
innovations for which Euripides is taken to task in *Frogs*.[14] Poetry and
music are politically dangerous not only for what they represent (although that is a constant worry for Plato and mimesis a problem in
itself within his ontology), but also for how they represent it. Plato
quotes Damon of Oa, a music theorist and prominent figure in the New
Music: "One must take care in changing to a new form of music, since
this creates risks for the whole; musical modes can never be altered
without altering the weightiest laws of the polis" (*Republic* 424c3–6).
Plato agrees: he subjects musical modes to minute legal regulation in
his *Laws* and bans poetry outright from the ideal city of his *Republic*.
The Athenians apparently also agreed—and ostracized Damon from
Athens.[15]

Aesthetic form, then, is never purely or abstractly formal for the
Greeks: it has real ethical and political effects. It achieves these effects
through its *psukhagōgia* or "leading of the *psukhē*" (soul, mind, psyche).

Acting on the *psukhē* as medicine does on the body, poetry injects "terrified shuddering and tearful pity and sorrowful longing," as Gorgias puts it, "and through words the *psukhē* suffers its own suffering at the successes and failures of others' affairs" (*Encomium of Helen* 9).[16] While all language has this magical force, tragedy is, of all genres, "most delightful to the masses and most able to move the soul" (*dēmoterpestaton te kai psukhagōgikōtaton*, Plato *Minos* 321a4–5). The pairing of *dēmoterpestaton* and *psukhagōgikōtaton* is not accidental. For Plato, tragedy arouses the inferior, irrational part of the soul against the superior and reasoning part, creating a state of psychic anarchy of which the political analogue was radical democracy (*Republic* 605a–c). In the *Timaeus* he imagines *psukhagōgia* working upon the appetitive part of the soul, the *epithumētikon*: locked away near the liver, far from the deliberating part of the soul so as not to interrupt its operations, the *epithumētikon* does not understand reason but is "soul-led by images and phantasms" (*hupo de eidōlōn kai phantasmatōn . . . psukhagōgēsoito*, 71a5–7).[17] Aristotle is more reticent, in the *Poetics* at least, about the political implications of tragic *psukhagōgia*, and more sanguine about its ethical value. There, a well-wrought tragic plot stimulates an intellectual response, encouraging the viewer to make ethical judgments about the relation between action and character and between virtue and happiness.[18] But even in Aristotle tragedy's *psukhagōgia* is not purely cognitive: his admission that theatrical spectacle, generally ignored in the *Poetics*, is psychagogic implies that tragedy's effect can work at a more immediate, visceral level that recalls Plato's *epithumētikon*, avidly consuming its phantasmatic images.[19]

These ancient theorizations of tragic *psukhagōgia* suggest that it is by operating on the psyche that dramatic form achieves political force. Aesthetic form provides a syntax for the imaginary articulation of the audience's real conditions of existence; it "leads the soul" to adopt certain subjective relations to that reality.[20] Ideology is not something that aesthetic form contains, then, but something it *does*. This book explores that premise. It seeks the content of the plays' political thought in their dramatic form, in their innovative use of the manifold generic resources of tragedy, and, especially, in their structuring of action (*muthos*), following Aristotle's insight that "*muthos* is the first principle and, as it were, the soul (*psukhē*) of tragedy" because its reversals and recognitions are the greatest vehicle for tragic *psukhagōgia* (*ta megista hois psukhagōgei hē tragōidia*, *Poetics* 1450a33–39). In *muthos*, soul and story move together, and they trace an ideological trajectory.

To the extent that it focuses on these formal elements of tragedy, this study is formalist. As should be clear already, this is not an empty formalism (although empty formalism and its political consequences will emerge as Euripidean themes). For the Greeks, as we have seen, aesthetic form was never ethically neutral, never purely abstract, never "empty." This is particularly true of Euripides, in whose plays form takes on a texture and materiality of its own. If, as James Porter puts it in a recent critique of formalism in the study of ancient aesthetics, "matter is the dirtiness of form, and it is visible whenever form's function becomes the object of perception instead of the mechanism that filters and guides perception," then Euripidean form is "dirty": we cannot help but notice it.[21] Moreover, as Aristophanes and the critics of the New Music show, it is "contagious," infecting the psyches of its citizen audience. These contemporary political epidemiologies of form suggest that Euripides' formal experiments, although self-conscious, are never merely or solipsistically self-referential.[22] When Euripides calls attention to the formal workings of his theater, it is not just to remind his audience that they are watching a play (something of which they were presumably well aware), but to invite them to consider the active force of the play's form: what it makes thinkable or unthinkable, what contradictions it mediates or calcifies, what political and ethical attitudes it commits them to—in short, where its *psukhagōgia* is leading them. In this sense, Euripides' formal reflection—thinking *in* form *about* form and its political entailments—anticipates my own, proving once again Nicole Loraux's thesis that there is nothing about ancient Greece that the Greeks have not already thought before us—and Euripides perhaps more than most.[23]

• • •

In the rest of this chapter, I would like to elaborate what I mean by the politics of form by way of a brief illustration. *Alcestis* is Euripides' earliest surviving play, produced in 438 BCE. The hero, Admetus, has obtained a reprieve from death: he can live on if he can convince someone else to die in his place. His mother and father refuse, but his wife, Alcestis, agrees, and the first half of the play stages her noble self-sacrifice and pathetic death, complete with mourning servants and weeping children. Admetus grieves extravagantly after she is gone: he swears never to remarry and renounces all pleasure. In the midst of his mourning an old friend happens to stop by, Heracles, en route to one of his labors. Admetus conceals his grief to offer his guest hospitality, but

Heracles discovers the news from one of the servants. Touched by his host's generosity and moved by his sorrow, Heracles wrestles Death and brings Alcestis back to life, handing her over to her husband in the final scene.

This play is odd, even for a Euripidean tragedy. The City Dionysia featured three days of theatrical productions. On each day, a different playwright presented three tragedies followed by a satyr play, a short burlesque piece featuring a chorus dressed as the eponymous satyrs. The plays were written in tragic language and featured the same sort of mythical heroes that we find in tragedy, but the tone is generally light and the humor tends (as one might expect of satyrs) toward the obscene. *Alcestis* was staged as the fourth play of its day, in the slot usually reserved for a satyr play. We know this from the ancient hypothesis (a brief synopsis from the third century BCE), which also comments that the play is "rather like a satyr play (*saturikōteron*) because, unlike a tragedy, its reversal is toward joy and happiness."[24]

Alcestis does, indeed, stage a reversal from bad fortune to good and ends with what seems, at least at first blush, like a happy ending, the long-awaited reunion of husband and wife. And the play does have some light—even funny—moments, as when a drunken Heracles, ignorant of Alcestis's recent death, carouses around the house, much to the disapproval of the slaves. But despite its light tone, this play is still far from the vulgar slapstick of a typical satyr play, and it lacks the satyr play's defining feature, satyrs. *Alcestis* has a thoroughly proper chorus of elderly citizens. Moreover, the very features that made *Alcestis* seem *saturikōteron* also characterize many other Euripidean plays whose tragic pedigree is unquestioned. The hypothesist himself notes that *Orestes* also features a reversal from misfortune to good fortune and a happy ending; so, too, do *Helen* and *Ion* and *Iphigeneia among the Taurians*. Aristotle allows that tragic reversals can move in either direction—from good fortune to bad or from bad to good—and implies that popular tastes in his day favored the latter, although he himself judges plays that end in misfortune the most tragic (*tragikōtatai*) in performance, and notes, ironically, that Euripides is on this score the most tragic of poets (*tragikōtatos ge tōn poiētōn*, *Poetics* 1453a23–30; cf. 13–15). Likewise, the sort of comic touches that we find in *Alcestis* occur in other plays as well, like the decrepit Iolaus excitedly arming himself for battle in *Heracleidai*. It is possible that in 438 this sort of thing seemed too outré to be staged under the heading of "tragedy" but that over the next three decades Euripides' experimentation expanded the definition of the genre. At any rate, while *Alcestis* is institutionally anomalous, its formal peculiarities are in fact typical of Euripidean tragedy as a whole.

The play opens with a prologue scene between the god Apollo and Thanatos, Death, who has come to fetch Alcestis to the underworld. The conversation between the gods lays out the premise of the play—that Alcestis has agreed to die in place of Admetus and her time has come—and also predicts its happy conclusion: Apollo announces that Heracles will come and steal the woman back, laying out the plot (65–71). This sort of plot prolepsis is quite common in Euripidean prologues, and, as we shall see in future chapters, it is not always to be trusted. Here, though, Apollo's role as god of prophecy might give us confidence (despite Death's objections) in his promise of a happy ending. That promise helps us to watch the suffering of Alcestis's death and Admetus's grief: we can enjoy their anguish knowing—or at least hoping—that all will be well that ends well. In this sense the prologue signposts the drama's psychagogic trajectory, setting the direction not only of the action but also of our affective response to it.

The play unfolds much as Apollo predicts. Alcestis's death is staged in poignant detail. A servant describes her preparations for death within the house and reports her final tearful apostrophe to the marriage bed: "Oh bed where I gave up my maidenhood to this man for whose sake I die; farewell. . . . Some other woman will possess you now, luckier than I perhaps but not more virtuous" (177–82). We hear of her young children hanging from their mother's dress sobbing, and how she comforted them, taking them in her arms and kissing first one then the other, on the very verge of death (189–91). Everyone is in tears: Alcestis, Admetus, the children, the servants (192–203). The vivid pathos of this messenger speech is amplified when Alcestis herself is carried onstage "to see the light of the sun, one last time and then never again" (206–7). As she sees winged Death coming for her and feels her eyes dimming, she says her final goodbye to her husband, making him promise not to remarry and take a stepmother for her children. She dies before our eyes, the only onstage natural death in Greek tragedy. In fact, she dies not once but twice, first in intensely imagistic lyrics, then in a long *rhēsis* (speech), prolonging the crucial moment and exploiting to the full the formal possibilities of tragic expression. Her little children wail over their dead mother and beg her to come back to them (393–415), another dramatic amping-up of pathos, as children, too, are very rare on the tragic stage. Admetus's grief is hyperbolic: he will never remarry, he will mourn for the rest of his days (328–42). There will be no more parties and drinking, no more flutes or lyres: all plea-sure will die with Alcestis (343–47). After she is gone, he mourns in high lyric style: he envies the dead, he threatens to hurl himself into the grave alongside his dead wife (865–67, 895–902). He imagines his bar-ren future—the lonely house, empty bed, and crying children—and wishes he were dead (935–61).

The emotional demand of such scenes is not subtle. We are told early on that a good man will grieve with the sufferings of the good (109–11), and the play's pathetic onslaught leaves us little room to re-sist. How can we not be sad, seeing Admetus's grief? Likewise, how could we not share his joy at the end, when he finally takes his revived wife by the hand? That end comes only after we have witnessed Adme-tus's remorse, his too-late (and thus quintessentially tragic) realization that he should not have asked his wife to die for him and that the life he thereby gained is not worth living (935–61). It comes only after Her-acles has teased both him and the audience, refusing to tell Admetus that the veiled woman he offers him—whose identity we already know—is actually his wife. The ironic gap between his ignorance and our knowledge further heightens the dramatic tension, as Admetus begs Heracles to take the strange woman away, "for looking at her I seem to see my wife and it roils my heart and the tears break from my eyes" (1066–68). Finally, reluctantly, he lifts the veil and recognizes Alcestis. "Oh gods," he cries, "What am I to say? This is a miracle beyond all hope. Is it truly my wife I see? Or is some divine joy mocking me and driving me mad?" (1123–25). She is yours, Heracles says; take her. "You have everything you wanted" (1132). So the play ends with Ad-metus ordering choruses and sacrifices to be set up throughout the city to celebrate his good fortune. The dead house returns to life, as Adme-tus announces his happy reversal, his "change of tune" from bad for-tune to good (1157–58).

With this summary I've tried to convey the basic emotional trajec-tory of the play and to suggest that the psychagogic force it exerts over its audience is hard to resist. Our sympathetic involvement is solicited, first by the protagonists' suffering and then by their joy. The vivid de-scription of the scene inside the house, with its touching details and reported speech; the prolonged horror of Alcestis's onstage death; the crying children and heightened language of grief; the choral odes laud-ing the unprecedented heroism of Alcestis's sacrifice and the unprece-dented pain of her loss—Euripides deploys all the resources of the genre to orchestrate an extravaganza of pathos. Likewise, the suspenseful buildup to the couple's reunion intensifies the *peripeteia* and the ultimate fulfillment of the happy ending that we were promised by Apollo at the very start.

Some who resist a historicizing approach to drama have argued that tragedy's aim was simply to give pleasure by arousing the audience's emotions. *Alcestis* would seem a prime example of this "emotive hedonism."[25] Placing formal technique in the service of pathos, it makes us feel Admetus's sorrow and his joy. But as we do so, do we commit ourselves to more than mere emotional catharsis? Is there a politics to the play's pathos? On the surface, *Alcestis* is pointedly apolitical. Set in the mythic kingdom of Pherae, the drama seems distant from the political concerns of democratic Athens. The form itself—the folktale encounter of Apollo and Thanatos and Heracles' wrestling match with Death, the romantic plotline of loss and recovery, the happy ending—would seem to discourage any political interpretation. Its "prosatyric" position may likewise have prompted an audience to experience the drama as simple fun, an escapist fantasy or emotional joyride.[26] And yet, I would like to suggest that there is a politics implicit in the very structure of this ostensibly apolitical plot, one that we take on almost despite ourselves when we succumb to the play's compelling *psukhagōgia*.[27]

One of the key themes of the play, reiterated time and again by the characters and the chorus, is the universality of death: everyone must die, there is no escaping death, death is the one ineluctable necessity (112–31, 418–19, 782–86, 962–94). This is virtually the play's motto and it contributes to the sense of mythic distance: the play purports to be about general human verities, life and death, love and loss. But this universal law is explicitly politicized in the opening scene. Apollo tries to persuade Thanatos to defer Alcestis's death, reminding him that if she dies an old woman her burial will be wealthier (*plousiōs taphēsetai*, 56) and therefore a greater honor for Thanatos. The latter replies, "You are establishing a law for those with means"—literally, "for the haves" (*pros tōn ekhontōn*, 57)—since "those who could would buy the right to die at a ripe old age" (*ōnoint' an hois paresti gēraioi thanein*, 59).

Apollo dismisses this claim as so much sophistry (58), but in fact it resonates with the play's broader thematics. All mortals must die: this iron necessity applies equally to rich and to poor. The chorus try to console Admetus at several points by reminding him that he is not the only person to have lost a loved one (416–18, 892–94). They tell of a kinsman of theirs who lost an only son and yet, old and childless though he was, he bore this loss stoically (903–10). Typically, tragic choruses generalize in the direction of mythology: Niobe lost seven sons and seven daughters in a single day; imagine her grief and bear up under your own. But this comparison to the chorus's anonymous cousin, instead of mythologizing Admetus's grief, democratizes it. Death is the great leveler, no less painful for the average citizen than for the king in his palace. Thus, when Thanatos resists Apollo's suggestion of "a law (*nomos*) for the haves," he establishes mortality as a sort of *isonomia*, the equality of and before the law that was one of the fundamental premises of Athens's democracy.

So, on the one hand, we have the democratic equality of death. On the other hand, though, royalty does seem to have its benefits, for Admetus has escaped death's necessity and broken its universal law not once but twice, first evading death himself and then regaining his dead wife. The king seems to be above the law, an exception to a mandate that we are told has no exception. This is undemocratic enough in itself, but the play is quite clear that what allows him to transgress this unbreachable law is his aristocratic status and connections. Admetus had been able to evade death in the first place because of his friendship with Apollo, who tricked the Fates into agreeing to the exchange of bodies. His life is saved a second time by another friend, Heracles. This theme of friendship is prominent in the play, and is generically marked by allusions to sympotic literature. The role of Heracles is often pointed to as one of the "satyric" features of this play, as Heracles was a popular figure in satyr plays. But here Heracles, for all his drunken carousing, is less satyric than sympotic:[28] he sports the paraphernalia of the symposium (756–60), and his drunken speech (773–802) is full of the diction and tropes of sympotic poetry, where the brevity of life is compensated by the pleasures of convivial companionship.

In sympotic literature, originally the product of the Archaic period and its powerful oligarchies, that companionship is aristocratic, and in *Alcestis* it is no less so. Both Apollo and Heracles are bound to Admetus by a relationship of *xenia*, which refers not to personal bonds of affection but to an institutionalized relationship of guest and host. In the Archaic period, aristocratic houses across Greece maintained *xenia*-bonds—hosting one another, exchanging gifts, intermarrying—and the institution has been seen as instrumental in the consolidation of a Panhellenic elite during this period. In Athens, the democracy attempted to limit such extra-polis alliances but never fully did away with them or the elite class that formed them, and the theme of *xenia*, like the genre of sympotica, continued to carry oligarchic associations.[29]

For Admetus, *xenia* has been a saving grace time and again. Apollo saved Admetus from death the first time in thanks for his hospitality (*xenōi*, 8). Heracles likewise undertakes to return Alcestis to life in gratitude for Admetus's *xenia* at such a difficult time (68, 854–60). Who in all of Greece is a more devoted host, more *philoxenos?* (858) Heracles asks. We see that *philoxenia* firsthand in Admetus's dilemma over whether to entertain Heracles despite his grief. When Heracles first arrived and saw the house in mourning, he offered to leave, "For a *xenos* is a burden to those in mourning" (540); but Admetus insisted he stay and even lied, leading Heracles to believe that the dead person was not someone close to him. The chorus are outraged that Admetus would entertain a guest at such a time (*xenodokein*, 552; cf. 809), but Admetus defends himself on the grounds of *xenia*. Would you praise me if I drove away a *xenos?* Sending away Heracles would not lighten my grief but would only add to it by earning me a reputation for being a bad host (*axenōteros*, 556; *ekhthroxenous*, 558). No, he says, my house does not know how to dishonor a *xenos* (566–67).

The chorus quickly come around and praise Admetus extravagantly in the ode that follows (569–605). "Oh ever-hospitable house of a liberal man!" (*ō poluxeinos kai eleutherou andros aei pot' oikos*, 569). They go on to explain how Admetus had offered hospitality to Apollo when he was living among mortals. This mythic backstory had been recounted by Apollo himself in the opening lines of the play: Zeus was punishing Apollo for taking revenge for Zeus's prior killing of his son Asclepius, who had created drugs that would allow mortals to escape death. The punishment of Asclepius is alluded to throughout the play as evidence of the ineluctability of death (121–31, 966–71). But where Asclepius failed to transgress that mortal law, his father Apollo seems to have succeeded, and he grants Admetus what Asclepius was forbidden to give all mankind, eternal life. His *philoxenia* has brought Admetus this special dispensation. It has also brought him wealth: as a result of his hospitality to Apollo, the chorus note, Admetus rules a house "supremely wealthy in flocks" (588–89) and a vast expanse of land (590–96). Finally, at the end of the ode, the *philoxenia* that has made him wealthy and powerful is praised as the product and proof of his own innate nobility: *to eugenes* (600), his good birth and good breeding, comes out in his hospitality toward Heracles, just as it did in his hospitality toward Apollo. "All wisdom is inherent in the noble," the chorus conclude (*en tois agathoisi de pant' enestin sophias*, 602–3).[30] *Xenia* is thus strongly marked as aristocratic: it is both result and cause of Admetus's elite status, both an inborn virtue and an ethical principle that governs his actions. It is this elite virtue and the elite friendships it seals that allow Admetus to defer his death and win back his wife.

To a democratic Athenian audience, Admetus's lofty social status and important social connections would have been crystal clear. But what, then, is the message of this play? Remember Death's worry that if he lets Alcestis go, that would mean establishing a law in favor of the rich, who would buy a deferral of their own demise. That is, in fact, precisely what Admetus has done, although he's paid for it in favors to influential friends, not in hard cash. Even as the play insists upon the universality of death, it insinuates that if you have the right connections and move in the right circles, you can circumvent that law—not once but repeatedly. Admetus closes the play marveling at his good luck (*eutukhōn*, 1158), and it is true that he seems to have done little to merit his happy reversal of fortune. He is reproached by his father Pheres as a coward who let his wife die for him (675–733), and by Heracles for lying to a friend and letting him revel while the house is in mourning (1008–18). He is a bad husband, a bad son, even a bad friend. All he seems to have going for him is his aristocratic connections. Lucky, indeed.[31]

The play thus induces a cognitive dissonance for its democratic audience. On the one hand, as spectators we are rooting for Alcestis's return and the happy ending: we wept to see Alcestis die, we will rejoice to see her return. The prologue's divine plot prolepsis, the narrative of loss and recovery, the play's dextrous deployment of pathos and suspense, even its prosatyric position with its anticipated *peripeteia* from bad fortune to good—all these formal elements conspire to make that emotional trajectory compelling and encourage us to join in Admetus's celebration at the end. But what exactly are we celebrating? The fact that the universality of death holds for the rest of us, but not for the elite? The fact that a good aristocrat has been rewarded for, essentially, being a good aristocrat? As democratic citizens committed to the egalitarian ideology of *isonomia*, the audience should be uncomfortable with the politics of this "fairy tale" ending.

Euripides in fact goes out of his way to emphasize this dissonance. Right before the final scene, with its joyous reunion, the chorus sing an ode to Necessity, Anankē: nothing is more powerful; no one can escape it, not even the gods. This ineluctable Anankē is none other than death itself, a force mightier than any song of Orpheus or drug of Asclepius (969–71). You cannot bring back the dead by crying, the chorus sing

(985–86). But in fact Admetus *will* bring back the dead by crying: we know that, even as the chorus are lamenting the inevitability of death, Heracles is wrestling Thanatos, and no sooner do they finish than he appears, as he had promised he would, with the silent Alcestis. This ode intensifies the dynamic of the play as a whole: we are told that there are no exceptions to the law of death, but we see with our own eyes that there is, in fact, an exception—for one who is, not coincidentally, extremely well-to-do. Moreover, this exception seems to be allowed, even decreed, by the very gods who bow to the will of Necessity, for Apollo's prediction in the prologue grants Alcestis's return divine sanction. The gods, themselves often imagined as the supreme aristocrats, enforce the iron law of mortality but seem willing to bend the rules when it comes to their own human *xenoi*.[32]

The play thus forces us into an emotional position that has uncomfortable political consequences for a democratic audience. Euripides doesn't spell out those consequences, but the discomfort they produce lingers to cloud the final reunion which, for all its superficial rosiness, contains a sub-current of coercion, deception, and betrayal. Heracles doesn't simply hand over the resurrected Alcestis, but plays a trick on his friend to pay him back for the concealment of his wife's death. Heracles pretends that the veiled Alcestis is just a girl he picked up as a prize in an athletic competition and wants Admetus to look after while he is off on his labors. Admetus is reluctant to take the veiled woman: he had promised his wife on her deathbed that he would not replace her, and this woman reminds him so uncannily of Alcestis (1061–67). He fears the justified reproaches of the servants and his dead wife herself if he betrays his oath and takes this stranger to his bed (1055–60). But despite his pleas, his good friend Heracles forces him to commit this betrayal. The scene is played for its irony—we know all along that the veiled woman is really Alcestis—but it still leaves a bitter taste in the mouth that mars the happiness of the happy ending.[33]

What are we supposed to feel, then, as we leave the Theater of Dionysus after *Alcestis* ends? And recall that we do leave after it ends, since *Alcestis* was the fourth and final play of the day. In fact, perhaps we can now understand this placement better in light of the play's emotional dynamics: the confused response the play induces, its tension between emotional satisfaction and political discomfort, is alleviated by its pro-satyric position, which tells us: don't take it all too seriously, relax and enjoy it, it's just a satyr play after all. And maybe that's good advice: maybe after suffering along with their grief, we should just enjoy the reunion of husband and wife, and not worry about the larger metaphysical or political implications of that happy ending achieved in breach of an ostensibly universal law. *Alcestis*'s generic indeterminacy thus smooths over the troubling dissonance between the play's action and its thematics, between its *muthos,* in Aristotle's terms, and its *dianoia* (thought). And so the tragedy closes with a bemused resignation at the unpredictability of the universe: "Many are the shapes of the divinities; many things the gods accomplish against all hope. The expected is not accomplished; for the unexpected the god finds a way. That's how this affair has turned out."

And yet that smoothing-over has a politics of its own, of course, for if *Alcestis*'s prosatyric position encourages us to take it as a simple fantasy of wish fulfillment, it also discourages us from asking precisely whose wishes are being fulfilled. Mark Griffith proposes that the ultimate message of the satyr play is that someone else will solve our problems; all we need to do is acquiesce and "the reward for our acquiescence will follow, in the shape of a miraculously happy ending."[34] *Alcestis* asks us to acquiesce in its romance of elite prerogative. A good man (*khrēstos*) grieves at the suffering of the noble (*agathoi*), says the chorus of Pheraean citizens, and shares like a loyal friend in his sorrow (109–11, 210–12, 369–70). We are asked to be loyal friends to this lucky king, to feel (as the chorus do) for his misfortune and to cheer at its reversal. As a reward for our acquiescence, we also get to share in his happy miracle: the choruses and sacrifices that Admetus proclaims "for the citizens and the whole region" (1154–56) at the play's close anticipate our own post-play celebrations, even as the final lines, with their universalizing wonder at the gods' inscrutable ways, generalize his unexpected reversal to all of us.[35] Thus the play's prosatyric good cheer contributes to the false consciousness the form itself generates. Meanwhile, if we leave the theater feeling grateful to that aristocratic hero for whom wrestling Death is all in a day's work—who solves not only Admetus's problems but (by loosening the dramatic bind) our own—we might also come to feel that he and his friends deserve whatever good luck happens to come their way.

What I hope to have shown in this necessarily sketchy reading is how a play's formal structure can bear political meanings, even in as pointedly apolitical a play as *Alcestis*. The way it sets up its plot, its use of language and song, its modulation of emotions, even its prosatyric position: these formal choices are informed by, even as they give form to, the political possibilities of the playwright's contemporary world.

Even a play that, on its surface, has nothing to say about contemporary politics contains and expresses these possibilities silently within its dramatic structure. Its specific message is hard to pin down, and in the end it's no doubt largely a matter of personal inclination whether one comes away from this play with a warm glow of love regained and prosatyric jubilation at the reversal from bad fortune to good, or with a vague sense of unease—or a more acute sense of class *ressentiment*—at the licensed transgression by which that reversal is achieved. The political force of the play—and, I propose, of Euripidean tragedy in general—is thus formal in two senses. It doesn't tell us what to believe but instead offers a framework, a form, for belief; and that framework is built into the very form of the play. Whatever messages the play may convey about elite exceptionalism, it conveys them not at the level of its explicit content, but in its most fundamental dramatic structure.

Aesthetic form and political meaning are not mutually exclusive, then, as the current critical impasse between formalism and historicism would suggest. Instead, they are indivisible: one cannot strip away the aesthetic form to get to a kernel of political content because the aesthetic form *is* the political content. It is this form of politics—this politics of form—that I propose to explore in the pages that follow, this mutual implication of poetic structure and political meaning that makes Euripides' tragedies, in Adorno's famous phrase, a "sundial telling the time of history."[36]

CHAPTER 1

Dramatic Means and Ideological Ends

We begin at the end. Endings are vital to the way we experience a play: how we interpret it as it goes along is determined in part by where we think it will end up, and our perception of its structure is shaped by our "anticipation of retrospection" from a fixed point of closure.[1] This is true of all drama, but especially of ancient drama, where the audience already knew the outcome of the myth. Athenian playwrights had quite a lot of freedom in presenting mythic material, but they seem rarely, if ever, to have changed a major plot point. So Euripides could set his *Electra* on a farm and have Electra married to a farmer, but apparently couldn't have the farmer kill Aegisthus and Clytemnestra: mythically speaking, that's Orestes' job. Greek tragedy is structured, then, less by the suspense of not knowing how things will turn out than by the suspense of not knowing how things will manage to turn out the way they have to, of fearing that we may not be able to get there from here—a suspense, in other words, between dramatic means and mythic ends.

This tension between means and ends generates for the spectators a desire that binds our attention and impels us through the temporal experience of watching the play. This desire, as Peter Brooks has argued, is essentially a desire for the end. We want the story to end, we want to know how it ends, but we don't want that ending to come prematurely: it has to feel right.[2] Closure, in this view, is more psychological than phenomenological, more feeling than thing. Brooks is writing about novels, but this teleological desire is even more definitive in the case of plays. With a novel you can flip forward or go back, pick it up and put it down, but the experience of drama is linear: a play builds toward a determinate endpoint and won't release you, if it can help it, until you get there. Aristotle says that a dramatic action must have a beginning, middle, and end (*Poetics* 1450b21–34). How the play gets from one to the next—the plot's enchainment—is key to its unity, its "wholeness," and its quality as an aesthetic experience. Aristotle favors tight logical enchainment: events should follow one another "according to probability or necessity" (*kata to eikos ē to anankaion*). He disapproves when things happen randomly or by chance (*tukhē*) since, he says, the greatest emotional impact is produced when chance events seem actually to have happened for a reason (*Poetics* 1451a36–1452a11).[3]

This explains in part why Aristotle so admires Sophocles' *Oedipus Tyrannus*. In that play, every individual event seems to happen according to *tukhē*: Oedipus happened to come from Corinth to Thebes, happened to kill an old man at a crossroads, happened to solve the riddle of the Sphinx and marry the widowed queen Jocasta. Likewise in the unfolding of the drama on stage: a messenger happens to come from Corinth telling Oedipus the man he thought was his father is dead; in the course of the scene he happens to mention that Oedipus was not really his son; and so on. Every event is linked to the prior one by chance, and yet all of them add up to the inevitable discovery that Oedipus killed his father and married his mother. In this play, probability takes on the force of necessity as the action moves ineluctably toward its telos—the revelation that the divine prophecy has been fulfilled—and its sweep is so forceful that it lends that ending a sense of finality even though the prophecy has not, in fact, been fulfilled entirely.[4] That telos is also the *arkhē* (beginning): the tragic action was completed before the play even began, and what unfolds onstage is its dramatic realization. This gives the play a feeling of inexorable teleology, an almost claustrophobically tight enchainment in which the means are always—whether Oedipus knows it or not—defined by the end.

Contrast Euripides. In Euripides' plays, as in *Oedipus Tyrannus*, the end is often known from the beginning. Many of his plays open with an extradiegetic prologue, delivered more or less directly to the audience, often by a god, telling us from the start how things will end.[5] In these proleptic prologues, the play's beginning anticipates its telos, and yet the route from the one to the other is so circuitous and indirect that for much of the play we are uncertain where we are headed and whether we will ever actually get there. Between beginning and end, events are enchained not by a probability that verges on necessity, as Aristotle prefers, but often by pure accident, *tukhē*. Episodes are linked by chance events or the random comings and goings of the myriad characters; actions do not follow one another in a clear and singular path, but double back and repeat themselves, stop and start and head off down dead ends. And whereas in *Oedipus Tyrannus* these random acts of *tukhē* all contribute to the final *anankē*, in Euripides means and ends seem never to fully cohere. In fact, sometimes the plot goes so radically askew that it takes a deus ex machina to bring it back into line. So, in *Orestes*, as we shall see in chapter 5, Apollo has to come down at the last minute to ensure that the plot ends the way, mythically, it has to. The necessary telos is accomplished, but it requires some mechanical tweaking to make it happen. In place of an adamantine teleology, we are left with a sense that the end doesn't fully circumscribe the means nor the means fully justify the end.

This non-congruence of ends and means is part of what Donald Mastronarde terms the "open structure" of Euripides' dramas. In contrast to the inexorable progression of a play like the *OT*, in Euripides events are juxtaposed without explicit ligatures, just as at the thematic level, conflicting viewpoints are presented without being reconciled. This thematic and formal openness, Mastronarde argues, produces a sense of disequilibrium that poses a "challenge to the audience to make sense of the whole," and in this way to participate actively in the interpretation of the play's action and the construction of its meaning.[6] Euripides' open structure has seemed to many to be a particularly suitable aesthetic for Athens's radical democracy. Forcing the citizen-spectators to weigh different positions and reach their own conclusions, this way of structuring action seems to confirm the claim of the character Euripides in Aristophanes' *Frogs* that his tragedy is the most democratic because it teaches the demos to think (952–79). In its gleeful break from traditional mythic and narrative probabilities and its openness to contingency and reversal, Euripidean tragedy seems to mirror contemporary democracy, its structural freedom a mimesis of the democracy's *eleutheria*.[7]

This idea is exceptionally appealing to us today. As postmodern democrats, we like the thought of political and literary openness, the sense of freedom and infinite possibility that comes with the loosening of formal constraints. But openness can generate anxiety as well as exhilaration, and an open structure can produce a paradoxical longing for closure, both dramatic and ideological.

This is what I think happens in Euripides' *Ion*. In this play the tension between means and ends is particularly strained and the political stakes particularly high, for its telos is the *arkhē* of Athens's *arkhē*, the origin of its imperial power. The play stages Ion's assumption of his

identity as forebear of Athens's pure autochthonous lineage and Ionian empire. The *muthos* is governed by *tukhē*: a circuitous tale of abandoned babies, mistaken identities, and failed murder plots. Indeed, the
play contains more occurrences of the word *tukhē* than any other extant Greek tragedy and it marks all the key moments in the plot.[8] But
the telos is pure *anankē*: no less than in Sophocles' *Oedipus Tyrannus*,
that end is written from the start. We know all along that Ion is really
the progenitor of Athens and its Ionian empire: his destiny is fixed in
advance and the only question is how he will fulfill it. The play thus
pits the ideological certainty of the end against the contingency of the
dramatic means: we know where we have to end up, but we spend most
of the play uncertain that we will ever get there. It is precisely this uncertainty, however, that makes us determined to reach that telos and
makes us so invested in it as a telos. It makes the audience long for
their own national and imperial destiny even as they are shown its essential contingency. What ultimately secures this precarious destiny is
their own spectatorial desire, the longing for an ending that the play
induces through the openness of its structure and contingency of its
plotting.

In this way the play's formal structure leads the audience toward a
psychic attachment that withstands any critique, even those the play
itself poses. It is in this formal *psukhagōgia* that I locate the play's ideological force, not in what it says about Athenian citizenship and imperialism (although, as we shall see, it has much to say on those topics), but
in the way it makes us feel about them, in the imaginary relation it
produces toward them. This shift of focus from ideology as determinate
content to ideology as affective structure allows us to move beyond a
critical impasse in political approaches to this play and to tragedy as a
whole, that is, the debate as to whether tragedy celebrates or contests
Athenian ideology. *Ion* has provided support for both readings. To
some its patriotic myth and explicitly political ending make the play a
glorification of Athenian unity and imperial power in harmony with the
overall ideological tone of the City Dionysia.[9] Others stress the violence
and deception necessary to secure this glorious future, and take *Ion* as a
trenchant critique of Athens's foundation myth and the civic self-image
and imperial policies built on it.[10]

But if ideology is less a determinate set of beliefs than an affective
relation to those beliefs, then these seemingly contradictory readings
are in fact mutually compatible, for the affect may be sustained even if
the beliefs are demonstrated to be ungrounded, false, or pernicious.[11]

Ion shows the Athenian ideologies of autochthony and imperial hegemony to be arbitrary and contingent, as all ideologies are. But it makes its audience long for those ideologies nonetheless, and all the more so the more arbitrary they are shown to be. With its digressive plot and happy ending, *Ion* has sometimes been labeled a "romance."[12] We might consider it an ideological romance. Its *muthos* not only depicts the passionate attachment of ideology; it psychagogically enacts it, as its drama of *tukhē* and telos arouses a spectatorial desire that makes the contingent seem destined and transforms luck into necessity.

• • •

Ion is a story of reunion between a boy and his mother. Creusa, daughter of the Athenian king Erechtheus, had been raped by Apollo and in shame had exposed the baby, leaving him in a cave to die. But Apollo had taken care of his child: he sent Hermes to transport him from Athens to Delphi, where the boy, Ion, grew up as a temple servant, ignorant of his true parentage. In the first scene we meet Ion, a charming naif whose joyful devotion to his holy duties is tinged with the melancholy of an orphan. It just so happens—the first of many such lucky coincidences—that Creusa and her husband Xuthus have come to Delphi to inquire of the oracle how they can remedy their childlessness. Creusa and Ion happen to meet, and mother and son feel an immediate sympathetic bond, although they do not know the other's identity. Xuthus, meanwhile, has received an oracle that, unbeknownst to him, he already has a son, and that son will be the first person he meets as he is going out of the temple. Who would that be but Ion, whom Xuthus names "Ion" from the verb "to go": "I name you Ion, a name fitting this lucky encounter" (*Iōna d'onomazō se tēi tukhēi prepon*, 661). Xuthus, overjoyed at his newfound heir, plans to take Ion back to Athens to establish him in the seat of power. This false recognition, based on a false prophecy, sets in motion a series of near catastrophes: Creusa, in despair at her own ostensible childlessness and the thought of this intruder on her family throne, tries to kill Ion. She poisons his wine, but when a bird dies after it chanced to drink some of the spilt liquid, the plot is discovered. Pursued by the Delphians, Creusa takes refuge at the altar of Apollo, where Ion finds her and is about to kill her. But just at that moment—lucky timing—the Priestess who had raised Ion reveals the tokens she had found with the abandoned baby: a young girl's weaving, a golden snake necklace, and a garland of olive leaves, still green after all these years. These items identify Ion as Creusa's long-lost child, and the play ends (or, as we'll see, almost ends) with the joyful reunion of mother and son.

A happy ending, then, and for the Athenian audience a necessary one, for they would have known that this is not just any ordinary mother and son. Creusa, as the play constantly reminds us, is the daughter of Erechtheus whose father Erichthonius was Athena's offspring, born from the very soil of Attica. The Athenians claimed descent from this original monarch and through him they imagined themselves as autochthonous, born of the earth, and brothers united by this royal lineage.[13] This autochthonous origin was vital to the Athenians' communal identity, rooting it in the soil and the blood, and was codified in the Periclean law that defined an Athenian citizen as the son of two Athenian parents. "Athenian-ness" was not just a legal status but a matter of *phusis* (nature, birth, heredity), a point on which the play insists by emphasizing the outsider status of the Euboean Xuthus, who is *eugenēs* but not *engenēs*, noble but not native (291–93). This autochthonous Athenian bloodline is nearly broken by the separation of Ion and Creusa and is resecured—along with the civic identity it entails—in their reunion. At the same time, Athenian audiences would have known that Ion was not just the simple boy we see happily sweeping the temple steps, but the progenitor of Ionia, the Greek area of Asia Minor that formed the core of Athens's empire in the fifth century.[14] So when they heard the name Ion, they would have thought not of the chance encounter of Xuthus going out of the temple, but of Athens's imperial destiny, a destiny inherited along with their pure autochthonous blood from this early Athenian king. Ion's name thus encapsulates the play's paradox of means and ends, bringing together the pure contingency of the former—"I name you Ion, a name fitting with *tukhē*"—and the historical necessity of the latter.

Ion opens with a proleptic prologue delivered by the god Hermes, who tells us in advance how everything will work out. He tells of Apollo's rape of Creusa and her exposure of the child, affirming both his divine paternity (35) and his relation to "the autochthonous people of famous Athens" (29–30; cf. 9–11, 20–26). Hermes presents the background to the plot—Ion's upbringing in the temple, Creusa and Xuthus's longing for children—and concludes: "Apollo is driving *tukhē* to this point, and it has not escaped his notice, as it seems" (*Loxias de tēn tukhēn es tout' elaunei, k'ou lelēthen, hōs dokei*, 67–68). He then sets out Apollo's plan and, we presume, the play's plot: Apollo will tell Xuthus the child is his, Xuthus will take Ion back to Athens where he will be recognized by Creusa and will come into his rightful inheritance without their secret affair ever being made public. "Thus he will name him Ion, founder of the Asian land, a name famous throughout Greece" (74–75). The prologue ends with a patriotic flourish and Hermes withdraws to watch the action unfold.

So we know how the play has to end and we're told from the beginning how it will end. And in fact that is, more or less, how it does end. After mother and son are reunited, Athena appears to put the play's events in their larger civic context, an ideological epilogue, as it were. She confirms Ion's divine paternity and the autochthonous maternity that, she says, make him worthy to rule over Athens and famous throughout Greece (1573–75). She also predicts the civic destiny that will be his legacy to the Athenians: Ion will have four sons who will give their names to the four tribes of Attica; their descendants will settle the islands of the Aegean and the coast of Asia Minor that, Athena says, "give strength to my land" (1584–85). "The Ionians, named for Ion, will have glory" (1587–88). The ideological consequences of the story are spelled out in no uncertain terms: in fact, we are rather hit over the head with them.[15] The telos is thus heavily overdetermined in every way: ideologically, dramaturgically, even theologically, as Athena reaffirms the justice of Apollo, which has been openly questioned throughout the play. Her brother, Athena tells us, has "managed everything well" (1595). And so she bids Ion and Creusa farewell and proclaims "a happy fate for you after this cessation of suffering" (1604–5).

The goddess assures us of the happiness of the happy ending. This divine assurance—or reassurance—is needed because that telos has been undermined continually throughout the play. First, it has been undermined by the myriad alternate possible endings the play imagines. These constitute a series of counterfactual histories of Athens, or rather anti-histories of an Athens that never came to be. Baby Ion dies in the cave. Adult Ion dies at the hands of his mother, or she at his. Ion goes back to Athens with Xuthus, and Creusa kills him there. Or nothing happens: Creusa and Ion fail to recognize one another, Xuthus crosses paths with some other temple servant and adopts him as his son, and Ion continues his peaceful existence in Delphi, never learning his true identity. Any one of these narratives would derail the play's patriotic telos: Ion would fail to become Ion and Athens would fail to become Athens. These counterfactual narratives and alternate possible endings are the work of *tukhē*, but so, too, is the fact that they don't pan out. The fact that Ion does not die from his mother's poison, for instance, is a double stroke of luck: when they are raising the libation that Ion is to drink from the poisoned cup, one of the servants curses, and Ion, taking this as an ill-omen, orders a fresh cup of wine. He pours out the first cup on the ground, where a bird drinks it and immediately dies (1187–1215). Ion's survival is a matter of luck and Athens's glorious history the result of *tukhē*, just one possible telos among many others.

But maybe it only seems like *tukhē*. The bird that drinks the poison meant for Ion is sacred to Apollo (1197–98), and the messenger credits the god with averting the murder (1118). Likewise, it is Apollo who prompts the Priestess to reveal the tokens of Ion's identity, which she has kept secret all these years, just in the nick of time to prevent him from killing his mother (1342–53). Many readers have seen the god's hand behind these strokes of fortune and have taken this as the play's message: what looks to mortals like *tukhē* is, in fact, divine *anankē*.[16] As Hermes says in the prologue: "Apollo is driving *tukhē* to this point, and it has not escaped his notice, as it seems" (67–68). But how are we to understand this "as it seems" (*hōs dokei*)? Is it Apollo's neglect that is only apparent or his control over *tukhē*? This equivocation injects a note of uncertainty that lingers until the end. Is Athens's glorious destiny a matter of divine necessity or is it just plain luck?

Apollo's plan, Hermes told us, was for Ion and Creusa to be reunited back in Athens and his own involvement in the affair to remain secret. But as it turns out, Creusa recognizes Ion in Delphi, not in Athens, and only after the two have nearly killed one another. The divine plot prolepsis is misleading. Perhaps this is no more than we should expect from the god of thieves and tricksters, but it also implicates Apollo, whose divine providence supposedly governs this *muthos*.[17] The god's plan and the play's plot don't fully match up, and Euripides goes out of his way to remind us of this at the end, when, instead of Apollo, the *deus* we expect *ex machina*, we get the *dea* Athena. Immediately preceding the goddess's appearance, Creusa tells Ion that Apollo is his father; Ion, still mistrustful, is about to go into the temple to ask the god himself for the truth. Athena's appearance prevents Ion—and us—from securely ascertaining that truth. She affirms that Apollo is his father (1560), but we never hear it from Apollo himself, and her excuses merely call attention to his evasiveness: Apollo didn't come himself, she says, because he did not want to face Creusa and Ion nor for their reproaches to become public (1557–59). Athena then repeats Hermes' account of their brother's original plan: Apollo had intended to have

Ion discover his identity once he was back in Athens, "but when the matter was disclosed, fearing that you would die by your mother's plotting and she by yours, he saved you by his own devices" (*mēkhanais*, 1563–65). Athena's appearance *apo tēs mēkhanēs* is but the latest of those devices. The god's ultimate goal is obtained—Ion does come to know his identity—but not in the way he had intended. Athena commends the god for "managing everything well" (*kalōs d'Apollōn pant' epraxe*, 1595). And yet amid the play's twists and turns, the god of prophecy seems to lose control over his own plan, to fall victim to a *tukhē* that nearly derails the telos of his divine will.

In fact, even after the god's will is done, it isn't really done, and there is still a chance that things might go wrong. Even as she promises Ion and Creusa a "blessed fate" (1605), Athena warns them not to tell Xuthus that Ion is her son, "so that he may remain happy in his belief [that the boy is his] and you may go and enjoy your prosperity" (1602–3). Even after they have succeeded, they could still fail, the divine father's plan overturned by the jealous human father and Athens's glorious history cut short before it even begins. So Ion's identity is exposed in Delphi but will remain a secret in Athens: there the affair will seem to have concluded with one of the alternate endings the play imagined but rejected, and Ion himself will be known as the product of a Delphic one-night stand (545–55) found in a lucky encounter outside the temple. The deception and concealment, the mistaken identities and failed *anagnōriseis* that nearly drove this play off course will continue even in Athens. The end is thus not really the end, and as the characters head off home, we can expect more detours and false turns along the way.

On the one hand, then, with the reunion of Creusa and Ion the audience get the ending they are expecting, the one they were promised in the prologue and knew, as Ion's Athenian descendants, was historically probable and necessary. On the other hand, as I have been suggesting, the lingering force of *tukhē* is still felt in this final scene, undermining its finality and its necessity. The god's plan is fulfilled, but not as he expected, and it could still fail; the play's plot has reached its telos, but it is only one possible telos and maybe not even the final one. The play's means destabilize its end, leaving us with a nagging sense of irresolution as we look backward at the meaning of the play and forward at its future consequences for the polis.

In this unsettled and unsettling finale, is Euripides challenging his Athenian audience to acknowledge that their national myth is built on violence and deception, that their imperial power is a matter of sheer luck, not divine necessity? Many scholars have thought so and have read the play as a pointed critique of Athens's most cherished ideologies. Its multiple near misses and strokes of fortune undercut any simple conviction of Athens's destined greatness. At the same time, the vivid horror of Creusa's rape and the murder by which, spurred on by the vicious chauvinism of the chorus and her old tutor, she plans to avenge her misery expose the violence and xenophobia behind the city's ideology of autochthony. The happy ending may suggest the political necessity of these flattering myths of divine favor and racial purity, but it also emphasizes their inherent fictionality, their limitations, and their high cost, especially for women.[18]

I basically agree with these readings, but I think they tell only half the story. In fact, I think they miss something fundamental about the experience of watching or even reading this play, and that is our desire for the reunion of Ion and Creusa. This intimate *anagnōrisis*, this private "romance" of separation and reunion, is the narrative engine of the play, and it is propelled by a pathos so intense that the desire for recognition becomes a palpable yearning.[19] In the first episode Ion and Creusa learn of each other's loss, not realizing that each is the object of the other's longing. Their corresponding melancholy, emphasized by the tight responsion of the dialogue, creates an immediate bond between them, a "harmony of pathos" (*prosōidos . . . t'ōmōi pathei*, 359; cf. 312, 320). The language used to describe their relationship, intensely desiderative and markedly physical, heightens the pathos. After the encounter with Xuthus, Ion is pleased to have found his supposed father but still yearns for his mother: "Oh dear mother," he cries, "when will I see you too? Now I long (*pothō*) to see you even more than before, whoever you are. But perhaps you are dead and I could not see you even in my dreams" (563–65). Likewise, when Creusa hears the false oracle that she "will never hold a child in her arms nor embrace it to [her] breast" (761–62), she responds "Oimoi, let me die" (763), and longs to escape into the air (796–99), a fantasy that marks the extreme of tragic duress. She relives the abandonment of her infant over and over again, remembering him stretching out his tiny hands for her embrace (961–63; cf. 1458–61, 1491–95), and laments his assumed death in the emotional lyrics for which Euripides was famous (897–904, 916–18). As Ion sums up their separate fates just before the final recognition: "I shed wet tears when I think about the woman who bore me. . . . For all the time

I should have been warmed in my mother's arms, delighting in life, I was deprived of my dearest mother's care.[20] And the poor woman who bore me! She has suffered the same sorrow, losing the pleasure of her child" (1369–79). For both mother and son, a life of separation from the other is unlivable (*abioton*, 670, 764).

The characters' visceral yearning for reunion is mimetically reproduced for the audience by the play's structure. The *anagnōrisis* comes unusually late in this play, one of its most striking structural features. Usually in Euripides' plays of recognition and intrigue, the recognition precedes the intrigue.[21] So, for example, in *Helen*, first Helen and Menelaus recognize one another, and then they plot their escape. But in *Ion*, the recognition is delayed and comes only after Creusa and Ion, in their ignorance, have reached a murderous pitch of hostility. This delay turns the *anagnōrisis* into the play's telos, not a means toward the end but the end itself. From the prologue on, this is the moment we are waiting for, and Euripides makes innovative use of tragedy's formal elements to heighten the suspense. The first episode features a long dialogue between Ion and Creusa in the rapid question-and-response format of stichomythia.[22] Euripides often uses stichomythia to lead up to a recognition scene, and this one is replete with ironies that build our anticipation, as when Creusa first congratulates Ion's mother for having such a son (308), then pities her for losing him, "whoever she was" (324). But the stichomythia teases our expectations.[23] Instead of the anticipated reunion between mother and son, we get a false recognition, the parodic *anagnōrisis* between Xuthus, ebullient at the thought that he's found his son, and a very bewildered Ion. The scene is played for humor: Xuthus is buffoonish, and when he greets Ion at first sight and tries to embrace him, Ion thinks he is out of his mind or possibly coming on to him (518–30).[24] Xuthus eventually explains the prophecy—that the first person he met on leaving the temple would be his son—and Ion reluctantly embraces him as his father. This false recognition sets in motion the train of events that nearly derails the real recognition as Creusa, in despair, tries to kill her own son. The suspense is sustained up until the final scene. Just as Ion is threatening to kill Creusa at the altar of Apollo, the Delphic priestess fortuitously enters, carrying the chest containing the tokens she had found years before with the baby Ion. Ion tearfully takes the chest in the hope that he will finally be able to find his mother, but then decides instead to dedicate it, unopened, to Apollo. We are made to wait one more painful minute—

thinking the recognition may still fail at this eleventh hour—before he changes his mind and decides to open the chest.

Just when we feel we can't bear it any longer, Ion reveals the birth tokens and the recognition comes like a bolt of lightning. Creusa immediately recognizes the chest; Ion, initially suspicious (as in the earlier false recognition with Xuthus), is quickly convinced as she describes the recovered tokens. "Oh my dearest mother," he cries, "I fall upon your joyful cheeks in my joy at seeing you." "Oh child," she replies, "oh light greater than the sun's to your mother . . . I hold you in my arms, a discovery I didn't dare hope for" (1437–41). With this emotional reunion, everything comes together. "I am no longer barren and childless," Creusa sings. "The house has a hearth, the land has rulers. Erechtheus is young again!" (1463–65). *Tukhē* has been transformed into *eutukhia*, good fortune, and *eudaimonia*, blessed happiness (1456–57, 1501–14).

The play thus uses all its structural and poetic resources to make us yearn for the *anagnōrisis*, and to make that recognition feel, when it finally comes, emotionally satisfying. Every delay and detour—and the whole play is essentially delay and detour—merely intensifies our longing for this reunion of mother and son and makes it seem natural and necessary, even as we have seen the strokes of luck by which it is reached. Ion and Creusa's recognition is also the audience's own, both as spectators and as Athenians. As spectators, we recognize their reunion as the play's proper ending, the ending promised from the start, anticipated by Creusa and Ion's immediate and symmetrical sympathy, sustained through the play's multiple repetitions and reversals, and clinched with the last-minute revelation of the birth tokens mentioned by Hermes in the prologue (21–27): the golden snakes of Erichthonius, as well as Creusa's girlhood weaving of the Gorgon and the evergreen garland from Athena's sacred olive. Hermes' emphasis on the Erechtheid snakes at the start primes us to expect their return at the end—to expect, in fact, that their return will signal the end—an expectation kept alive by the recurrent chthonic imagery that runs throughout the play.[25] With this structural and thematic closure, we have the satisfaction of recognizing the design of the whole, a pleasure in the play's aesthetic form heightened by that form.[26] That formal pleasure is also ideological, of course, for the tokens are symbols of Athens's unbroken autochthonous lineage and eternal flourishing, and this recognition of mother and son is also the Athenian audience's self-recognition as their blessed heirs.[27] Spectatorial satisfaction and ideological satisfaction arrive together in this final scene, driven by the play's wave of pathos. Athena's appearance at the end merely states aloud what the viewers have already been made to feel in their hearts: that Ion and Creusa's *eudaimonia* is that of Athens and her citizens as well.

The play's swell toward emotional closure is so strong that it sweeps away everything in its path. One of the things it sweeps away, ironically, is actual politics. When Xuthus had planned to take his newfound son back to Athens to a life of wealth and power (581), Ion resisted, condemning the frenetic competition of Athenian political life in terms familiar from fifth-century anti-democratic discourse: the competitive rough-and-tumble of Athenian democracy, with its class resentments and overbearing mob, is not for him (585–647). Contemporary democratic politics are depicted in considerable detail, only to be cast aside as one of the play's rejected counterfactuals. Associated with the false recognition, the reunion with a false father who is also a false Athenian (63–64, 290, 589–92, 813), they are a narrative dead-end. They are repudiated in favor of a myth explicitly acknowledged as such, for, as Xuthus pragmatically remarks, "The ground does not bring forth children" (542).[28]

That myth had a politics of its own, of course: Creusa is not just a bereft mother but also an Erechtheid, and her barrenness means the end of her royal line. From Hermes' first mention of the golden snakes, Athena's gift to her son Erichthonius, we know that the positive resolution of the *muthos* will coincide with the restoration of the dynasty, and our narrative expectations are closely bound to the fortunes of this aristocratic house.[29] *Ion* thus opens itself to the sort of reading I offered of *Alcestis* in the introduction, where the play's happy ending was shown to come at the price of acquiescence to elite exceptionalism, to the fact that Admetus, unlike the rest of us, does not have to die. *Ion*, too, asks us to cheer at the restored good fortune of an elite family. But in this case, that family is *our* family and its good fortune our own. The perpetual rule of an aristocratic dynasty is euphemized in the politically acceptable form of the autochthony myth that made every Athenian citizen a trueborn aristocrat. At the same time, it is depoliticized, segregated from the unsavory political realities back in Athens, which are figured as no more than a momentary interruption in the timeless cycle of this elite bloodline. With the return of the birth tokens, structural repetition creates a dramatic closure that projects a horizon of genealogical repetition stretching far beyond the play, as the Erechtheid dynasty will be reborn with each new generation of Athenian citizens. "Erechtheus is young again!"

In this juxtaposition of true and false recognition, of repetition and detour, Athenian identity is freed from democratic politics; it becomes instead an essence, unchanging and eternal. That essence transcends all concrete political positions. Many Athenians sitting in the audience of this play—not to mention the numerous non-Athenians present at the City Dionysia—were no doubt uncomfortable with the claim that Athens was destined for imperial rule: we hear in contemporary sources vehement debate over precisely what Ionian kinship entailed in terms of actual imperial policy. Likewise, many good democrats in the audience would have found both Ion's elitist distaste for the mob and the idea that the future of the democratic city depends on the continuity of an aristocratic bloodline politically objectionable. The date of *Ion* is disputed, but it was likely produced in the late 410s, a period (as we shall see in chapter 5) of intensifying class conflict, in which the genealogical purity and inherited rule of a birth elite may not have struck all citizens as desirable ends. But in a sense, none of that matters here. Yoked to the romance of Ion and Creusa's reunion, Athenian ideology is stripped of any contention or contestation—any real politics. It becomes as simple and as pure as a mother's love.[30]

The very structure of this play is thus ideological, not only in that it leads to a specific vision of Athens but more importantly in the way it induces in its audience a certain imaginative relation to that vision. The more the *anagnōrisis* is delayed—the more *tukhē* threatens to derail the telos—the more invested we become in the play's reaching that end. This tension between dramatic means and ideological end transforms our relationship to that end, changing us from ideological tourists into participants. That may seem a strange way to put it, but tourism is a recurring theme in the play, beginning with the entrance of the chorus. These Athenian serving women of Creusa have accompanied their mistress to Delphi and are excited to see all the famous sights. Their entrance song takes the form of a touristic ekphrasis, as they point out to one another the beautiful temples and the mythological scenes engraved on them. "Look, see here: it's Heracles slaying the Hydra! . . . And I see Pallas Athena, my own goddess!" (190–92, 211).[31] This ekphrastic ode situates the chorus as spectators of the Delphic drama, in contrast to Creusa, who closes her eyes and cannot bear to look at the temple of the god who has brought her so much suffering (241–51).

But as the play progresses, these tourists lose their spectatorial distance and become more and more involved in the action. In fact, they take on an extraordinarily active role in the play. They tell Creusa about the oracle that Xuthus had received, despite his command, on pain of death, that they remain silent (666–67). They even elaborate on this oracle, not only relating Xuthus's discovery of his son, but also reporting that Creusa was destined never to have a child of her own (761–62). This unusual choral intervention precipitates the events that will lead to Creusa's attempt on Ion's life, a murder they both anticipate and incite with the violent fantasies of their odes—"May the boy die before he ever comes to my city" (719–20)—and for which they will share the punishment (1229–49). Swept up by their sympathy for Creusa's suffering and their devotion to her royal house, they are transformed from spectators—mere tourists—into bloodthirsty agents in the play's disastrous action.

Meanwhile, Ion himself undergoes a similar transformation. When we first meet him, Ion is a contented, albeit orphaned, Delphic temple servant. When he encounters Creusa and discovers that she is the daughter of Erechtheus, he questions her about her family's mythic history with the eager curiosity of a tourist: tell me, stranger, is it true, the story people tell, that your ancestor was born from the earth? Did Athena really give him to the daughters of Cecrops to raise, as it is shown in paintings? (265–83). His relation to his own family history is ekphrastic: he knows of it from stories and paintings and asks about it as an outsider, little realizing that it is in fact his own. "What concern is the daughter of Erechtheus to me?" he asks. "She is no relation" (433–34). Likewise, when Xuthus takes Ion back to Athens, he plans to spare his wife's feelings by introducing the boy as a foreign guest (*xenos*) and a tourist (*theatēs*, 654–60). But of course we know all along what Ion will eventually discover: he is no stranger—either to the bloodline of the Erechtheids or to the city of Athens. The questions he poses to Creusa are answered by the *anagnōrisis*, as he himself becomes the living proof that the tales of Athenian autochthony are true.

Like Ion and the chorus, we too are transformed from spectators to participants in this ideological romance. At first we watch the action onstage with a detached spectatorial pleasure. Like the chorus picking out Athena on the Delphic frieze, we know this Delphic story is our own, but we can watch it unfold with a certain ironic distance because we, unlike the characters, know how it is going to end. Indeed, this irony is pervasive at the start of the play and is a large part of its pleasure. Ion's monody, for example, as he sweeps the temple steps, derives much of its charm from the fact that we know this humble servant is in truth the future king of Athens. The tension between the song's elevated hymnic form and its quotidian contents adds to this enjoyable irony, casting Ion's lowly chores in a sacral light. Thus, when Ion sings "Phoebus is the father who bore me; I praise the one who nurtures me and call my benefactor by the name of father" (136–40), we can smile at the irony, confident (because we've been assured by Hermes in the prologue of this divine parentage and the Ionian destiny that rests upon it) that by the end Ion will know the truth.[32] Likewise, the ironic near-recognitions between Ion and Creusa are poignant without being painful because we know they are only temporary. Our patriotic certainty of the outcome thus allows us to enjoy the dramatic *desis* (bind) in the comforting knowledge of its eventual *lusis* (resolution).

But this changes as the play progresses: the romance of separation and reunion initially secured by our certainty of its end now threatens to forestall that end. We lose our touristic distance from the action. As we are drawn into Creusa's suffering, it becomes harder and harder to remember that all will be well that ends well. In this play full of repetitions, the scene of Creusa's rape and infanticide is repeated again and again: in Hermes' matter-of-fact account in the prologue, in Creusa's disguised narrative of her "friend" in the first episode, in her desperate monody and the painful unfolding of its compressed trauma in the ensuing dialogue.[33] Each reiteration draws us closer to the action, diminishing our spectatorial distance and the comfort of our superior knowledge.

The turning point comes in the moving lyric monody in which Creusa recalls the scene of her rape and laments with stark despair the presumed death of her child (859–921). Structurally this ode mirrors Ion's monody in the first episode, but its intense subjectivity—announced in the opening apostrophe to her own *psukhē* (859)—deprives us of the ironic distance of that ode, with its pleasant discrepancy between lofty form and humble content. Like Ion's song, Creusa's is framed as a hymn, beginning with an invocation to Apollo as god of the lyre and "the beautiful-resounding hymns of the Muses" (881–86). Instead of calling on the god to come to her, though, this bitter hymn describes how he came:

> ἦλθές μοι χρυσῶι χαίταν
> μαρμαίρων, εὖτ' ἐς κόλπους

κρόκεα πέταλα φάρεσιν ἔδρεπον
†ἀνθίζειν† χρυσανταυγῆ·
λευκοῖς δ' ἐμφὺς καρποῖσιν
χειρῶν εἰς ἄντρου κοίτας
κραυγὰν Ὦ μᾶτέρ μ' αὐδῶσαν
θεὸς ὁμευνέτας
ἆγες ἀναιδείαι
Κύπριδι χάριν πράσσων.

You came to me, hair glimmering with gold,
when I was gathering saffron into my lap,
the petals reflecting gold on my veils.
Gripping me by my white wrists
into the cave-chamber,
uttering a cry—Oh Mother!–
my divine bedmate,
you led me,
gratifying shameless Aphrodite. (887–96)

The sustained second-person address lends a terrible intimacy to the mythic setting (an allusion to the paradigmatic rape of Persephone by Hades), as we move slowly, the main verb delayed, from the hymnic epiphany, through the golden beauty of the meadow into the cave filled by her choked cry, and finally to the dreadful, euphemistically bland act. She goes on to describe the birth of the child in that same miserable cave, and her exposure of the infant "with a mother's shudder" (898): "And now he is gone, snatched up as a feast for birds, my child and yours. But you, wretch, you keep on playing your lyre and singing your hymns" (902–6).

Perhaps, as some readers have suggested, the hymnic form of this song reminds us that Creusa's reproach is groundless, that the child she thinks is dead is really alive, and that Apollo will make good her grief in the end.[34] But in the immediate dramatic moment, the ode's tension between form and content ironizes not the content but the form. In Ion's monody, the hymnic form cast a sweet irony over the humble chores of Apollo's secret son. But now theological form—both the aesthetic structure of the hymn and the structure of faith in benevolent gods—no longer provides a reassuring framework for the dark substance of human suffering nor the guarantee of a divinely ordained telos, either for the characters (whose loss of faith precipitates the murderous action to follow) or for us in the audience.

Without that guarantee, the ironies that were poignant and pleasurable at the beginning become excruciating by the end, as when Creusa, clinging to the altar of Apollo, begs for her life in the god's name and Ion responds, "What do you share in common with Phoebus?" (1284); or when Ion demands she leave the altar and Creusa taunts him to "go and tell it to your mother" (1307). The drama of the means makes us lose sight of the end. The ideological telos becomes a point of anxiety, not security, precarious in itself and too fragile to allow us a safe touristic distance from the action. Will mother and son be reunited? Will Ion return to Athens to guarantee our autochthonous bloodline and imperial future? Will Athens become Athens? The audience become as uncertain of the end as the characters themselves. And so when that happy ending comes—with a final reiteration of Creusa's trauma as she recounts the story of his birth to her newfound son—we welcome it, as they do, as a miracle. That miraculous closure is not the work of divine necessity, though, as the prologue asked us to believe. Instead, it is the product of our own spectatorial desire, which is to say, of the drama that produces that desire. Athens's glorious history, which at the beginning of the play we confidently took for granted, by the end emerges as an object of our longing, a longing the play generates, frustrates, and finally satisfies.

Or at least mostly satisfies. Maybe one is left worried, given all that's gone before, about the continued deception of Xuthus and Ion's future in Athens. Maybe one wishes for more certain proof of paternity for Ion, who at the end still doubts the veracity of the oracle and is heading to seek confirmation when Athena appears (1437–48). Maybe one feels cheated of justice for Creusa, for even if Apollo is proved innocent of letting his son die (1600), he never addresses her recrimination that he unjustly deprived a mother of her child (357–58, 384–89), and in his guilty absence her larger theological question—"Where should we appeal for justice if we are to be ruined by the injustices of our divine lords?" (253–54)—is left hanging.[35] But if the end doesn't leave us completely satisfied, Athena consoles, or at least distracts us with her promise of Athens's future glory. The ideological desire produced by the plotline of separation and reunion smooths over any remaining rough edges in that plotline, both for us in the audience and for the characters, who forgive Apollo on the spot and proclaim his beneficence. Ion accepts his divine paternity, which even before, he says, "was not implausible" (1606–8). Creusa, who had earlier said that the god could never make amends for his sins against her (425–28), now applauds him for returning the child he had neglected, "although I did not do so before" (1609). And so they all head off to Athens, praising both the gods and the polis. If the characters' immediate acquiescence and sudden belief seems forced, the Athenian viewer's own sense of the obvious rightness of this patriotic ending covers over the discrepancies, and his relieved self-recognition as its fortunate beneficiary proves the truth of Athena's closing assertion: "The god's will takes time but it is not without strength in the end" (*es telos*, 1615).

In this way civic ideology is transformed from something external to the drama, enabling its ironies and guaranteeing in advance its happy conclusion, to something that emerges from its very structure, from its tension between *tukhē* and telos, means and ends. In this ideological romance, ideology figures less as the object-cause of desire than its product. For if at the end, despite any niggling doubts, we celebrate the inauguration of Athens's autochthonous dynasty and future imperial might, it is because the play's contingencies have made us long for that final certainty and welcome it as we would a mother's loving embrace.

• • •

The character Euripides in Aristophanes' *Frogs* claims that his tragedy is the most democratic because it teaches the demos to think, to challenge, to ask questions (952–79). Many have seen that education at work in the open structure of Euripides' dramas. This interpretation kills a lot of birds with one stone: it promises to explain the difficult aesthetics of Euripidean tragedy and its seeming indifference to dramatic unity or coherence; it chimes with contemporary Athenian reception of Euripidean drama, at least as Aristophanes represents it. Most importantly, it reinforces a vision that we hold dear, of Athenian democracy as a regime that thrived on questioning and challenging by its citizens, and a vision that we hold equally dear, of tragedy as the genre that provoked that democratic questioning and challenging.

I don't really dispute this view, but I hope to have shown that for all their openness and questioning, Euripides' plays also produce a kind of closure, an investment in a secure dramatic and ideological end. That closure should not be moralized as the antithesis of democratic freedom; instead, it should be imagined as the passionate attachment to certain ideological tenets that is essential to any political system, even one as relatively open as Athens's radical democracy. *Ion* shows how that attachment not only survives critique—including the play's own—but is in fact strengthened by it: the more contingent ideology is shown to be, the more necessary it becomes. Thus it makes little sense to ask whether tragedy supports or subverts Athenian civic ideology: simultaneously denaturalizing Athens's civic myths and naturalizing the audience's attachment to them, *Ion* shows that it may do both at once. In the process, it suggests that ideology is less a determinate content than a "structure of feeling," in Raymond Williams's famous phrase,[36] and that tragedy's ideological force lies not in its mimetic representation (positive or negative) of the former but in its psychagogic manipulation of the latter.

Ion allows us to see how this "structure of feeling" emerges out of the formal structure of the play, through its repetitions and reversals, its arousal and satisfaction of desire, its pacing of suspense and resolution. The play's tension between means and ends stages the process by which the psychic attachments of ideology are generated and sustained. Thus we might consider dramatic form as a mode of political theory: a way of thinking about, and getting the audience to think about, the imaginary relations that subtend the real relations of the polis. But ultimately I hope to have advanced a stronger claim, for I've suggested that *Ion* not only represents the process of ideological attachment but enacts that process. Sweeping its audience up in its swell of emotion, this romance invites them to experience that passionate attachment even as it allows them to think critically about it. To say this is to suggest that ideology is not something tragedy depicts but something it *does*, and that aesthetic form is not only a kind of political theory but a mode of political practice, not just a *mimēsis* of a political *praxis*, but that *praxis* itself.

CHAPTER 2

Beautiful Tears

This chapter starts from a simple observation and a simple question. The observation is that the essence of Greek tragedy is the staging of beautiful suffering. Tragedy shows its protagonists in situations of extreme duress: grief, destitution, madness. But they express their misery in meter and ornament their despair with poetic imagery. Tragedy makes suffering beautiful. That is the observation. The question follows immediately from this: what is the effect of watching this beautiful suffering? What does listening to tragedy's "songs of sorrow" do for us—and to us?[1]

It may seem jejune to talk of beauty, and especially the beauty of Greek tragedy. After all, one of the great advances of the New Historicist approach to tragedy, with its emphasis on the text's political meaning, was to move beyond a New Critical hermeneutic that, at its worst, seemed to do nothing more than document the beauty of the beautiful. But aesthetic judgments bring with them questions of ethics and politics. This was certainly true for the Greeks. Theirs was a culture that used the same word, *kalos*, to refer to physical attractiveness, ethical virtue, and social standing, and for which a well-governed city could be described as a thing of beauty. Or think of Plato's ladder of enlightenment in the *Symposium*: one starts by appreciating the physical beauty of a single handsome youth; from there one goes on to be a lover of all physical beauty; then of beauty of the soul; then beauty in practices, laws, and sciences; and finally of the Absolute Beauty accessible only to the philosopher (*Symposium* 210b–c). Beauty, for Plato, drives us toward the Good.

This attractive theory has recently been revived by Elaine Scarry, in her essay *On Beauty and Being Just* (1999). Scarry argues that seeing beauty in the world makes us aspire to justice. Looking at the symmetry of a butterfly or a palm tree makes us want to find the same symmetry in social relations. If that symmetry is absent in society, beauty spurs our aspiration to create it. Thus, she concludes, "It is the very symmetry of beauty which leads us to, or somehow assists us in discovering, the symmetry that eventually comes into place in the realm of justice."[2]

But what about tragedy? Tragedy would seem to put tremendous strain on this theory because its beauty is so often the aestheticization of human misery. What happens when we look at the beautiful spectacle of tragic suffering? Does this beauty make us just? Plato, ironically, thought not. Ever a literalist when it came to mimesis, he feared the degrading effects of tragedy's scenes of woe: watching heroes moaning and weeping onstage will encourage men to give way to such base and immoderate behavior themselves (*Republic* 603e–606e); poetry's "sweetened muse" (607a5) should accordingly be banned from the ideal city. For Aristotle, by contrast, tragedy's beautiful suffering is redeemed through the emotional response it produces in its audience: the clarification, or catharsis, of pity and fear. For Aristotle, this response was cognitive and ethical, not purely emotional. Pity, in particular, was for Aristotle—and it seems for the Greeks in general—a discerning emotion, reserved for unmerited suffering.[3] When we pity the suffering we see on stage we are making cognitive judgments about the ethics of the action and the moral responsibility of the agents. And that emotional-cognitive process is aroused by beauty—for Aristotle the beauty not of lyric lamentation, to which he is notoriously indifferent, but of an exquisitely unified plot—and it produces an experience that is both pleasurable and morally beneficial. For Aristotle, then, tragedy's formal beauty, by arousing our pity, might in fact make us just.

Yoked to questions of justice, tragic pity is a fundamentally political emotion. This is especially obvious in the plays I will discuss in this chapter. War plays (or, as many critics argue, antiwar plays) produced while Athens was at war, they depict with tremendous pathos exactly the sort of suffering that Athens was itself inflicting on others—and continued to inflict still after watching these pathetic performances. The Athenians prided themselves on their pity, and they remarked upon this disconnect between their emotions in the theater and their responses in real life.[4] If pity did not translate into concrete ameliorative action, what good are tragedy's displays of beautiful suffering? Worse, if mimetic artistry can make us take pleasure in normally painful things, as Aristotle proposes (*Poetics* 1448b10–12), might not the pleasure of watching tragic suffering in fact prevent action?

At stake in the response to tragic suffering, then, is the question not solely of tragedy's ethical consequences but of its political impact, its actual effect in and on the city. Readers often assume that tragedy's pathetic spectacles made its Athenian audience more discerning judges of suffering in real life, and therefore more just, even more humane. This is an appealing idea, but Euripides himself challenges it with his scenes of aestheticized suffering. These scenes yield an abundance of pity and pleasure, but they do not necessarily yield justice. They thus raise questions about the ethics of pathos and the politics of pity: in short, does tragedy's beautiful suffering make us just?[5]

These questions are raised not only in the plays' verbal and thematic content but also in and by their aesthetic form. This is ironic, since the form of Euripidean drama has often been considered distinctly *un*beautiful. The structural features I am exploring in this book—the fragmented plots, the spasmodic pacing, the inconsistencies of tone—are often condemned as aesthetic embarrassments. This condemnation originates in an Aristotelian aesthetic that prizes unity and consistency above all other qualities.[6] But Euripides pointedly eschews structural unity in favor of variety and surprise: his plays are—by these criteria, not in any absolute sense—"ugly." I use this loaded term not as an aesthetic criticism but as a formal description. Unity is obviously only one among many possible criteria by which to judge a play (and in fact one not much valued by our own postmodern sensibilities), and this chapter will suggest that Euripides poses an ethical critique of the aesthetics of unity by means of his own "ugly" counter-aesthetics. Likewise, "beauty" in what follows is not a subjective quality of the text but shorthand for a set of specific aesthetic options—structural symmetry, lush poetic language, rich visual imagery, intense music—that the poet can deploy when he wishes, and the deployment of which bears significant ethical and political consequences. These consequences are particularly clear in Euripides because his plays denaturalize their own aesthetic form. Their disjointed, ungainly structure throws the strategic moments of beauty into high relief. This makes us aware that beauty is itself a resource for *psukhagōgia*, and forces us to ask—in a way a more formally "perfect" play might not—where we are being led. If this is true, then perhaps it is ugliness, not beauty, that makes us just.

This chapter treats two plays in which the relation between ethics and aesthetics—the justice of beauty and the beauty of justice—takes center stage. The first, *Trojan Women*, presents a tale of unmitigated misery and renders it self-consciously beautiful. But how are we to watch this sublime suffering? The play won't let us maintain a safe spectatorial distance; it demands that we watch with pity, but also suggests the insufficiency of that response. Our tears do no good. The insufficiency of pity is also a central theme of the second play, *Hecuba*. Here pity is shown to be not only politically ineffectual, but in fact morally dangerous: the beauty of tragic suffering generates a perverse investment in that suffering itself, and our longing for the beautiful symmetry of justice makes us complicit in a vicious act of injustice. Both *Trojan Women* and *Hecuba* thus propose that aesthetic judgments bear ethical and political consequences, but neither play takes it for granted that beauty will make us just.

It's not insignificant, of course, that the suffering in both plays is paradigmatically elite: the tragedy of Hecuba is, above all, her *peripeteia* from queen to slave. The class status of these fallen princesses, as we shall see, contributes to the beauty of their misery for a culture in which beauty was class-coded, and their enduring nobility of character, emphasized in both plays, intensifies pity for them by showing the undeservedness of their situation. This chapter does not pursue the class implications of this dynamic (tragedy's class politics are the focus of chapter 3). Instead, we will examine the broader ethical and political questions raised by Euripides' deployment of beautiful pathos. As we do, though, we should bear in mind that both that beauty and that pathos bear specific class associations, and that their combination, here and throughout Greek tragedy, is not fortuitous, but the product and perpetuation of specific hegemonic relations. We should also note that the *peripeteia* of kings and queens is not the only, or even the worst form of human misery, and remember all the other less glamorous or dramatic tribulations—including social inequality itself—that tragedy does not aestheticize or invite us to lament.[7]

• • •

Trojan Women stages the extreme of beautiful suffering: in fact, it consists of virtually nothing but, and is often condemned as a drama devoid of event. Troy has recently fallen, and the captured Trojan women are awaiting assignment to their new Greek masters. The action of the play—such as it is—is the gradual piling on of misery upon misery. The play opens with Hecuba, once the queen of Troy and now a ruined old woman, lying on the ground, bitterly lamenting: "Aiai aiai! What is there that I do not groan for in my misery, my fatherland gone, my children gone, my husband gone?" (105–7) Then Cassandra appears, dressed in her bridal gown, singing a deranged hymeneal in preparation for the marriage-to-death that, with her second sight, she can envision all too clearly. Then there is Andromache, whose superlative virtue as Hector's wife has earned her a place in the bed of his killer's son. This alone is enough to make her envy the dead, but then she learns that her young son Astyanax is to be killed, thrown from the walls of the city. The play rises to its most agonizing pitch of pathos as the child is ripped from his mother's arms. The final hundred lines are one extended wail of grief as his grandmother prepares the boy's broken body for burial in a land already in flames and soon to be reduced to dust.

This unremitting woe is presented in self-consciously aestheticizing terms. Near the end of the play, Hecuba comments that "If the god had not overturned the land entirely, we would become obscure and would not be hymned, the subjects of songs for muses in generations to come" (1242–45). This sardonic consolation is a double poetic allusion: first to the *Iliad*, where characters console themselves for their present hardships by imagining their future immortalization in epic, and second, to the play itself, which continues that epic heroization. The chorus, too, allude to this poetic tradition in the first stasimon, which begins *Amphi moi Ilion, ō Mousa*: "Sing to me, Muse, of Ilion, a funeral song of new hymns accompanied by tears" (511–14). These lines conflate the opening of the *Odyssey* (*Andra moi ennepe, Mousa*) and the theme of the *Iliad* to create a new song to rival the bard's.[8]

Euripides deploys all the resources of tragic language to sing this *Iliad* of suffering. We might observe, for instance, the brilliant use of naval metaphors. Hecuba rocks back and forth in grief like a ship (116–19); the Trojan Horse is compared to a great wooden ship come to harbor in the city (539–41); Andromache's heaving chest is described as "the oaring of the breast" (570); at the end of the play, Troy is set ablaze by "hands sweeping like oars, burning with torches" (1257–58), even as the Trojan women, in their parting lines, prepare to step onto the literal ships that will bear them to slavery (1331–32).[9] Or note the extended use of *antilabe*, the breaking of one metrical line between two speakers, a mark of extreme agitation (577–96).[10] Or the insistent trope of polyptoton to convey the piling up of sorrows: "grief is laid upon grief" (*epi d'algesin algea keitai*, 596); "tears pour from tears" (*dakrua t'ek dakruōn kataleibetai*, 605). There is Cassandra's spectacular monody—a mad lament sung in the form of a wedding song—and the visceral anguish of Andromache as her son is ripped from her breast: "Oh child whom I hold in my arms, most beloved to your mother. Oh, the sweet smell of your skin. It was for nothing, then, that I nursed you at this breast. . . . Now embrace your mother for the last time, throw your arms around my neck and press your lips to mine" (757–63). The scene ends with her bitter cry: "Take him, carry him away, hurl him from the walls if that is your decision. Feast on his flesh! I am destroyed and I cannot save my child from death" (774–77). Euripides pulls out all the poetic stops to construct this sublimity of sorrow.

Trojan Women thus offers an abundance of tragedy's characteristic pleasure—its *oikeia hēdonē* (Aristotle *Poetics* 1453b11), the arousal of fear and, especially, pity. But how are we to watch such pitiful suffering, much less take pleasure in it? The play itself poses this question in the chorus's third stasimon, which begins with an anguished cry to Zeus: Have you really so betrayed the temples and altars of Troy? Have you just looked on while the city was destroyed, its ritual choruses abandoned, its men left unburied, its children crying out as they are torn from their mothers? "I am anxious, I am anxious whether you care about these things, lord, as you mount your ethereal seat in the heavens, while the city is destroyed, undone by the blazing blast of fire" (1077–80). Is Zeus watching this spectacle of suffering? How could he watch and do nothing?

That horrifying possibility is imagined in the second stasimon. Troy was once honored by the gods; the chorus sing of Ganymede, the Trojan prince whom Zeus loved and made his cupbearer on Olympus. Does that love count for nothing now?

> μάταν ἄρ᾽, ὦ χρυσέαις ἐν οἰνοχόαις ἁβρὰ βαίνων,
> Λαομεδόντιε παῖ,
> Ζηνὸς ἔχεις κυλίκων πλήρωμα, καλλίσταν λατρείαν.
> ἁ δέ σε γειναμένα πυρὶ δαίεται,
> ἠιόνες δ᾽ ἅλιαι
> ἴακχον οἰωνὸς οἷ-
>   ον τέκνων ὕπερ βοῶσ᾽,
> ἇι μὲν εὐνάς, ἇι δὲ παῖδας,
> ἇι δὲ ματέρας γεραιάς.
> τὰ δὲ σὰ δροσόεντα λουτρὰ
> γυμνασίων τε δρόμοι
> βεβᾶσι, σὺ δὲ πρόσωπα νεα-
>   ρὰ χάρισι παρὰ Διὸς θρόνοις

καλλιγάλανα τρέφεις. Πριάμοιο δὲ γαῖαν
Ἑλλὰς ὤλεσ' αἰχμά.

Is it in vain, then, oh child of Laomedon,
that you walk delicately among the golden cups,
filling Zeus's vessel, an exquisite servitude?
The city that gave you birth is burning.
The shores groan
like a bird
shrieking for its young:
here husbands, here children,
here aged mothers.
Your dewy baths
and race courses
are gone. And you sit
with pleasure by the throne of Zeus,
with your beautiful-calm young face.
The Greek spear has destroyed Priam's land. (821–38)

Troy is a scene of devastation, but the Trojan Ganymede watches serenely from Zeus's side. The young Ganymede's face is described as
kalligalana. This startling compound adjective, apparently invented by
Euripides, combines *kallos*, beauty, and *galēnē*, calmness at sea. This
evocative word contrasts with the seashores groaning with dead and
with the ships—literal and metaphoric—that symbolize the Trojan
women's doom. Divinely remote and tranquil amid his golden cups,
this beautiful boy sits impassive in the face of the Trojans' groaning,
chaotic destruction.[11]

The Olympian "beautiful-calm" of Ganymede finds its human embodiment in Helen, who comes onstage in the next scene, dressed in
finery, to defend herself before her husband Menelaus, her untarnished
beauty an insult amid the devastation that beauty has wrought (1022–
28). Herself driven wild by the "exceptional beauty" of Paris (*kallos
ekprepestatos*, 987), Helen has destroyed Troy "with her most beautiful
eyes" (*kallistōn . . . ommatōn apo*, 772–73). Her disastrous beauty also
renders her immune to disaster. When Menelaus enters the scene, determined to punish his unfaithful wife, Hecuba warns him not to look
at her lest he be seized by longing (*pothōi*, 891) and shaken from his just
intent: such is the baneful spell (*kēlēmata*, 893) of her beauty. The extended debate (*agōn*) on Helen's guilt that follows explores the force of
desire in human affairs and also illustrates it.[12] At the end of this pseudo-

trial, Menelaus judges Helen guilty of starting the war by her infidelity and sentences her to death. But he defers that punishment until they get back to Greece, and Hecuba's parting warning to him not to ride on the same ship with her because "a lover loves forever" (1051) leaves us with the distinct impression that Helen will escape the war unscathed.[13] That impression is bitterly reinforced by the chorus who, in the third stasimon, picture her onboard her husband's ship heading home, gazing into a golden mirror, while they themselves are taken on the same ship to "a servitude full of tears in Greece, far from my land" (1105–6).

Helen becomes a latter-day Ganymede; serene in her gold and beauty, she is untouched by the misery of the Trojan women or their call for retribution. Beauty engenders a desire that is impervious to argument and indifferent to questions of justice—and this not only in weak-willed mortals, but in the heavens, too, where Eos makes love with her Trojan husband Tithonus while his city is destroyed (847–58). The gods' love once raised up Troy's towers (841–45). Now, that love is gone, the chorus conclude (857–58); but the truth may be far worse. Are the gods themselves so seduced by beauty's spell that they can watch the Trojans' anguish and do nothing? Has desire rendered them, too, morally apathetic?

As Menelaus leads his beautiful wife off to her uncertain fate, the third stasimon begins, with its cry to Zeus: O Zeus, have you really betrayed Troy's temples and altars? That ode ends with the chorus's fervent prayer that the god smite Menelaus's ship with lightning, that the Greeks never reach their homeland (1100–17). But in the present moment all they can see is "new disasters following one upon another for Troy" (1118–19), as the Greek herald enters with the body of the dead child Astyanax. Is there nothing but suffering? Is there no compensation, no justice for their suffering?

We in the audience know that there is, or will be. The play opened with a prologue in which Athena and Poseidon discuss the Greek victors' fate. Athena, previously a supporter of the Greeks, has turned against them after Ajax raped Cassandra in her temple, an act of impious violence (hubris, 69) that functions as a traditional metonym for all the brutality of the war. As punishment for this hubris, Athena asks Poseidon to stir up storms for the Greeks and deprive them of their homecoming. Thus we know, as the Trojan women themselves cannot, that their prayer to Zeus will be answered: their suffering will be compensated, at least in some measure. Their Greek destroyers will eventually be destroyed in turn, and their violent aggression—the effects of which the play stages with such extreme pathos—will eventually be punished. Zeus on his ethereal throne *is* watching the spectacle of Troy's demise, and he is not indifferent to the captive women's misery.

This prologue grants us the gods'-eye view that lets us watch the scene of suffering onstage with some degree of distance. For the Trojan women there is nothing but unmitigated grief: "what I suffer and have suffered and will suffer," as Hecuba says (468); within their traumatic present, this future justice can appear only as the hallucinations of a mad Cassandra. But we can put their misery into a larger perspective, knowing about the *peripeteia* to come. This knowledge affords us the spectatorial distance that enables us to watch their suffering and enjoy its pathos without being crushed—as they are—under its weight.

And yet, that sense of serene distance is false because the future *peripeteia* that makes their suffering bearable is in fact our own. Not only is there an automatic affinity between Athenian audience and Greek heroes in a play structured by a polarity between Greek and barbarian, but this play goes out of its way to emphasize the analogy between imperial Athens and the conquering Greeks. The second stasimon, with its images of golden Ganymede and the groaning shores of Troy, opens with an address to Telamon, the mythic hero who, along with Heracles, sacked Troy the first time it fell. Telamon is addressed as king of Salamis, the island off the coast of Attica, and this occasions a brief encomium to "the holy mount where Athena first revealed the sprig of gray olive, a heavenly crown and glory for shining Athens" (801–3). This encomium to Athens, which comes right after Astyanax has been torn from his weeping mother's arms, implicates the Athenians themselves in the destruction of Troy. "You Greeks who have invented barbarian evils, why do you kill an innocent child?" cries Andromache (764–65). Are we those barbaric Greeks? Even as we enjoy the pathos of Andromache's laments, this ode forces us to acknowledge that we bear some responsibility for them—whether as imperial Greeks, who that very year reduced the island of Melos to ruins, killing all the men and enslaving all the women, or as spectators for whose theatrical pleasure this mother's anguish is staged.[14]

We cannot watch with the beautiful-calm of Ganymede, then, or with the remote omniscience of Zeus, for we are morally implicated in the play's misery. *Trojan Women* solicits an ethical response: its pathos demands our pity. But is pity enough? We are offered a model for sympathetic spectation in the Greek herald Talthybius, who delivers the army's devastating orders with increasing reluctance. That man would be shameless, he says, who could deliver such commands without pity (786–89). This pity even moves him to wash the body of the dead Astyanax and dig the child's grave himself (1151–55). It doesn't move him, however, to resist the Greeks' cruel orders. Shedding tears of sympathy, he leads Astyanax to his death and lights the fire that will reduce Troy to ash.[15]

Scholars have argued that tragic pity had a humanizing effect on its viewers, that it "enlarges our sympathies and so our humanity," as Charles Segal put it.[16] Talthybius—a Greek soldier moved to grief as he watches the suffering of the barbarian enemy—would seem to illustrate this humanizing effect. Pity would seem to transcend politics, crossing the boundaries of ethnicity and gender to forge a bond of shared pathos, *sumpatheia*, between the Greek (mostly, if not exclusively) male audience and the barbarian women onstage. And yet for all his sympathy Talthybius still carries out the Greeks' commands. What good, then, are his tears? Human sympathy fails to translate into justice or tragic pity into political effect. Indeed, to the extent that it allows us to feel complacent about our inaction, pity may even impede the impetus toward justice: we can watch this beautiful suffering and cry our humane tears and feel that we have done enough.[17]

But if we think our pity is enough, the prologue disabuses us of this comforting notion. It shows us our own implication in the suffering of the Trojan women and suggests that the compensation for that suffering will be our own tragic *peripeteia*. To really do justice to this suffering, the prologue suggests, it is not enough to weep. We must accept our responsibility for it and embrace our own eventual shipwreck. Artificially attached to and weakly integrated with the action that follows, this prologue has been condemned as an aesthetic flaw.[18] But it is precisely this "ugly" *décalage* between play and prologue that forces us to examine our moral response to the aestheticized misery on stage. Structurally enacting the gap between suffering and compensation, it demands that the audience bridge that gap themselves. That demand is substantial. Francis Dunn notes that *Trojan Women* is extraordinary in ending without any of the usual formal generic markers of closure: there is no deus ex machina, no prophecy for the future, no general moral reflection. Instead, these closural gestures come in the prologue, a plot inversion that, Dunn argues, makes dramatic development impossible.[19] By transposing the divine prophecy of future retribution to the beginning and refusing to remind us of it, either in the course of the play or, more pointedly, at the end, Euripides leaves it up to us to remember. We must hold on to that future justice amid all the beautiful lamentation and our own cathartic tears. We must hold on to it even though it will come at our own expense.[20]

By projecting retribution beyond the end of the play, Euripides makes us take responsibility for the suffering we have watched and enjoyed. Justice is not passive: it makes serious moral demands on us, and to that extent can never be satisfied by merely watching, even with tears in our eyes. If pity is to be translated into *praxis*, this will happen not in the Theater of Dionysus but beyond it, and we ourselves will be its *prattontes* (agents). This theory of justice emerges not from the play's exquisite suffering, though, but from its unlovely structure; if we take it to heart, then it is the play's ugliness, not its beauty, that has made us just.

•••

Trojan Women shows that we cannot watch tragedy's spectacle of suffering with divine indifference: its beautiful lamentation demands our pity. But the play also suggests the inadequacy of that pity as an instrument of justice. Euripides' *Hecuba* likewise solicits our pity and simultaneously indicates its insufficiency: pity for beautiful suffering expressly fails to translate into justice. Worse, pity in this play entails an injustice, a sadistic enjoyment of beautiful suffering that is, the play suggests, part of tragedy's *oikeia hēdonē*. Like *Trojan Women*, *Hecuba* juxtaposes this dynamic of pity with a larger scheme of retribution, the balancing of crime by punishment. The promise of retributive justice hinted at in *Trojan Women* is fulfilled in *Hecuba* in an act of bloody vengeance the play represents as *dikē*, justice. This symmetrical *dikē* has a beauty of its own and it seems to offer a morally and aesthetically pleasing closure. But its beautiful symmetry will turn out on closer examination to be illusory and to conceal a deeper injustice. Beauty in this play may make us long for justice; but it does not make us just. In fact, as we shall see, the opposite may be the case.

Aesthetically, *Hecuba* is an "ugly" play with some beautiful moments. Its ugliness is both structural and ethical: an ungainly divided plot, and a corrupt and violent world in which nearly all the characters are morally unappealing. Like *Trojan Women*, *Hecuba* is set in the aftermath of the Trojan War. The Greeks are now heading home with their Trojan captives, but they have stopped en route in Thrace, stalled by adverse winds. The action again focuses on Hecuba and her suffering. First, she learns that her daughter Polyxena is to be sacrificed at the tomb of

Achilles; and next, that her son Polydorus—the only one of her dozens of sons to have survived the war (or so she thought)—has been murdered by the Thracian king Polymestor. The play falls into two distinct halves. The first depicts Polyxena's sacrifice and Hecuba's pathetic lament for her daughter; the second deals with the discovery of Polydorus's body and Hecuba's brutal revenge for her son. This bifurcated plot has come in for much criticism and the play is often deemed an aesthetic failure. Add to this the corruption of the Greeks and their leaders, the barbarity of Polymestor, and the savage vengeance of Hecuba, and one might be tempted to concur with Ann Michelini that "The watchword of [*Hecuba*] is ugliness, *to aischron.*"[21] The play's beauty, to the extent that critics are willing to recognize any, lies in its laments— the laments of the chorus of captive Trojan women over their sorrowful fate; the laments of Hecuba over the noble self-sacrifice of her daughter—as well as in that sacrifice itself. The relation between the play's ugliness and its beauty is not simply an aesthetic question, though; as we shall see, it is inseparably bound up with the play's imagination of justice.

Halfway through the play, Hecuba discovers the mutilated body of Polydorus, and begs Agamemnon for help in avenging the death of her son.

> Pity us: standing back like a painter,
> look at me and observe what I suffer.
> Once a tyrant I am now your slave,
> once blessed with children, now a childless old woman,
> without a city, bereft, most miserable of mortals. (807–11)

Hecuba seeks to engage Agamemnon's pity by means of an artistic image that figures him as a painter and herself as a spectacle of suffering.[22] That spectacle, despite Agamemnon's painterly eye, is actually more theatrical than graphic, for what she wants him to see is precisely the tragic *peripeteia* that the play stages: once a queen, Hecuba is now a slave. This appeal demands an aesthetic and an emotional response. It also demands an ethical and political response: Hecuba is asking this political authority to translate pity into just retribution for her dead child. In this case the child is Polydorus, but earlier in the play she makes a similar appeal to Odysseus on Polyxena's behalf. "Do not rip my child from my arms. Do not kill her. . . . In her I take joy and forget my woes. She is my consolation for so much, my city, nurse, staff, guide on my road. . . . I was prosperous once but now am no longer: one day has robbed me of all happiness. . . . Pity me" (*oiktiron*, 277–87). Hecuba paints a picture of her suffering—her anguish for her beloved daughter and her own tragic *peripeteia*—and asks Odysseus to look on her with pity. She pleads her case through the beauty of her language, with its asyndetic string of pathetic metonyms: "my city, nurse, staff, guide on my road" (*polis, tithēnē, baktron, hēgemōn hodou*). The poetry evokes pity; pity calls for justice.

The play asks us, as Hecuba asks Agamemnon and Odysseus, to look upon all she has suffered and pity her. It makes this appeal through the gorgeous lyrics that dominate the first half and that deploy in service of that appeal all the resources of tragic pathos. Consider (to choose an example almost at random) Hecuba's intense and broken lyrics the moment she first learns her daughter is to be sacrificed:

> οἲ ἐγὼ μελέα, τί ποτ᾽ ἀπύσω;
> ποίαν ἀχώ, ποῖον ὀδυρμόν,
> δειλαία δειλαίου γήρως
> <καὶ> δουλείας τᾶς οὐ τλατᾶς,
> τᾶς οὐ φερτᾶς; ὤμοι μοι.
> τίς ἀμύνει μοι; ποία γενεά,
> ποία δὲ πόλις; φροῦδος πρέσβυς,
> φροῦδοι παῖδες.

> Oh miserable, what cry am I to utter?
> What sound, what lament,
> wretched in my wretched old age
> and my slavery, unbearable,
> unendurable. Oimoi moi!
> Who protects me? What family,
> what city? Gone my old husband,
> gone my children. (154–61)

Polyptoton and isometry, rhetorical questions and metrical effects, anadiplosis, alliteration, anaphora, asyndeton—all work here to arouse pity for Hecuba's plight. Poetic beauty becomes a kind of jurisprudential rhetoric pressing the cause of justice.

This rhetoric is heard loudest in the descriptions of the sacrifice itself. The order that Polyxena will be sacrificed is first announced by the chorus, who envision "the virgin facedown on the tomb, scarlet with blood in a dark-gleaming stream from her gold-bound throat" (τύμβωι προπετῆ φοινισσομένην αἵματι παρθένον ἐκ χρυσοφόρου δειρῆς νασμῶι μελαναυγεῖ, 150–52). With the lush aestheticism of their visual imagery and compound adjectives, the eroticism and elitism of the maiden's gold-necklaced throat, and the metapoetic allusion to the sacrifice of Iphigeneia in Aeschylus's *Agamemnon* (*propetē*; cf. Aeschylus *Agamemnon* 233), these three lines contain *in nuce* all the features of the sacrifice scene to come.

That scene, as the herald describes it (518–82), is almost unbearably beautiful. Amid the flash of golden implements (528, 543), we see the beautiful young virgin. We catch glimpses of her flank and "most beautiful chest" (*sterna kallista*) and extended throat (559–61). We also hear her glorious speech: "I die of my own will. . . . I will offer my neck without flinching. Let me die free, since I, a princess, am ashamed to be called a slave among the dead" (548–52). The overtly elitist tenor of her self-sacrifice—as *kalos* socially as it is ethically—adds an aristocratic luster to the episode. The enduring nobility of these fallen queens, both Polyxena and Hecuba, has been a central theme throughout the play, magnifying the pathos of their *peripeteia* and the splendor of their suffering.[23] Here that nobility is combined with Homeric heroism to produce a spectacle of self-sacrifice so magnificent that the crowd of Greek soldiers roar their approval (553) and praise the girl as "outstandingly brave and noble in spirit" (579–80).

The reaction of the spectators makes the entire scene self-consciously theatrical, as does the comparison of Polyxena, her breast bared to receive the fatal blow, to a statue (*hōs agalmatos*, 560). Like Hecuba's painter simile, this comparison spotlights Polyxena not just as an artistic but as a specifically theatrical spectacle: the phrase is another allusion to Aeschylus's Iphigeneia, described at the moment of her death as "conspicuous as in a painting" (*prepousa t'hōs en graphais*, *Agamemnon* 242).[24] This simile transforms the described narrative into an inset tragedy. It focuses our spectatorial gaze upon the doomed virgin and demands our emotional response. As in *Trojan Women*, here too the Greek herald Talthybius offers a model for that response with his sympathetic tears. He begins his report of the sacrifice: "You wish me to reap a double profit of tears, woman, in pity for your child. For now I will wet my eyes as I recount her suffering, just as I did by the tomb when she died" (518–20). But again, as in *Trojan Women*, Talthybius's pity changes nothing. Nor does that of Neoptolemus, who, we are told, performs the sacrifice "both unwilling and willing through pity for the girl" (566). Willing or unwilling, he still slits her throat.

Polyxena's sacrifice is hyper-aestheticized, encrusted with layer upon layer of beauty: golden implements, tender flesh, heroic speeches. But this hypertrophic beauty does not lead to justice: the pity of the spectators, their admiration for the girl's noble bravery, has no effect. In the *Agamemnon*, Iphigeneia's sacrifice prompts a call for justice (*dika*, *Agamemnon* 250) that will unfold over the rest of the trilogy as Clytemnestra gets brutal revenge for her daughter's death. This virgin sacrifice, by contrast, concludes with philosophical reflections on the pain wrought by divine necessity and the vanity of human happiness (627–28). And that's that: no demand for retribution, just a sublime resignation that suggests that dying beautifully is its own revenge.

At the end of Hecuba's appeal to Odysseus before her daughter's sacrifice, the chorus had said to her, "There is no human nature so rigid that it would not shed tears hearing the lament of your wails and long cries" (296–98). But Odysseus remained unmoved by her pleas. If you suffer, he says, there are Greek mothers who suffer no less than you. His callous response marks the limits of tragic pity; it does not translate into political action or serve as an impetus toward justice. This indifference is consonant with the play's generally bleak view of politics. The violent and corrupt political establishment of the Greek army is one of the "ugliest" elements of this play. Driven by a demagogic rhetoric of expediency, it is unable or unwilling to entertain considerations of justice. Agamemnon speaks against Polyxena's sacrifice, motivated by his sexual relationship with Cassandra; but that same relationship discredits his position (121–29), and Odysseus wins over the assembly. For this "shifty-hearted sweet-talking crowd-pleasing liar" (131–32), the sacrifice of Polyxena does not involve a question of justice but is simply a matter of military pragmatism: if the Greeks don't honor their fallen heroes, how will they motivate soldiers to fight in future wars? (303–20). His refusal to do justice to Hecuba's pitiful suffering highlights not only the iniquity of the political but also the futility of pity: neither Hecuba's beautiful pleas before her daughter's death, nor her beautiful laments after, translate into a political response.

But what about us in the audience? The political debate that results in the "vote" (*psēphos*, 196, 259) for Polyxena's death is described in terms that assimilate it disturbingly to contemporary Athenian democratic practice; as in *Trojan Women*, here too the Athenians themselves are implicated in the guilt of this bloody vote.[25] Surely we are not as indifferent as Odysseus to the suffering it entails. Surely our own nature is not so rigid that it does not shed tears at the daughter's death and the mother's grief. We can enjoy the complacent catharsis of our own beautiful tears, knowing that they make us better than the cold-hearted Odysseus or the craven, self-serving Agamemnon.

Yet as we do, the play hints at the perversion of this tragic pleasure-in-pity, an active investment in suffering that its aestheticization both masks and excites. This perverse investment is suggested by the sadism that pervades the sacrifice scene.

> λαβοῦσα πέπλους ἐξ ἄκρας ἐπωμίδος
> ἔρρηξε λαγόνας ἐς μέσας παρ' ὀμφαλὸν
> μαστούς τ' ἔδειξε στέρνα θ' ὡς ἀγάλματος
> κάλλιστα, καὶ καθεῖσα πρὸς γαῖαν γόνυ
> ἔλεξε πάντων τλημονέστατον λόγον·
> Ἰδού, τόδ', εἰ μὲν στέρνον, ὦ νεανία,
> παίειν προθυμῆι, παῖσον, εἰ δ' ὑπ' αὐχένα
> χρήιζεις πάρεστι λαιμὸς εὐτρεπὴς ὅδε.
> ὁ δ' οὐ θέλων τε καὶ θέλων οἴκτωι κόρης
> τέμνει σιδήρωι πνεύματος διαρροάς·
> κρουνοὶ δ' ἐχώρουν. ἡ δὲ καὶ θνήισκουσ' ὅμως
> πολλὴν πρόνοιαν εἶχεν εὐσχήμων πεσεῖν,
> κρύπτουσ' ἃ κρύπτειν ὄμματ' ἀρσένων χρεών.

> She grabbed the peplos from the top of her shoulders
> and ripped it to the mid flank near the navel,
> and revealed her breasts and her bosom, beautiful
> as a statue's. She dropped to her knee on the ground,
> and uttered the bravest speech of all:
> "See, strike here, young man, if you are eager to
> strike my breast; or if you want to strike beneath
> my neck, here is my throat ready for you."
> And he, both unwilling and willing through pity
> for the girl, severs with iron the channels of breath.
> Streams of blood flowed. And she, even as she died,
> was careful to fall decorously: she hid what should
> be hidden from the eyes of men. (558–70)

The shocking exposure of Polyxena's body, the girl's offer of her chest or throat to Neoptolemus's sword, the coy play of revelation and con-cealment as she falls: the scene offers an eroticized female body as an object of aesthetic pleasure. This is part of its hyperbolic beauty and thus part of its claim to justice. But that pleasure is predicated on the girl's suffering and climaxes in a spurt of blood.[26]

This sadistic aesthetics sits uncomfortably with the pity that suffuses the scene. It is uncomfortable for Neoptolemus, "both unwilling and willing through pity for the girl" (566), but also for the audience, whose view of this spectacle is focalized through the avid gaze of the Greek army, the "eyes of men" (570).[27] Neoptolemus's conflicted desire encapsulates the perverse specular dynamic of the episode, which demands that its audience invest simultaneously in the pity aroused by beautiful suffering and in the suffering that arouses that pity. Hecuba's appeals propose that pity can fuel the drive for justice by making us feel the iniquity of this girl's undeserved and lamentable death. But if we are aroused by the scene of Polyxena's sacrifice (and it seems clear that we are meant to be), then we become complicit in its injustice. We, like the Greek army, derive pleasure from the girl's murder, and that pleasure is only increased by the beautiful pathos of the event.

This investment in exquisite suffering is generalized through the play's choral odes. In these odes, the suffering of the Trojan women, aestheticized in the high lyric style for which Euripides was famous, is presented both as a pitiful spectacle and as a source of pleasure for the audience. Thus, in effect, they turn the whole play into the sacrifice of Polyxena—beautiful, pathetic, unjust, and profoundly enjoyable. The third stasimon (905–52), for example, depicts the night Troy fell:

> μεσονύκτιος ὠλλύμαν,
> ἦμος ἐκ δείπνων ὕπνος ἡδὺς ἐπ' ὄσσοις
> σκίδναται, μολπᾶν δ' ἄπο καὶ χοροποιὸν
> θυσίαν καταπαύσας
> πόσις ἐν θαλάμοις ἔκει-
>   το, ξυστὸν δ' ἐπὶ πασσάλωι,
> ναύταν οὐκέθ' ὁρῶν ὅμιλον
> Τροίαν Ἰλιάδ' ἐμβεβῶτα.
>
> ἐγὼ δὲ πλόκαμον ἀναδέτοις
> μίτραισιν ἐρρυθμιζόμαν
> χρυσέων ἐνόπτρων λεύσσουσ' ἀτέρμονας εἰς αὐγάς,
> ἐπιδέμνιος ὡς πέσοιμ' ἐς εὐνάν.
> ἀνὰ δὲ κέλαδος ἔμολε πόλιν·
> κέλευσμα δ' ἦν κατ' ἄστυ Τροίας τόδ'· Ὦ

παῖδες Ἑλλάνων, πότε δὴ πότε τὰν
Ἰλιάδα σκοπιὰν
πέρσαντες ἥξετ' οἴκους;

λέχη δὲ φίλια μονόπεπλος
λιποῦσα, Δωρὶς ὡς κόρα,
σεμνὰν προσίζουσ' οὐκ ἤνυσ' Ἄρτεμιν ἁ τλάμων·
ἄγομαι δὲ θανόντ' ἰδοῦσ' ἀκοίταν
τὸν ἐμὸν ἅλιον ἐπὶ πέλαγος·
πόλιν τ' ἀποσκοποῦσ', ἐπεὶ νόστιμον
ναῦς ἐκίνησεν πόδα καί μ' ἀπὸ γᾶς
ὥρισεν Ἰλιάδος
τάλαιν' ἀπεῖπον ἄλγει.

In the middle of the night I was destroyed,
when after dinner sweet sleep spreads over the eyes,
and my husband, come from the song
and dance of the feast,
lay in the bedchamber,
his spear on a peg,
no longer watching for the throng of ships
that had invaded Troy.

And I was arranging my hair
in its binding hood,
gazing into the endless gleams of the golden mirror,
preparing to fall into the covers, into bed.
A cry came up to the city.
This exhortation went through the city of Troy:
"Sons of the Greeks, when, when
will you destroy the Trojan citadel
and go home?"

I left my beloved bed
in a single shift like a Doric maid
and sat in supplication to holy Artemis, in vain, alas!
I am led—I see my husband dead—
upon the open sea.
Gazing back at my city, since the ship has
started its journey home
and separated me from the land of Troy,
I faint from grief. (914–42)

The ode takes us into the bedroom of a Trojan woman as she combs her hair and prepares to join her husband in bed. This intimate domestic scene is ruptured by the war cry of the Greeks. The woman rises from her "beloved bed" in a single peplos; the pathos of her unanswered prayers to Artemis anticipates her pathetic future: her husband dead, she is led away, over the sea, gazing back upon her receding homeland. The ode solicits the listener's pity (*oiktrotatan*, 912) and also his aesthetic appreciation, with its Homeric echoes (*ēmos*, 915; *xuston*, 920), lush visual imagery (e.g., 923–26), and soft-focus eroticism. The ode focalizes the events through the woman's eyes, but even as it invites identification with her suffering, it also turns it into an aesthetic object for our enjoyment. If we derive pleasure from the ode's terror and pathos, its sudden *peripeteia* from serenity to violence, the visual details of its intimate setting, and the lyricism of its lament, we are emotionally invested in that violence—no less than the Greek soldiers are in the slit throat and flowing blood of the beautiful Polyxena. Can we really be confident that beauty makes us just?[28]

Polyxena is never avenged. There is pity but no justice for her beautiful death. Instead, there is a jarring break in the action. Hecuba goes into her tent, leaving the stage briefly empty, which is very rare in Greek tragedy. The play essentially starts over, with a new dead child and a new demand for justice. Hecuba returns to the stage to discover the mangled body of her son, Polydorus. Now, we in the audience have known about his death from the beginning and have been anticipating this moment. The play opened with a prologue delivered by the ghost of Polydorus, unable to rest so long as his body remains unburied. The ghost explained the backstory: his parents had sent him to the Thracian king Polymestor, along with a sum of gold, for safekeeping during the war; after the fall of Troy this supposedly loyal friend had stolen the gold, killed the boy, and thrown his body out to sea. Polymestor is represented here and throughout the play as a thoroughly wicked character. A barbarian who is often described in bestial images, he has violated the trust of guest-friendship and killed a child, all for the love of filthy lucre. He has committed an act that is, as Hecuba says, "unspeakable, unnameable, beyond amazement, unholy, unbearable" (714–15). "Where is the justice among guest-friends?" she asks (*pou dika xenōn*, 715). This crime demands punishment, *dikē*, and by the end of the play it will get it.

Hecuba again appeals to the political authorities for justice, begging Agamemnon to help her avenge her son. She entreats him, in the passage quoted earlier, to look at her with a painter's eye and pity her tragic suffering (807–11). But to this now-familiar appeal for tragic pity, she also yokes a claim to a different sort of justice.

> We may be slaves and powerless,
> but the gods are strong, as is the law (*nomos*) that
>   governs them.
> Because of law (*nomōi*) we believe in the gods
> and live distinguishing injustice (*adika*) from justice
>   (*dikaia*).
> If the law, referred to you, is corrupted
> and those do not pay the penalty (*dikēn*) who kill guests
> or dare to plunder the temples of the gods,
> then nothing is equitable (*ison*) in the affairs of men.
>
> (798–805)[29]

With this new appeal, we seem to shift to a different model of justice, a *dikē* based not on pity but on retribution. Closely aligned with the power of the gods, with the law (*nomos*) both as universal precept and as judicial practice, and with the democratic ideal of *isonomia* (equality before the law), this *dikē* has a symmetry as perfect as a palm tree's. It figures justice as an equation of crime and punishment, the negation of suffering by equal suffering, an eye for an eye. It rests upon a principle of moral and aesthetic balance, the principle, as Agamemnon says, "common to all, individuals and cities alike, that the bad man will suffer something bad, and the good will prosper" (902–4).[30]

This symmetrical *dikē* governs Hecuba's revenge. Luring the evil Polymestor into the tent on the promise of more gold, she puts out his eyes and kills his children. This gruesome deed is presented to us as an act of *dikē* and deserved retribution for Polymestor's undisputed *adikia*. Thus, while Hecuba is inside the tent taking her revenge, the chorus warn the barbarian: "You have not yet paid but perhaps you will pay the penalty (*dōseis dikēn*). . . . For where Dikē's guarantee coincides with the gods', there is deathly deathly destruction" (1024–31). Hecuba echoes their words as the tent opens to reveal the blinded Polymestor and the bodies of his two slain children: "He has paid the penalty to me" (*dikēn de moi dedōke*, 1052–53). His dead children balance hers and his grief equals hers (1254–56). *Dikē* is achieved in the form of a symmetry both equitable and beautiful.

The exquisite symmetry of retributive justice is sealed in the trial scene at the end of the play. Revenge and law, so often opposed in

Greek thought, are here reconciled as Agamemnon, echoing the fifth-century Athenian jurors' oath, undertakes to listen to plaintiff and defendant in turn and deliver a just judgment on Polymestor's suffering (1130–31). His verdict: the savage Thracian got what he deserved. "Since you dared to commit ugly acts, endure unwelcome results in return" (*all' epei ta mē kala prassein etolmas, tlēthi kai ta mē phila*, 1250–51). In this ostensibly equitable judgment, Polymestor's criminal daring (*etolmas*) is answered by punishment (*tlēthi*); his ugly acts (*ta mē kala*) are balanced by unwelcome results (*ta mē phila*). The symmetrical chiasmus of the verdict mirrors the symmetrical justice it purports to enact.

Thus the play seems to close with both aesthetic and ethical catharsis, a sense that balance has been achieved, closure reached, and justice done. With Agamemnon's verdict, the play would seem to have moved beyond tragic pity to a new and more productive model of justice. The cynical, murderous politics of its first half is apparently redeemed by the justice of the law, which is both efficacious and humane. This legal judgment also seems to bring dramatic closure: the dead boy whose ghost opened the play has been avenged; the murder he revealed in the prologue has been punished in kind. Now the winds that have kept the Greeks stalled in Thrace begin to blow once more (1289–92): the Greeks can take their Trojan captives and leave, and the play can end. All the play's ugliness—its violence and sadism and injustice—seems to be redeemed in a vision of *dikē* that is morally equitable, aesthetically pleasing, and dramatically satisfying.[31]

But the play does not in fact close with Agamemnon's verdict. Polymestor decries the iniquity of the judgment and prophesies further retribution: Agamemnon will be killed by his adulterous wife upon his return to Greece, while Hecuba will jump to her death from the mast of the ship and be transformed into a fiery-eyed dog. These bizarre prophecies unbalance the beautiful equilibrium of the legal verdict, suggesting that justice has not, in fact, been done, but is still to come, and will come in the form not of lawful punishment but of bloody murder and bestial mutations. Polymestor says he learned these predictions from Dionysus, "who is a prophet among the Thracians" (1267). In this unsettling ending the god of tragedy himself seems to deny us the dramatic closure and ethical satisfaction the verdict had promised and to reopen the case it had closed.

This deferral also hints at an injustice papered over by the legal judgment, namely, Agamemnon's complicity in the crime he is judging. Hecuba, as we have seen, had begged Agamemnon to help her get vengeance for her son's death, appealing both to the equity of law and to his sense of pity. He had refused to help her directly: Polymestor, for all his savagery, is a Greek ally. But Agamemnon did pity Hecuba. He acknowledged that she had suffered an injustice (850–53), and so agreed not to stop her from taking revenge herself. This craven compromise marks once more the gulf between tragic pity and political justice. On the one hand, Agamemnon's pity does not translate into action. Fearing the army's disapproval, he refuses to take a stand against an act that he himself acknowledges is an injustice. Political expedience trumps the claims of justice, and Hecuba calls this what it is, slavish cowardice (864–69). On the other hand, that same pity implicates Agamemnon in the deception and savagery of Hecuba's revenge, undermining his promise to judge impartially and thus the justice of his "just" verdict.[32]

The play's ragged ending disrupts the beautiful balance of *dikē*, and not just for Agamemnon's verdict but also for the act of retribution that verdict had legitimated. Hecuba, Agamemnon, and the chorus all insist that Hecuba's retribution is *dikē*, a punishment equal to the crime and consonant with the law: an eye for an eye. But to Polymestor it is an act of sheer *hubris* (1257). He accuses Hecuba of taking pleasure, *kharis*, in the deed—a charge she does not deny (1257–58). The play's sadistic pleasure-in-pain here finds its outlet in Hecuba's gloating vengeance and legitimation in Agamemnon's legal verdict.[33] In a lyric monody that echoes Hecuba's at the opening of the play, Polymestor mourns his children, sacrificed by this "bacchant of Hades" (1076–78). This formal repetition implies a formal symmetry between Polymestor's suffering and Hecuba's, and yet the pathetic content of the barbarian's lament suggests that this symmetry is *purely* formal and invites us to ask whether the punishment does in fact fit the crime. Hecuba's one dead son is avenged by the death of Polymestor's two. Instead of eye-for-an-eye justice, this is two eyes for an eye, plus two more literal eyes thrown in for good measure. This surplus of suffering, as Polymestor puts it (*pēma pēmatos pleon*, 1168), breaks the symmetry of the play's *dikē*; and Hecuba's revenge, instead of being the lawful recompense everyone pretends it is, starts to look like an excessive and unbalanced act of savagery.

Perhaps the symmetry of justice can be saved, though, if we see the murder of Polymestor's two sons as revenge for the death of Polyxena as well as Polydorus. Polyxena's death, as we saw, was never avenged: her murder aroused our pity but never satisfied our desire for justice. Polyxena is not mentioned by name in the second half of the play, but

Hecuba speaks of revenge for "her children" (*teknoisi tois emoisi*, 749–50); the two children have been paired throughout (not least by their names), and their double burial is stressed at the end (894–97, 1287–88).[34] So perhaps we can imagine Polymestor's suffering as indirect compensation for Polyxena's undeserved death, as well. By the same token, the involvement of the Trojan women in Polymestor's blinding turns that act into retribution for their suffering, too, the beautiful suffering described in the third stasimon that directly precedes the Thracian's entrance; and the intimate feminine scene of the revenge, with its juxtaposition of serene domesticity and sudden violence (1160–64), echoes that ode's scene in the Trojan woman's bedroom.[35] Polymestor's shrieks of pain recall for Agamemnon the terror at Troy (1111–13): the punishment of this hateful character seems to provide a compensation for all the loss and misery of the war. The pity aroused in the first half of the play by Polyxena's sacrifice and the choral odes appears finally to be converted into justice; tragic pity seems to be aligned with legal recompense in the perfect symmetry of *dikē*.

But of course that sense of symmetry is false, since Polymestor's blinding is not fair retribution for the fall of Troy or the death of Polyxena, any more than is Polyxena's murder for the death of Achilles.[36] In the avaricious, child-murdering barbarian, the play offers us a convenient scapegoat for our emotional catharsis, a displaced victim to satisfy pity's longing for justice for Hecuba and the Trojan women. But has our pity made us complicit in a new injustice? Have our own beautiful tears blinded us to the ugliness of the justice the play actually enacts: an exhausted old woman mutilating a bestial foreigner for, among other things, a crime he did not commit?

In *Hecuba*, beauty, far from making us just, seems to involve us over and over again in injustice. Our pleasure in the play's beautiful suffering becomes a sadistic investment in injustice; our pity for Polyxena's beautiful death makes us take satisfaction in the punishment of a man who bears no responsibility for it, even as our desire for the beautiful symmetry of *dikē* helps us to accept the corrupt verdict that judges this brutal vengeance just. If we are left uncomfortable about this judgment and unsatisfied by the fairness, moral or aesthetic, of the play's ending, it is not beauty that makes us so, but, as in *Trojan Women*, ugliness— here the formal "ugliness" of the play's divided plot. It would have been simple for Euripides to build stronger thematic, structural, and even causal bridges between the two stories, binding them together into a single action. But he does not do so. Indeed, he widens the rift between them by emptying the stage between the two halves of the play and draws attention to the discrepancy through pointed doubling and repetition, like the chiastic repetition of the two victims' names and the echo of Hecuba's lament in Polymestor's.[37] This refusal to synthesize the two plotlines holds open the gap between tragic pity and legal recompense and makes us aware, in a way a more unified plot would not, of the non-communication between the two. At the same time, in the ragged and inconclusive ending, with its Dionysiac predictions of future retribution, the god of theater himself warns us that the play's closure is more illusory than real and that its superficial symmetry may conceal deeper injustices, including our own.

Beauty, then—the beauty of tragic suffering or of legal recompense—may make us long for justice, but it does not in itself make us just; and it is Euripides' pointed refusal of the particular beauty of formal unity that reminds us of the crucial difference between the two. Denaturalizing tragic form—revealing it as something artificial not organic—Euripides alerts us to the ethical snare of pleasing symmetries and to the iniquities that can be concealed beneath the smooth surface of formal unity. In *Hecuba* as in *Trojan Women*, Euripides' aesthetics of disunity provokes a sort of "alienation-effect," forcing us to look anew not only at the aesthetics of dramatic unity but also at its politics.[38] And not just to look, but to act: as these plays have shown, aesthetic contemplation, however critical, is not enough.

That imperative to action marks the practical limit of tragic justice but also its point of entry into the political. If, as Derrida has argued, justice is defined by its futurity—"the very dimension of events irreducibly to come"[39]—then Euripides' plays enact a sort of justice precisely through their formal "ugliness." Their lack of symmetry and closure defers justice beyond the bounds of the play and into the real world, where it becomes not the characters' responsibility or the playwright's but the audience's own. If, as the Athenians walked home from the Theater of Dionysus through the Agora, past the council hall and law courts, they felt dissatisfied by the resolution, dramatic and ethical, these plays offered, perhaps that dissatisfaction served as a provocation, a reminder that justice is yet to come and that the burden of pursuing it rests with them.

CHAPTER 3

Recognition and Realism

In a provocative essay on the sociology of tragedy, Edith Hall proposes that Athenian tragedy is "a supreme instantiation of what Marxists call art's 'utopian tendency.'" This expression, she writes,

> Denotes art's potential for and inclination towards transcending in fictive unreality the social limitations and historical conditions of its own production. To put it more simply: Greek tragedy does its thinking in a form which is vastly more politically advanced than the society which produced Greek tragedy.

The form of tragedy's progressive thinking, for Hall, is precisely its form. Its multi-vocal structure and heterogeneous casts granted a voice and perspective to individuals like women and slaves who had none in contemporary Athenian democracy, and in this way enacted a radical egalitarianism that went beyond the "dominantly hierarchal world-view of [tragedy's] content" and of its historical context. "In tragedy the Athenians created a public dialogue marked by an egalitarian *form* beyond their imagination in actuality."[1]

This appealing notion finds support (as Hall notes) in Aristophanes, who associates it particularly with Euripides. In the infernal poetic contest of *Frogs*, as we have seen, his Euripides boasts that his tragedy is "democratic" (*dēmokratikon*, 952) because it gives everyone a chance to speak, the slave no less than the master (948–49). His Euripides shows a preference for lower-class characters over the "noble and four-square" soldiers of Aeschylean tragedy (1014–17, 1039–44, 1069–73), for "men as they are" over "men as they should be" (Aristotle *Poetics* 1460b34). This egalitarian realism extends beyond his characters: the comic Euripides is proud to depict *oikeia pragmata*, "things we know about and have experience with" (959), a claim that is turned against him in the parody of his lyric monodies, a high-tragic lament over a stolen chicken (1331–63).[2]

If any play exemplifies tragedy's formal egalitarianism, it would seem to be Euripides' *Electra*, with its "realist" mise-en-scène, its lower-class characters, and its depiction of the *oikeia pragmata* of agrarian poverty. Scholarly consensus views the play as an attack on the mythic heroic tradition from the perspective of grubby, unglamorous modernity, as Orestes and Electra are stripped of their heroic pretensions and forced to exist in the inhospitable atmosphere of the audience's contemporary reality.[3] The drama's ostentatious intertexuality is often seen as part of this same demythologization: the constant allusions to the *Orestia* and the *Odyssey* present a model of heroism that highlights by contrast the failure of these characters and their heroic action. This assault on the heroic tradition is often understood, implicitly or explicitly, as Euripides' attack on the elite and their values in the name of the demos and *dēmokratia*.[4] The play's realism, intertextuality, and demythologization are thus offered as prime examples of the sort of radicalism of form that the comic Euripides boasts of and that Hall sees as part of tragedy's "utopian tendency."

There is much truth to this reading of *Electra*, and in fact, as we shall see, the play itself encourages us to read it this way: with its insistence on the class politics of its realist scenario and the class identity of its everyman characters, *Electra* is not shy about proclaiming its "utopian tendency." But as noteworthy as the play's noisy radicalism is the way this radicalism is silenced and its utopian potential thwarted. The play offers us a vision of egalitarianism premised on the claim that a man's virtue cannot be judged by his wealth or birth but only by his own *ēthos* (character). It associates that democratic vision with "reality." But as the play unfolds that vision is prevented from realization and indeed is de-realized, as we are led to abandon this reality—our own democratic reality—for an illusion explicitly recognized as such.

This process of de-realization proceeds alongside the play's demythologization. The myth is shown to be implausible, an empty form. And yet we are asked to accept this mythic form in place of "reality" and its ethical and political content. This deal is sealed in the famous recognition scene. This ostentatiously metatheatrical *anagnōrisis* reveals Orestes not only as Electra's long-awaited brother but also as the heroic agent of the revenge plot that is this play's tragic *praxis*. But that recognition is staged as a misrecognition, based on a set of stale tragic conventions and secondhand quotations. What we recognize in the recognition scene, then, is the force of the *anagnōrisis*, that is, of tragic form itself. Recognizing Orestes entails accepting empty forms—theatrical and social—in place of ethical content and, ultimately, disavowing the reality of our own world, along with its radical egalitarian ethos and utopian possibilities.

The rest of the play elaborates the consequences of this choice: an impious murder is hailed as a glorious victory and matricides are rewarded by the gods. The result of misrecognizing tragic form for real content is an evisceration of both tragedy and reality, as we are asked to believe in a narrative structure that ill fits the events actually described and that reduces the play's "reality" to a temporary disruption of normalcy, both generic and social. The play is thus built upon a kind of structural bad faith. Its generic form—its *anagnōrisis*, the structure of its *muthos*, the choices it offers us and makes for us—works against the egalitarian possibilities of the "reality" it presents. To say this is to suggest that in *Electra* tragic form, far from enabling radical thought, as Hall proposes, in fact constrains it, preventing it from being realized in any meaningful way within the tragic scenario. This tragedy raises egalitarian ideas that cannot be developed within its own generic structure, and it is the structure itself, the deadweight of tragic form, that prevents their development.

In this way, *Electra* stages the genealogy of an elitism that we have already seen at work in Euripides' plays. Tragic beauty, as we saw in the last chapter, glows with an aristocratic luster: in *Hecuba* and *Trojan Women*, as in so many dramas produced in democratic Athens, the fall of the noble is the paradigm of suffering and affords the widest ambit for its aesthetic and ethical expression. Likewise, the romance of *Alcestis* and *Ion* (as we saw in the introduction and chapter 1) is not only the joyful reunion of loved ones but also the miraculous consolidation of a royal household or dynasty: the happy endings of these plays invite us to celebrate the *eudaimonia* of the *eudaimones*, the prosperity of the prosperous. Euripides is not unique in this regard. Aristotle makes a prescription of tragic practice when he asserts that tragic characters should be men of "great reputation and good fortune, like Oedipus and Thyestes, and extraordinary men from such families" (*Poetics* 1453a10–12). Predicating the audience's emotional satisfaction, whether jubilation or cathartic tears, on the fortunes of the rich and famous, tragedy would seem to reinscribe elite hegemony within its very structure.[5]

Electra stages the generic exigencies that subtend tragedy's structural elitism; it also dramatizes its political costs and contingencies. As it moves from egalitarian utopia to elite *eudaimonia*, the play both enacts and reflects upon the different political possibilities inherent in tragedy's form and the pressures, political and generic, that govern their realization. In the process, it exposes both the utopian potential of tragedy and its limits, and challenges us in the audience to recognize our own role in both.

• • •

The audience would have known the story going in: Orestes returns from exile and he and Electra kill their mother Clytemnestra and her lover Aegisthus in vengeance for the murder of their father Agamemnon. Perhaps some were old enough to have seen Aeschylus's classic treatment of the story in *Choephoroi*. If so, they were in for a surprise, for the action is set, not before the doors of the royal palace, like *Choephoroi* and almost all other tragedies, but in front of a poor farmer's hut in rural Argos; and the prologue is delivered by the Farmer himself.[6] He explains the extraordinary circumstances: after the murder of Agamemnon, Aegisthus feared retribution by his children. He killed Orestes—or thought he did: the baby was secretly saved by his father's tutor to be raised in exile. As for Electra, fearing that she would raise an avenger, he planned to kill her too, but instead was persuaded by Clytemnestra to marry her to a poor man—the Farmer—on the assumption that "by giving her to a weak man (*asthenēi*), he would weaken his fear, for if a man of rank married her, he would arouse the sleeping murder of Agamemnon and then justice would come for Aegisthus" (39–42; cf. 267–69). Aegisthus's social logic, which is the premise for the play's rural setting, reiterates the logic of tragedy itself, following Aristotle's observation that tragic protagonists are always men of "great reputation and good fortune" and lofty mythic pedigree. Equating birth and wealth with social and dramatic agency, Aegisthus assumes that only a nobleman will have the "strength" to carry out the revenge plot that constitutes the play's *praxis*.

Now, we may suspect that Aegisthus will ultimately be proved right, that the action will be performed not by a farmer or his son, but by Orestes and Electra, who will thus prove themselves the true offspring of Agamemnon and true scions of this royal house. Going in with this expectation, we may experience this rustic setting as a temporary suspension of the normal world of tragedy, an inversion caused by the illegitimate tyranny of Aegisthus and Clytemnestra that will end with their deaths. This narrative arc of inversion and restoration is, in broad strokes, the plotline of the *Oresteia*, and it is reinforced here by frequent allusion to the *Odyssey*: Orestes, like Odysseus, will return home, oust the interlopers, and restore order in the end. But while we wait for that anticipated restoration, we are allowed to dwell in the humble world into which Electra has been exiled, and to dwell here for a good long while: the recognition scene in *Electra* comes late relative to its Aeschylean prototype, and its delay extends the opening sequence to some 430 lines, a full third of the play. Some of this opening sequence is necessary for the plot of recognition and revenge that follows—to establish character and motive, for instance—but much is not, and it seems that Euripides has some other reason for lingering in this unusual landscape.

That landscape is unusual for tragedy, but not for us in the audience. For us, it would be something like our everyday lives: this is the play's celebrated "realism." We see a scene of rural poverty and its all-too-familiar hardships: the Farmer's labor in the fields, Electra fetching water from the spring, the embarrassment of the couple with nothing to offer the well-dressed strangers who arrive at their door. The austerity of this life is emphasized in particular by the princess suddenly dropped in its midst. Electra laments her impoverished existence, the menial tasks she must perform, the cropped hair and ragged dress that make Orestes mistake her for a slave (107, 110). But this existence has its pleasures, too, like the rural festival of Argive Hera to which the chorus of country girls invite Electra in the *parodos*; they even offer to lend her something when she complains that she'd have nothing to wear, "a pleasantly mundane detail," as Martin Cropp puts it.[7]

Needless to say, this "reality" is heavily stylized. What the chorus offer to lend Electra is described as "fine-woven veils and golden accessories to charming adornment" (191–92), language that paints this "pleasantly mundane detail" in the rare colors of tragedy's loftiest lyric style.[8] Likewise, when the Farmer complains about yoking his oxen and sowing his fields at daybreak (78–79), he does so in the same iambic trimeters and specialized tragic diction used by the most blue-blooded of tragic heroes, complete with Hesiodic allusions (80–81).[9] So we wouldn't mistake Euripides' realist scenario for reality itself. Instead, it is tragedy's gesture toward something outside its own mythic world: "reality" in tragic quotation marks.

Even so, it is the longest such quotation in all of extant tragedy and is quite atypical of the genre. Indeed, many readers have noted that this opening scenario is more like something from fourth-century New Comedy, with its rural settings, miscegenated marriages, and quotidian domestic dramas.[10] While it isn't particularly funny, it is true that this episode also doesn't feel typically tragic: in fact, it seems to present a specifically non-tragic world, marking it off *a contrario* by the unhappy presence of the mythic princess in its midst. We might note the way myth and reality collide, for instance, when Electra enters with the pitcher (*khoes*) that in *Choephoroi* bore libations for her father's tomb, here used to haul water from the spring.[11] As she bemoans her fate in high lyrics full of Aeschylean echoes, we feel a tension not only between myth and reality but between tragedy itself and (what tragedy presents as) reality.

But what are we to make of this "reality," this world of peasants and rural poverty? As it happens, the play tells us in no uncertain terms what we should make of it. Toward the end of the episode, the Farmer returns from the fields and sees the disguised Orestes and Pylades before his hut. Upon being told that they are messengers from Orestes, he immediately offers them such hospitality as his house affords. "I may have been born poor," he says, "but I will not show myself to be ill-bred in character" (*to g' ēthos dusgenes*, 362–63). This launches Orestes on a disquisition on the nature of nobility:

> φεῦ·
> οὐκ ἔστ' ἀκριβὲς οὐδὲν εἰς εὐανδρίαν·
> ἔχουσι γὰρ ταραγμὸν αἱ φύσεις βροτῶν.
> ἤδη γὰρ εἶδον ἄνδρα γενναίου πατρὸς
> τὸ μηδὲν ὄντα, χρηστὰ δ' ἐκ κακῶν τέκνα,
> λιμόν τ' ἐν ἀνδρὸς πλουσίου φρονήματι,
> γνώμην δὲ μεγάλην ἐν πένητι σώματι.
> πῶς οὖν τις αὐτὰ διαλαβὼν ὀρθῶς κρινεῖ;
> πλούτωι; πονηρῶι τἄρα χρήσεται κριτῆι.
> ἢ τοῖς ἔχουσι μηδέν; ἀλλ' ἔχει νόσον
> πενία, διδάσκει δ' ἄνδρα τῆι χρείαι κακόν.
> ἀλλ' εἰς ὅπλ' ἐλθών; τίς δὲ πρὸς λόγχην βλέπων

μάρτυς γένοιτ' ἂν ὅστις ἐστὶν ἀγαθός;
κράτιστον εἰκῆι ταῦτ' ἐᾶν ἀφειμένα.
οὗτος γὰρ ἀνὴρ οὔτ' ἐν Ἀργείοις μέγας
οὔτ' αὖ δοκήσει δωμάτων ὠγκωμένος,
ἐν τοῖς δὲ πολλοῖς ὤν, ἄριστος ηὑρέθη.
οὐ μὴ ἀφρονήσεθ', οἳ κενῶν δοξασμάτων
πλήρεις πλανᾶσθε, τῆι δ' ὁμιλίαι βροτῶν
κρινεῖτε καὶ τοῖς ἤθεσιν τοὺς εὐγενεῖς;

Ah!
There is no precision when it comes to judging a good
    man (*euandrian*).
Men's natures are in confusion (*taragmon*).
For before now I have seen the son of a noble father
turn out worthless, and good children from bad parents,
famine in a rich man's intellect,
and a great mind in an impoverished body.
How, then, might one judge rightly, taking these things
    one at a time?
By wealth? He'll be using a poor criterion.
Or by lack of means? But poverty brings a sickness:
it teaches a man to be bad through want.
Then by turning to war? But when a man is facing the
    enemy's spear,
how can he testify who is courageous?
It's best just to let all that go.
This man here is not a big man in Argos
nor does he swell with the reputation of his house:
one of the many (*en tois pollois*), he has turned out super-
    lative (*aristos*).
Stop being such fools, you who go around full
of empty beliefs (*kenōn doxasmatōn*); by their company
judge noble men (*eugeneis*) and by their character
    (*ēthesin*). (367–85)[12]

Orestes is shocked to discover that wealth, birth, and virtue are not the
same, that a poor man can have a good heart and a well-born man can
be morally worthless. His world is turned upside down by this sudden
revelation: there are no clear signs by which to judge individual worth
(*euandria*), and human nature is thrown into chaos (*taragmos*). *Eugeneia*

(noble birth) is no indication of *eugeneia* (moral worth). Wealth, ancestry, military prowess are all just empty beliefs or fancies (*kena doxasmata*[13]), and the only true measure of a man is his own *ēthos*. A commoner (*hoi polloi*) can be a great man.

These should hardly have been shocking revelations in democratic Athens. That wealth and birth were not reliable markers of virtue was admitted already by Theognis, and even the Old Oligarch must have known a crook or two among his oligarchic friends. By the same token, the premise that *hoi polloi* can be *agathoi* was staged regularly in comedy, whose poor farmers are invariably better citizens than the wealthy politicians or well-born generals. These observations are trite enough that some have seen them as part of the characterization of Orestes as a slightly dense and out-of-touch aristocrat.[14]

But the lesson Orestes is so surprised to learn is one the play has been teaching us, too, in the person of the Farmer, who is conspicuously a "poor but noble man" (*penēs anēr gennaios*, 253). The Farmer introduced himself in the prologue as "born from Mycenean parents . . . illustrious in ancestry (*lamproi gar es genos*), though in wealth poor, which undermines *eugeneia*" (35–38). Though impoverished, the Farmer claims a kind of nobility as a citizen: his "illustrious" Mycenean ancestry is probably meant to be an Argive version of the Athenian ideology of autochthony that figured all Athenian citizens as an elite. He also claims nobility on moral grounds: he has not touched his royal bride because, he tells us, he is "ashamed to commit an outrage (*hubrizein*) and take the child of rich men when I myself am not worthy by birth" (45–46). This extraordinary self-restraint is duly lauded by Electra (67–70, 253–57), Orestes, and above all the Farmer himself, who notes defensively that some would call him a fool for failing to take full advantage of his unusual situation (50–53). The Farmer is thus presented to us, as well as to Orestes, as the prime example of the proposition that a poor man can be virtuous. "Ah!" says Orestes, when he learns of the Farmer's exceptional *sōphrosunē*, "The man you have described is noble (*gennaion*) and deserves to fare well" (262).

Here we seem to get an inkling of what Hall terms tragedy's "utopian tendency." The play stages a "reality" in which a man's worth is judged only by his character, not by external tokens like wealth or birth; these are "empty fancies" (*kena doxasmata*) trusted only by fools and contradicted by the very reality the play presents. This ethical essentialism implies a social and political egalitarianism that jibes with the fundamental principle of Athens's radical democracy, that every

Athenian citizen, however low-born or poor, is capable of benefiting the city. At the same time, its separation of birth and wealth from virtue takes aim at one of the traditional props of elitism in Athens, the misrecognition of class status for moral superiority. The belief that aristocratic birth predicted moral worth and wealth was its divine reward was still widely held in Euripides' Athens. Many elites felt that their political authority under the democracy was incommensurate with their true value, an imbalance they sought to rectify in the oligarchic coup of 411, not long after *Electra* was produced.[15] So in this mythic aristocrat's discovery of ethical egalitarianism, we would seem to have a clear example of tragedy thinking ahead of its time—thinking both expressed in the play's content and enacted in its form, its choice of character and setting.

This is an enticing idea, but there are reasons to be wary. Start with the realist scenario. Ernst Bloch argued that realism is intrinsically ideologically conservative: limited to depicting what is, it cannot think about what might be, and thus ends up reaffirming the very social realities that it imitates.[16] From this perspective one might argue that in representing "reality" in the form of agrarian poverty, the play naturalizes that poverty as the condition of all mortals not fortunate (or unfortunate) enough to be born into the House of Atreus or one of the other great mythic families. Moreover, this "reality" has a distinctly retrograde cast. The virtue for which the Farmer is so roundly praised (and ultimately rewarded by the gods) is knowing his place, feeling the "shame" (*aiskhunē*, 44, 45) appropriate to a poor man in relation to a rich man, and refraining from committing the *hubris* of touching a woman of whom he is not worthy by birth (*ou kataxios gegōs*, 46). That virtue rules out from the start the most extreme "utopian" possibilities of this scenario: social mobility, class miscegenation, the son of a peasant avenging his royal grandfather and laying claim to his throne. The Farmer guarantees in practice the theoretical principle of Aegisthus (and Aristotle) that only extraordinary men from elite families can enact a tragic *praxis*, and he clears the way for Orestes to do so. The resulting narrative of inversion and restoration of order brackets this agrarian scene and its egalitarian ethos: that reality turns out to be nothing but a *taragmos*, as Orestes put it (368), a temporary confusion that will be resolved with the overthrow of the tyrants and the restoration of normalcy under the rule of the legitimate monarch.

This is what I meant by the play's structural bad faith: the play's form will not let its utopian content develop. It doesn't allow us to pursue the implications of the egalitarian ethics it so loudly proposes, to find out what it might mean, for the tragic world or our own, for a poor man to be *aristos*. *Electra*'s dramatic structure, the basic emplotment of its central *praxis*, constrains its more radical thought. In fact, it makes it difficult even to decide how radical that thought is. How seriously should we take this episode and its class ideology? Perhaps it is just a generic experiment, and the language of class should be seen, like the psychological realism and the mildly comic tone, as Euripides playfully testing the limits of the genre before getting down to the real business of the tragic action. Perhaps, in other words, this reality is itself just an empty form, with no real social consequences, utopian or otherwise.[17]

These questions will prove unanswerable, and the play's pointed refusal to answer (or really even to ask) them will be part of its drama. But for the moment, at least, Euripides seems to want us to take this reality seriously, for the ethical and social lessons of the first episode seem to be repeated and extended in the second. The Farmer has offered *xenia* to the strangers. His generosity wins him praise from Orestes, as we have seen, but a sharp rebuke from his wife, since they have nothing in the house to give. She sends him off to borrow provisions from the Paidagogos, the loyal slave who raised Agamemnon and saved the infant Orestes. The next episode begins with the arrival of the Paidagogos carrying not only provisions for dinner, but also mysterious offerings he found at the grave of Agamemnon.

This precipitates the play's *anagnōrisis*, probably the most innovative in extant tragedy. The old man describes a lock of hair he found at the tomb. Perhaps Orestes has secretly returned and left this offering? Hold it up against your own hair, he tells Electra, and see if it matches. Electra rejects this idea as idiotic: a man's hair will be different from a woman's, she says, and anyway, many locks of hair look the same. Well, then, step in the footprint left by the grave, proposes the Paidagogos, and see if it matches your foot. Again Electra scoffs: even if there were a clear print on the rocky soil, a man's foot would be bigger than a woman's. Finally, the Paidagogos holds up a piece of cloth he found at the spot and asks her to recognize Orestes' baby-blanket, woven by her own hand. A third time, Electra mocks him: she was just a child when Orestes left Argos, too young to weave anything; and even if she did, how could he still have that ancient garment "unless it grew along with his body" (544)?

The scene enacts a tragic *anagnōrisis* and, simultaneously, a mimesis of a tragic *anagnōrisis* in its extended allusion to the famous recognition scene in Aeschylus's *Choephoroi*.[18] There Electra herself finds the lock and footprint, so like her own that they can belong to no one but Orestes. Her brother immediately appears to claim them, and overcomes her hesitation by presenting the weaving; the two are instantly and joyfully reunited (*Choephoroi* 166–237). Euripides mocks the logical implausibility of the Aeschylean scenario and of the tragic *anagnōrisis* as a whole, showing it to be just an artificial literary convention.[19] Euripides' Electra, unlike Aeschylus's, has lived too long in the real world to be fooled by such implausible and stagy artifice. She knows that in reality one lock of hair looks much like another and a man's footprint is bigger than a woman's.

Electra's skepticism seems to repeat the lessons of the first episode. Just as you cannot judge a good man by his wealth or birth, you cannot judge a brother by his footprint. These contrived tokens are just "empty fancies," *kena doxasmata*: they do not reveal a man's true identity or nature. The connection between the two scenes is underlined by their socioeconomic language. The Paidagogos catches sight of Orestes and Pylades, who are still in disguise: the young men are evidently *eugeneis*, the slave remarks, but that can be deceptive (*en kibdēlōi*), since many *eugeneis* are scoundrels (550–51). This is precisely the language, as well as the message, of Orestes' earlier speech. The class connotations are foregrounded through a coinage metaphor: *kibdēlos* literally means "counterfeit." A few lines later Orestes asks why the old man is looking at him "as if he were examining the shining stamp (*kharaktēr*) of a silver coin" (558–59; cf. 572). The metaphors evoke the elitist ideology in which the superior *ēthos* of the genuine nobleman is accurately represented in the *kharaktēr* of his social status and a bad nobleman is a counterfeit coin.[20]

Electra's repudiation of the artificial tokens of recognition thus seems to reinforce both the ethical essentialism of the opening scene—the notion that a man should be judged only by his *ēthos*, not by external signs—and its egalitarianism, its rejection of the elite's equation of social status with moral excellence. Our Electra, the wife of a noble pauper, has learned the lessons of the reality in which she now lives, and carries them over to the myth. To judge a man by his footprint is as foolish as judging him by his wealth: it is to mistake artifice for essence, social or literary forms for ethical content. Electra, for one, won't make that error.

At stake in this refused *anagnōrisis* is not only Electra's recognition of Orestes as her brother, but our recognition of Orestes as the hero who will kill his mother and avenge his father, the *prattōn* of the play's *praxis*. The myth dictates that Orestes perform these acts, but from what we have seen of the character so far, he hardly seems up to the task.[21] Virtually the first thing we learn about him is that he is there in secret (88, 93) and lurking on the outskirts of Argos so he can escape over the border if he is recognized (96–97). This apparent cowardice is in fact part of the reason why his sister refuses to believe that the tokens are his: it seems impossible that "my brave brother would come to this land in secret through fear of Aegisthus" (524–26). As an exile he is, as he himself says, "weak" (*asthenēs*, 236, 352). Will he confirm Aegisthus's assumption that a "weak" man cannot exact vengeance? Orestes is not *asthenēs* in the way Aegisthus meant: he is the son of a king. But he must show himself worthy of that noble lineage; as Electra remarks, "It would be shameful if his father captured Troy but he cannot even kill Aegisthus, one on one, especially as he is younger and born of a better father" (336–38). The revenge thus becomes a test of his *eugeneia* in both the literal and figurative sense of the word, and it is not at all clear that he passes: he will need to be coached through the planning by the Paidagogos (599–639) and reminded by his sister to "be a man" (693, 982). Orestes himself had proposed that *euandria* must be judged not by the external tokens of wealth and birth, those empty *doxasmata*, but by a man's own *ēthos* (385). By this standard, Orestes would seem to be a failure. Are we, then, going to recognize this character as our hero based on a lock of hair, a faded footprint, and a tattered rag?

The answer, it turns out, is yes. Euripides goes out of his way to show these tokens as implausible, unrealistic, artificial. Nonetheless, they work: they really do belong to Orestes. Again Euripides emphasizes the artificiality of the moment: what finally persuades Electra is not the Aeschylean tokens but an equally contrived and secondhand sign, a scar Orestes received as a child chasing a deer in his father's house (573–74). This playful allusion to Odysseus's scar, the memento of an early heroic boar hunt (*Odyssey* 19.390–475), is of a piece with the previous tokens, but whereas they are rejected as laughably unrealistic, this scar is accepted as a plausible imprint (*kharaktēr*, 572), sure proof (*tekmērion*, 575), and convincing sign (*sumbolon*, 577) of Orestes' identity. The language of signs and the literary allusion denaturalize this marker of identity, even as it is stamped on Orestes' skin.[22] The artificial becomes natural as Electra embraces her long-lost brother.

We were told in the first episode not to judge a man by external tokens. Here we are given the most ostentatiously external tokens, yet they turn out to reveal Orestes' true identity. This Orestes really is *the* Orestes, the son and avenger of Agamemnon, the *prattōn* of the tragic *praxis* to which he turns as soon as the recognition is complete. You may not be able to tell a good man from his wealth or birth, but apparently you can tell a brother from a footprint. And maybe, after all, you *can* tell a good man from his social status as well, since the man we have just recognized as the play's hero just happens to be a prince in disguise. He just happens to be *eugenēs* in the literal sense of the word, and if he is poor, it is only because the tyrant Aegisthus has deprived him of his rightful property, a temporary dispossession that will be rectified with his murder. "Embrace your dear treasure (*philon thēsauron*), whom the god reveals!" the Paidagogos tells Electra (565). This suspect coin is discovered to be solid gold—a royal treasure—on the basis of these dubious stamps, the faded echo of literary conventions no longer in currency.

The *anagnōrisis* that seems at first to confirm the lessons of the first episode in fact annuls them, as we recognize—or misrecognize—Orestes as a nobleman and a hero. The substantive ethics and politics of the play's "reality" are abandoned. Orestes' heroic status is shown to be empty, based not on *ēthos* but on literary allusions and theatrical clichés. His social status is likewise empty, based on the accident of birth and devoid of ethical content. Elitism, like heroism, is just an empty form. These two misrecognitions, the social and the dramatic, are mutually reinforcing.[23] Orestes inherits his dramatic status from his royal father: the right to avenge Agamemnon—and thus to be the protagonist of this revenge drama—is a kind of theatrical wealth passed down from father to son in this illustrious tragic *genos*. At the same time, as we shall see, it is Orestes' enactment of the tragic *praxis* that will secure his social standing in Argos.

Euripides shows Orestes' identity to be based on *kena doxasmata*; nevertheless, he asks us to believe in these empty illusions—or at least pretend we do—since if we don't this tragedy is essentially over. There will be no reunion between brother and sister, no vengeance for Agamemnon, no punishment for Aegisthus, no matricide—all things we know, mythically and dramatically, "have to" happen, even if that necessity is itself just based on a set of mythic quotations and theatrical conventions. The structure of the *muthos*, both the myth and the plot, thus compels our recognition. But in fact it only asks us to recognize what we already knew, both from this play (where Orestes identified himself at line 80) and from tragedy as a whole: we recognize Orestes in part because we have seen him in other tragedies, including and especially the Aeschylean tragedies from which his recognition tokens are borrowed. His role is in that sense purely formal: he steps into a heroic footprint left by the buskins of past actors playing Orestes. It doesn't much matter whether his foot fits or whether he is worthy of his mythic part. If we want to see this tragic *praxis*—the tragedy of Orestes and Electra, the *praxis* we came to see—we have to recognize Orestes as the *prattōn*.

We get our play, then, but at the cost of "reality" and its egalitarian possibilities. With the recognition of Orestes, the reality so vividly introduced in the opening scene is de-realized. Whatever "utopian tendency" may have lain in the rocky soil of Argos will not be allowed to grow: we will not even be given a chance to decide how utopian it actually was. The recognition of this elite hero means we will never find out whether Aegisthus was right that a poor farmer is too "weak" to avenge Agamemnon or what it might mean, within the tragic scenario, for one of the *polloi* to be *aristos*. These questions cannot be answered—they cannot even really be asked—within the formal structure of this tragedy. It is not that the genre is incapable of asking them, for we have seen that the first episode does precisely that. Instead, *Electra* raises these questions only to stifle them. The *anagnōrisis* both enacts and exposes this stifling effect when it asks Electra—and us—to put faith in artifice, not essence, *kena doxasmata*, not *ēthos*. In making the recognition of Orestes a repudiation of the lessons of the first episode, this scene offers us a choice between "reality" with its potentially radical ethical and social contents, and tragic form: the tragic *anagnōrisis*, the tragic agent, the tragic *praxis*. But that choice is really no choice at all: we already made it the minute we walked into the Theater of Dionysus.

• • •

The second half of the drama plays out the consequences of this choice of form over content: the evacuation of content altogether. On the one hand, reality is lost, along with its egalitarian politics. On the other hand, tragedy itself is reduced to a collection of hollow conventions and quotations, unable to fully explicate the ethical implications of its action. The process begins immediately, in the ode that follows the recognition scene (699–746). The ode deals with an episode from the earlier history of the House of Atreus, Thyestes' seduction of Atreus's wife and theft of the golden lamb that symbolized his rule. In anger at Thyestes' crime, Zeus changed the course of the sun and stars, reversed the direction of the winds, and overturned the natural order of the cosmos.

The ode constructs a mythical framework for the action to follow. The rule of Aegisthus, Thyestes' son, is as illegitimate and unnatural as his father's was. Orestes' murder of Aegisthus will not only avenge his father and grandfather and thus restore order to this troubled house; it will not only depose a tyrant and restore order to the polis. It will also restore order to the very heavens, enacting the justice of Zeus.[24]

This is the mythic paradigm that we are asked to recognize in the murder of Aegisthus. But this recognition will turn out to be as implausible as Orestes' own. An apparition (*phasmata*, 711), "a story that persists among graying rumors" (700–701), the golden lamb is another mythic artifact, like Odysseus's scar or Orestes' lock of hair. It is hard to believe that the course of the heavens was changed because of this fantastic creature. And in fact the chorus do not believe it:

> λέγεται <τάδε>, τὰν δὲ πί-
>   στιν σμικρὰν παρ' ἔμοιγ' ἔχει,
> στρέψαι θερμὰν ἀέλιον
> χρυσωπὸν ἕδραν ἀλλάξαν-
>   τα δυστυχίαι βροτείωι
> θνατᾶς ἕνεκεν δίκας.
> φοβεροὶ δὲ βροτοῖσι μῦθοι
> κέρδος πρὸς θεῶν θεραπείαν.
> ὧν οὐ μνασθεῖσα πόσιν
> κτείνεις, κλεινῶν συγγενέτειρ' ἀδελφῶν.

> So it is told, but it holds little
> credence with me,
> that the sun left its warm abode,
> and turned away its golden face
> on account of man's misfortune
> for the sake of mortal justice.
> But stories men fear
> are profitable (*kerdos*) for the gods' worship.
> Ignoring them you killed your husband,
> sister of famous brothers. (737–46)

The story is unbelievable, but it is "profitable" to believe it. This belief in the implausible reiterates the dynamic of the recognition scene: its mythic tokens may have held "little credence" with us, but it was "profitable" to act as though they did and to recognize the hero they purported to identify. This same dynamic also governs all the action that will unfold in the second half of the play as we are asked to believe that a perverted sacrifice is the restoration of cosmic order.

As the ode concludes, we hear the death cries of Aegisthus, which the chorus compare to the "infernal thunder of Zeus" (748), thus connecting his death to the ode's story of cosmic disturbance. Their own ode has taught them how to interpret the meaning of these "not unintelligible blasts of wind" (749): all-seeing Dikē has come at last, as Electra says (771). Order is restored with the just return of the land's former rulers and the deposing of the tyrant (876–77). "Great is the strength of Dikē" (958; cf. 955).

But to interpret the killing of Aegisthus as a vindication of divine justice requires a suspension of disbelief as great as the chorus's toward the story of the golden lamb or Electra's toward the tokens, since this narrative frame ill fits the events the messenger actually describes. As he tells it, Orestes and Pylades come upon Aegisthus as he is in a meadow cutting myrtle sprigs for a wreath; he greets the strangers warmly and invites them to share his sacrifice. The accumulation of sacrificial details sets the stage for the perverted ritual to come: as Aegisthus is examining the animal's entrails, Orestes brings the meat cleaver down upon the king's spine. "He writhed, convulsed down the whole length of his body, dying a bloody, violent death" (842–43). The hero enters carrying the lifeless body of Aegisthus, which he invites his sister to desecrate (895–99)—a sacrilege from which even Electra shies, for all her bitter loathing of the man.[25]

Euripides spares no detail to show the gruesome impiety of the scene. Yet this horrific murder is hailed as a triumph. "Oh Mycenean maidens, glorious in victory," begins the messenger, "I announce to his friends the victory of Orestes! The murderer of Agamemnon, Aegisthus lies on the ground. Praise the gods!" (762–64). The chorus follow the messenger's lead with an ode whose language and meter strongly evoke epinician, the genre that feted archaic aristocrats and tyrants for their athletic victories.[26] They call Electra to join them in singing a "song of great victory" (kallinikon ōidan) in celebration of her brother's victory-crown (nikai stephanophora), greater than those won in the Olympic games (862–65). Electra's antiphonal prayer of thanks to "Light and the blazing four-horse chariot of the Sun" (866) ties the language of epinician back to the theme of cosmic restitution established in the second stasimon: the sun, restored to its proper place by Orestes' act, bears celestial witness to that act. Electra greets Orestes on his return as "Glorious victor, born from a father who bore victory from the Trojan war," (880–81) and binds his head with wreaths, "for you return to the house, not having run a useless footrace but having killed our enemy Aegisthus, who killed our father" (883–85). Orestes responds with a thanksgiving to the gods that recalls the return of his victorious father in Aeschylus's *Agamemnon* (890–94; cf. *Agamemnon* 810–11).

With the assassination of Aegisthus, we are told, order is restored to the universe. Orestes has proven himself worthy of his father, and has reclaimed his property and power. The evil tyrant has been ousted and the sun displaced by his father's crimes has returned to its proper path. The marked dissonance between this myth of cosmic restitution and the gruesome murder, between the structural form of the narrative and its actual contents, repeats the recognition-misrecognition of the *anagnōrisis* and the belief-disbelief of the second stasimon.[27] It tells us a manifestly implausible story and challenges us to believe it. But in fact it doesn't even matter whether we believe it: like the story of the golden lamb, this narrative delivers its profit whether we believe it or not.

That profit accrues particularly to Orestes, who is hailed not only as mighty victor, heroic avenger, and restorer of cosmic justice, but as king of Argos. After he killed Aegisthus, Orestes was about to be seized by the tyrant's attendants. "I am Orestes!" he cried out. "Do not kill me, old slaves of my father!" "And one of them, an old man who had served the house a long time, recognized him, and immediately they crowned [Orestes], wailing with joy" (850–55). The good news is spread by another faithful servant (*prospolon*, 766), the messenger who reports these events, and is celebrated by the chorus of country maidens, who dance in joy at the restored "tyranny" of their "dear" royal family (*philoi basilēs*, 876–77).

With this outburst of support, we are invited to see the assassination of Aegisthus as a victory for everyone: not only for our triumphant hero, but also for all the people of Argos, slaves and maidens and messengers, and even farmers. Throughout the play Aegisthus has been presented as the anti-type of the Farmer: his *hubris* in taking what doesn't belong to him is repeatedly paired with the Farmer's virtue in not doing so (46, 59, 68, 257, 266). In her *damnatio memoriae*, Electra reviles Aegisthus for, among myriad other offenses, "boasting that you were someone because your money made you strong" (*khrēmasi sthenōn*, 939). She elaborates in words that could come from the mouth of her husband: man's nature is sure and abiding, wealth is not, and particularly wealth unjustly gained (940–44). The reality in which Electra learned these truths was created by Aegisthus himself: it was the tyrant,

with his belief in the "strength" of the wealthy and wellborn, who introduced the Farmer into the myth and shifted its setting to the poor hovel
where his body now lies.

The tyrannicide seems to mark a new dawn in which the virtuous
poor will flourish, and the egalitarian principles discovered by Orestes
will finally become the law of the land. But if they do, it will be a land
ruled not by farmers but by a hereditary monarch. The radical political
possibilities of the play's realist opening are cut off at the very moment
they seem to be fulfilled, since the blow that kills Aegisthus also proves
him right: a farmer or his son *is* too "weak" (*asthenēs*) to exact revenge.
Instead, the aristocratic youth who does is enthusiastically crowned by
his father's loyal slaves. Meanwhile, the notional farmer's son is reduced to a prop in the revenge plan, as Electra uses the fiction of a
newborn child to lure Clytemnestra to her death.[28] In the recognition
scene, Orestes was hailed as a "dear treasure" by another loyal family
slave, the Paidagogos. That recognition is cashed out now, as the treasure is converted into royal power, acclaimed by the "dear" king's devoted subjects and celebrated in epinician, a genre that made an art
form of misrecognizing the wellborn and wealthy as "dear treasures."

Orestes never actually takes up his crown; after the matricide he will
leave Argos, never to return. The myth of cosmic restoration is an empty
form, a narrative structure divorced from real content, both in its unfolding and in its conclusion. The disconnect between the messenger's
account of Aegisthus's slaying and the characters' response shows this
narrative to be another *kena doxasma*, like the mythic tokens of Orestes'
recognition or the implausible story of the golden lamb. And like those
other empty tokens, this contrived *muthos* displaces reality: the rural
setting is just a temporary aberration, a *taragmos* both generic and social, brought to an end with Orestes' glorious coronation. And if you
don't believe this, it doesn't really matter: the play's faithful slaves will
do it for you. Their cheerful false consciousness assumes the heavy burden of recognition the play has laid upon the audience, as we are repeatedly asked to credit—or at least pretend to credit—the incredible.
They believe so we won't have to, and they pay the political price while
we enjoy the spectatorial profit.[29]

The misrecognition of Aegisthus's murder as an athletic victory fore-
closes any serious ethical analysis of the act: all the characters can do is
cheer. This misrecognition not only overwrites reality, as we have seen;
it also eviscerates tragedy as an imitation of an action in its full ethical
significance. We see this in the matricide that follows. Needless to say,

the matricide is presented as a highly ambiguous act.[30] Whereas Aegisthus's death was an epinician triumph, this murder is "a bitter and unpleasant contest" (*agōnisma*, 987) that yields as its trophy (*tropaia*, 1174) only suffering. As Orestes sees his mother approaching, he realizes the horror of the deed he is about to commit: "What am I to do, then? Will I really kill my mother?" (*Ti dēta drōmen? Mēter' ē phoneusomen?* 967). Like his heroic persona, his dramatic crisis is borrowed from Aeschylus's *Choephoroi*. At the crucial moment of that play, Orestes cries out, "What am I to do? Will I feel shame to kill my mother?" (*Ti drasō? Mēter' aidesthō ktanein?* 899). Like its *anagnōrisis*, *Electra*'s *peripeteia* is both a *mimēsis* of a *praxis* and a *mimēsis* of a *mimēsis* of a *praxis*, a staging of the tragic action "the murder of Clytemnestra." The moment borrows *Choephoroi*'s ethical urgency but also hollows it out, for Orestes' cry feel less like the anguish of a man caught between two impossible choices than the vacillation of a character seeking inspiration from his predecessor as to how to play his tragic part.

In *Choephoroi*, Orestes' anguished *ti drasō?* prompts an unambiguous response: "Where from now on are the Pythian oracles of Apollo, his oaths, trustworthy and truly sworn? Consider all men your enemies before the gods" (900–902). The oracle of Apollo has commanded Orestes to kill his mother; he believes the oracle and obeys. Euripides' Orestes, by contrast, obeys but does not believe. "Oh Apollo, what great stupidity (*amathian*) you have prophesied!" (971). "Where Apollo is stupid (*skaios*), who is wise?" counters Electra, but Orestes cannot credit the wisdom of a god who has commanded him to kill his mother. Maybe, he suggests, it was the work of an avenging demon masquerading as the god (979). Electra scoffs at this idea, but he persists: "I could not be persuaded that this prophecy is good" (981). He refuses to believe that Apollo's oracle is valid. He does not even believe that it is really Apollo's. Nevertheless, he obeys: "If this seems good to the gods, let it be" (986–87).[31]

Sustained by this obedience without belief, the word of Apollo becomes an imperative without moral grounding, an empty command. In the second stasimon the chorus suggest that stories of divine intervention are profitable whether one believes them or not. That empty belief pays dreadful dividends here as Orestes kills his mother in obedience to a "stupid" prophecy that he does not believe. Stripped of theological motivation or ethical commitment, the matricide becomes a purely formal exercise, just another mythic footprint into which the hero must place his foot.

The murder itself is recounted after the fact in a series of fleeting images drawn from Aeschylus's account: Clytemnestra, her breast bared in supplication; Orestes shielding his eyes with his cloak as he drives the sword into her neck (1206–26). This latter image (1221–23) elaborates Aeschylus's comparison of Orestes to Perseus, his eyes averted as he killed the Gorgon (*Choephoroi* 831–37). The myth of Perseus has been a recurring leitmotif throughout *Electra*. The hero first appears in the first stasimon in an ekphrastic description of Achilles' shield; among the signs (*sēmata*, 456) depicted on this famous Homeric object is Perseus holding aloft the Gorgon's severed head (459–60). Immediately preceding the recognition scene, the ode offers this multiply-mediated sign—a mythic exemplum on an artistic object that is itself a literary allusion—as a paradigm for Orestes' heroic action.[32] With the murder of Aegisthus, Orestes seems to follow this mythic model: he enters the stage, as the messenger says, "bearing not the Gorgon's head" but the dead Aegisthus (855–57). But if it strained credulity then, this icon of heroic endeavor now becomes devoid of all meaning, a *sēma* without referent. The chorus sing of justice (1169–71, 1189), of a "change of winds for the house" (1147–48) and the "reverse-flow of *dikē*" (1155). But even they are unable to sustain the pretense that this "exchange of evils" (1147) is the execution of divine justice or the restoration of cosmic order. It is simply, as Orestes says, a "bloody and polluted act" (*tad' erga phonia musara*, 1178–79).

As the siblings lament what they have done, their divinized uncles Castor and Polydeuces appear above the *skēnē*. Castor speaks for the pair and passes divine judgment on their sister's murder:

δίκαια μέν νυν ἥδ' ἔχει, σὺ δ' οὐχὶ δρᾷς.
Φοῖβος δέ, Φοῖβος—ἀλλ' ἄναξ γάρ ἐστ' ἐμός,
σιγῶ· σοφὸς δ' ὢν οὐκ ἔχρησέ σοι σοφά.
αἰνεῖν δ' ἀνάγκη ταῦτα· τἀντεῦθεν δὲ χρὴ
πράσσειν ἃ Μοῖρα Ζεύς τ' ἔκρανε σοῦ πέρι.

She now has justice but you do not do it.
It was Apollo, Apollo—but because he is my lord
I will keep silent. He is wise but his prophecy to you
    was not.
But one must (*anankē*) accept these things.
It is necessary (*khrē*) henceforth
to do what Fate and Zeus have ordained for you.

(1244–48)

In Aeschylus's *Choephoroi*, the conflict of *dikē* against *dikē* generates an examination of guilt on both sides that fills not only that play but the next as well, finally to be resolved in the court of Athena in *Eumenides*. Here that extended exploration of *dikē* and responsibility is compressed into an elliptical paradox—"she now has justice but you do not do it"—that encapsulates the moral ambiguity of the matricide without analyzing or resolving it. That same paradox characterizes the god: Apollo is wise but his prophecy is not. This contradictory theology simultaneously absolves Orestes by laying responsibility for the murder on the god and absolves Apollo by pointedly refusing to speak his guilt. Its compressed, almost oxymoronic formulation, like that concerning the justice of Clytemnestra's death, preempts serious thinking through of the questions of guilt, human and divine, that the matricide has raised. We are left with a theology in which the gods neither take responsibility for the acts they command nor demand responsibility from the humans who commit them.

This empty theology imposes upon mortals an empty necessity (*anankē, khrē*): one must accept the divine command and do what Zeus and Fate have decreed. The obedience without belief that drove Orestes to matricide becomes a categorical imperative governing all action, divine as well as human. When asked at the end of his speech why he and Polydeuces did not intervene to save their sister, Castor answers, "Fate and necessity (*anankē*) led to this necessity (*to khreōn*), and the sound of Apollo's tongue is unwise" (1301–2). The circularity of the expression mirrors the vacuity of this ethics: necessity (*anankē*) leads to necessity (*to khreōn*). Within that circle, it doesn't matter whether Apollo's command is wise or not; it is still "necessary" and must be obeyed.

Orestes and Electra's fated future will play out in obedience to this empty necessity. Electra will marry Pylades. Orestes will leave Argos: he will be hounded by the Furies until he reaches Athens, where he will be acquitted in the court of the Areopagus. He will then found a city in Arcadia that will bear his name. The bodies of Aegisthus and Clytemnestra will receive decent burial, the former by the citizens of Argos, the latter by the recently returned Menelaus and Helen (who, in a surprise twist, turns out not to have been in Troy after all). Even the Farmer is not forgotten: as the god tells Orestes, "Your brother-in-law in name shall go to Phocis with Pylades, who shall grant him deep wealth" (1286–87). Castor concludes with this parting promise: "When you have fulfilled your allotted fate for murder, you will be happy (*eudaimonēseis*), released from these labors" (1290–91).

These scattershot predictions and aetiologies fulfill the structural requirements of the *muthos*—everyone ends up where they need to be, mythically speaking, and all the loose ends are tied up—but in doing so, they void the contents of the play we have just seen. Aegisthus's burial by the citizens of Argos pretends that he was a beloved king, not a hated tyrant; at the same time, the permanent exile of Orestes from Argos deprives those citizens of the new king they had so enthusiastically crowned after Aegisthus's assassination. The triumphalist narrative of tyrannicide is evacuated of significance, dramatic or political: apparently it no longer matters who will rule Argos. The passing comment that Helen never went to Troy casually undercuts the rationale of the Trojan War and the glory of its hero Agamemnon: how this retroactively affects the question of Clytemnestra's justification for killing her husband, and hence the justification for her own death, is something the play evidently has no time or inclination to explore. Electra's marriage to Pylades annuls her marriage to the Farmer; it simply pretends that prior union never existed. The Farmer's reward meanwhile vitiates the entire ethics his character embodied, a point to which we will return shortly.

The god's prognostications do not engage the questions of guilt raised by the matricide, or pass judgment on its justice: the trial that is the culmination of the saga in Aeschylus's *Oresteia* here is just another item on Orestes' future itinerary. So ethically uncommitted is this closing prophecy that it is difficult even to tell whether the fate it describes is a punishment or reward: the matricides bemoan their separation and exile from their fatherland, but their uncle reassures them that their future is not after all so bleak (1311–13, 1319–20), and we might well think that they have gotten off relatively lightly, all things considered. The issues of responsibility, divine and human, that Castor pointedly declines to resolve are referred to the Areopagus, where Orestes will be acquitted on the basis of Apollo's prophecy (1266–67), that "stupid" prophecy he obeyed without believing, that Castor himself agreed was "not wise."

That prophecy will free Orestes of liability for the matricide. It will also cleanse him and Electra of blood pollution. The Dioscouroi do not speak to those polluted by murder, but Castor *will* speak to Orestes and Electra (1292–1302).[33] They are not *musaroi*, polluted, in his eyes, because the murder was Apollo's doing. As always, Electra is skeptical: *she* received no prophecy from Apollo to kill her mother (1303–4). She and Orestes had already acknowledged the defilement of their "bloody and polluted act" (*tad' erga phonia musara*, 1178–79) and accepted the consequences: life in exile from their city and from human society (1194–1200). But Castor insists on their purity. In the play's final and most disturbing misrecognition, polluted matricides are declared ritually clean on the basis of a token—Apollo's prophecy—that has been acknowledged to be stupid and implausible. The hero whose foot hardly fit the winged sandals of Perseus, whose Gorgon-slaying was in fact sacrilege and matricide, is now protected by the "Gorgon-faced" shield of Athena (*gorgōpa*, 1257). After his trial in blessed (*eudaimona*, 1289) Athens, the matricide himself will be blessed (*eudaimonēseis*, 1291). This *eudaimonia* is as circular and empty as fate's necessity, as the chorus's closing lines suggest: "Fare well. And whoever is able to fare well and is not worn down by disaster, that mortal is blessed (*eudaimona prassei*, 1359).[34]

With the deus ex machina, we get a formal conclusion to the drama. The gods' appearance is a generic sign that the plot has reached its telos and the play is over. But like all other generic signs in *Electra*, this one is void: it ends the play without providing resolution, ethical or dramatic. It fails to clarify the moral status of the act or its agents, either to themselves or to the audience, and instead blithely misrecognizes these bloody murderers as ritually clean. It fails to justify Apollo's command or to situate the matricide in a larger ethical or theological framework; instead, it reinforces the emptiness of the divine necessity that, however stupid, must be obeyed. Even Orestes and Electra cannot believe the god's prophecy; as a formal gesture of closure the divine speech fails, as they continue to interrogate their uncle about their ritual status, the role of Apollo, and the future he has promised.[35] Or rather, it succeeds only formally: it does bring the play to an end, but that end is devoid of significant content. It is just another hollow theatrical convention.

The inclusion of the Farmer in this final prophecy brings us back with a sudden jolt to reality, the reality of rural Argos so insisted on in the first third of the play and barely mentioned since. It makes us realize just how much we had forgotten this reality and seems to remind us of it now just to make sure we really have forgotten. How are we to understand the Farmer's fate? "Your brother-in-law in name shall go to Phocis with Pylades, who shall grant him deep wealth" (1286–87). This divine validation of the poor man's virtue seems to affirm the ethical lessons of the opening scene. "The man you have described is noble and deserves to fare well," Orestes said of the Farmer (262). Now he will get his just reward. At the same time, though, the nature of the reward undoes the social lesson of the play's opening sequence. There the Farmer taught us that wealth does not mark virtue, but his enrichment ensures that from now on, in his case at least, it will. Wealth and virtue are aligned at last, a happy end to the *taragmos* that so confused Orestes. The social order disrupted by the marriage of a princess and a farmer is resecured, as the man who had the good sense to remain Orestes' brother-in-law in name alone will now be supported in style by Electra's real husband, the aristocratic Pylades.[36] And if in the case of the Farmer the good man is made wealthy, in the case of Orestes and Electra the wealthy are made good, their crimes whitewashed by their deified uncle (and, we might recall, an erstwhile suitor for Electra's hand, 313). The elite status that was earlier shown to be an empty token here takes on real substance in the form of divinely guaranteed *eudaimonia*. Wealth and birth do turn out to have force (*sthenos*), as Aegisthus assumed, and the elite protagonists, those "dear treasures," find their proper fates: an aristocratic marriage for Electra, for Orestes the founding of a new city to call his own.

The Farmer's reward reminds us of a reality we abandoned when we recognized Orestes on the basis of an Aeschylean footprint and an Odyssean scar. That real world has been left behind, along with any radical possibilities it might have held: that a princess could find happiness as the wife of a farmer, that their son might avenge his royal grandfather and inherit his throne, that a man might truly be judged on his *ēthos* alone. Perhaps those "utopian" fantasies were just *kena doxasmata* from the start, but now we will never know: the potentially utopian consequences of the play's reality will never be realized. In fact, as we have seen, they are de-realized by a tragic illusion explicitly marked as such.

That de-realization of reality continues to the very end of the play and follows us out of the theater. The play concludes with Castor's speech of farewell as the Dioscouroi set off to bring aid to ships on the Sicilian sea (1347): "We will not help those who are defiled (*musarois*); but those who love what is holy and just, these men we save and release from difficult hardships" (1350–53). Scholars debate whether this is a reference to one of Athens's naval expeditions to Sicily: since the date of the play is unknown, it is impossible to tell. But regardless of whether it alludes to a specific contemporary event, the reference to a topical location jars us abruptly out of the mythical world of the play and into reality, our own "real" late fifth-century Athenian reality. But what are we to make of this offer of righteous support from gods who we have just watched wave off the defilement of matricide and promise murderers *eudaimonia*? Their offer is hard to believe, although maybe it would be profitable to do so. After all, we have already put our faith in equally implausible tokens.

• • •

Electra suggests that tragic form, far from instantiating a "utopian tendency," instead smothers it: radical egalitarianism remains a potential that cannot (yet) be realized. The play's utopianism, rather, lies precisely in staging this potential as unrealized. In the Marxist debate about the politics of realism, Georg Lukács argues, against Ernst Bloch, that "authentic" realism is ideologically avant-garde because it represents not only the material conditions of existence at a particular historical moment, but also the latent forces that will one day revolutionize those conditions. Realist writers, he proposes,

> Form the authentic ideological avant-garde since they depict the vital, but not immediately obvious forces at work in objective reality. They do so with such profundity and truth that the products of their imagination receive confirmation from subsequent events. . . . Great realism, therefore, does not portray an immediately obvious aspect of reality. . . . It captures tendencies of development that only exist incipiently and so have not yet had the opportunity to unfold their entire human and social potential.[37]

Lukács's insistence on the anticipatory nature of "authentic" realism helps us to understand better both the realism of Euripides' *Electra* and its utopianism. The play depicts not the immediate, surface elements of its historical reality, but the latent relation between the residual and the emergent that constitutes the deeper truth of that reality, a relation that involves real political struggle and entails real political consequences. *Electra*'s radical force, on this reading, lies less in its utopian imagination of full egalitarianism than in its representation of that egalitarianism as still to come, as emergent, not fully realized in the present. In staging both this not-yet-realized possibility and the formal structures, empty but efficacious, that prevented its realization, the play reflects its historical moment "not merely in the simple sense in which a successful photograph mirrors the original," but inasmuch as it "express[es] the wealth and diversity of reality, reflecting forces as yet submerged beneath the surface, which only blossom forth visibly to all at a later stage."[38] What allows art to express these subterranean forces is, as Adorno stresses in his critique of Lukács, its aesthetic form, the formal mediation that grants it a critical distance from its immediate reality.[39] Euripides' reflection *in* form *on* form and the social content it expresses and suppresses is the source of the play's true radicalism, and its truest realism.

CHAPTER 4

The Politics of Political Allegory

Euripides' *Suppliants* poses a particular challenge for a politics of form because its political content is so explicit. The play is often labeled a "political tragedy," and with good reason, since it is overtly, insistently political. Set in Attica, its plot celebrates Athens as the benevolent protector of divine principle and Panhellenic law. In extended passages of political theorizing, it virtually shouts the patriotic slogans of Athenian democracy. The hypothesist seems to hit the nail on the head when he writes: "The play is an encomium of Athens."

Suppliants has a lot to say about politics, then. But this noisy political content is complicated by the play's form, in particular by the lamentations of the Argive mothers who make up the chorus. In the tension between its ostentatiously political content and the "anti-politics" (in Nicole Loraux's phrase) of its choral laments, *Suppliants* stages a self-conscious meditation on the relation between politics and tragedy, and a critique of the very notion of "political tragedy." This play that seems, at first glance, to insist on tragedy as a mode of political discourse in fact reveals a gap between the tragic and the political and exposes the representational limits of each: tragedy cannot represent the realities of Athenian democratic politics; political discourse cannot represent the Real of death. Ultimately, the play does make a claim for tragedy's contribution to the polis; not, however, as a form of political discourse, but instead as a means of *psukhagōgia*: *Suppliants* leads the audience to a psychic space where politics and tragedy are one, and it is precisely in this synthesis that it locates tragedy's political efficacy. If the debate between historicism and humanism—between tragedy as politically engaged and tragedy as a vehicle for universal truths—has been one of the central fault lines in the history of scholarship on the genre, *Suppliants* offers an early and sophisticated intervention in this debate.

Suppliants dramatizes an episode from Athens's patriotic history, one that was recounted at the annual Funeral Oration among the other noble Athenian deeds of yore. In the battle between Polyneices and Eteocles for the throne of Thebes, the Argives had come to the aid of Polyneices, and seven of their generals had died fighting at the city gates. After the battle, the Thebans refused to return the bodies, in contravention of Greek religious custom. This play opens with the mothers of the dead sitting in supplication at the temple of Demeter, begging the Athenians to help them retrieve the bodies of their sons for burial. Theseus, the king of Athens, initially hesitates: he knows this will mean war with the Thebans; but his mother Aithra convinces him that it is the right thing to do. So the Athenians, champions of the downtrodden and defenders of Panhellenic law, do battle with the Thebans, roundly defeat them, and recover the bodies of the Argive heroes for burial.

The myth was familiar, but this play only barely maintains the mythic distance from contemporary reality that was a defining feature of tragedy. Set in Eleusis, just outside Athens, *Suppliants* is full of anachronistic references to the institutions and ideologies of the fifth-century Athenian polis. While such references are not uncommon in Euripides, the anachronism in *Suppliants* is unparalleled in its extent and explicitness; indeed, it is one of the play's most striking aesthetic features. Here mythic heroes speak in language imported directly from contemporary Athenian political discourse, like the funeral oration the Argive king Adrastus delivers over the dead heroes. Drawing overtly on the distinctive rhetoric of this Athenian institution, his speech paints the mythic Seven as the kind of men one might meet in the Agora. The play's Athens, though ruled by a mythic king, is also distinctly fifth-century: "a free city" (*eleuthera polis*), it is not governed by a single man; instead, as its king proclaims, "The people (*dēmos*) rule in turn (*en merei*) by annual rotation, not granting the greatest share to the wealthy man but the poor man, too, holds an equal share (*ison*)" (404–8). The mythic monarch uses specifically classical Athenian political vocabulary (*dēmos, en merei, ison*) and draws on specifically classical Athenian political theory (the sovereignty of the demos, the alternation of public offices, equality before the law). In the almost technical specificity of its references to democratic institutions and ideologies, *Suppliants* insists on its own political status. It presents itself as a kind of political discourse, and passages like this are often cited in the company of political thinkers like Thucydides, Plato, and the Old Oligarch. Likewise, with the ensuing *agōn* about the relative merits of democracy and tyranny, the play contributes to a contemporary theoretical debate about constitutional forms that we see in Herodotus and the Old Oligarch, and later in Plato and Aristotle.[1]

In its aggressive anachronism, *Suppliants* seems to be a formal experiment in staging contemporary politics. Ostentatiously collapsing the mythic and the modern polis, it presents its tragic action as political allegory. In so doing, it develops the allegorical potential inherent in the genre as a whole. Tragedy staged issues and situations that were presumably relevant in some regard to its fifth-century audience, but these are always presented at a distance. This structural feature of the genre was conspicuous enough to merit an origin myth: Herodotus recounts that when Phrynichus produced *The Sack of Miletus* just one year after the Persians' conquest of that city, he was fined by the Athenians "for reminding them of their own misfortunes" (*oikēia kaka*); and from then on, drama on contemporary subjects was banned (6.21). By law, if not by nature, tragedy seems to require distance in order to produce its characteristic pity and fear. Banned from speaking directly about contemporary realities, the genre can represent the Athenian self only through the medium of another (*allos*), through stories set in another place and time. In this sense, tragedy is intrinsically allegorical: it speaks otherwise (*all-ēgoreuein*).[2]

This allegorical nature is the grounding premise of historicizing approaches to the genre. While the hunt for direct and specific historical references has largely gone out of style, virtually all historicist (including New Historicist) readings are predicated on the same allegorical logic and the assumption that tragedy is "speaking otherwise" through the medium of its mythic scenarios about the *oikēia kaka*, the issues and concerns, of fifth-century Athens.[3]

Suppliants presents a marked example of this general feature of tragedy. Its mimetic compression, the insistent collapsing of the distance between mythic Athens and the contemporary city, seems not only to allow but indeed to demand an allegorical reading. That allegorical lure is all the stronger if we see in the plot an oblique reference to the Battle of Delium in 424 BCE, in which the Boeotians (including the

Thebans) defeated the Athenians and then refused to return the bodies of the dead. In *Suppliants* Athens would seem to reverse the outcome of that battle on appeal to the mythic past and claim the moral high ground over its enemies, to stage, as Angus Bowie puts it, a "mythical/ theatrical 'rectification' of recent events."[4] At the same time, the play draws up a fantasy treaty with current antagonist Argos, which abases itself before Athens's beneficent might and promises its eternal support in an oath that anticipates the one signed between the two states a few years later in 420 BCE. Through its insistent contraction of the mythic past and political present, *Suppliants* presents itself not just as political discourse, but as a political *praxis* that will repair the past and secure the future. Tragedy not only represents political events but makes them happen. It thus becomes, in effect, politics by other means, not just political allegory but allegorical politics.

In typical Euripidean fashion, though, the play both stages a "political tragedy" and simultaneously theorizes that hybrid creature, analyzing the implications of its own experiment in mimetic contraction. If tragedy, from Phrynichus on, was required to "speak otherwise" about Athenian realities, *Suppliants*'s anachronisms diminish that safe alterity: *Suppliants*'s Athens is too little different (*allos*) from contemporary Athens, and this loss of mimetic distance calls attention to the play's allegorical status and the politics of its political allegory. In the process, this "political tragedy" reveals the discursive distance between the tragic and the political and their non-congruity as ways of representing the world and acting upon it.[5]

My interest in this chapter is not so much in the content of the play's allegory, what it says (otherwise) about Athens and its imperial, domestic, or gender ideologies. Such issues have been well examined by others.[6] Rather, I am interested in the form of *Suppliants*'s allegory and allegory as a tragic form. If all tragedy is inherently allegorical, as historicist scholarship assumes, Euripides turns this generic feature into a resource for thought. His experiment in mimetic compression allows him to explore the nature of tragic mimesis as a mode of representation, both aesthetic and political.[7] The mimetic form itself becomes a kind of theoretical content: the doubleness of allegory offers not only a means of saying one thing through the vehicle of another, but also a way of thinking about the relationship between vehicle and tenor, tragedy and politics. By heightening tragedy's inherent allegorical potential, *Suppliants* challenges our historicist presuppositions, forcing us to rethink tragedy's role in and relation to the city and the possibilities and paradoxes of "political tragedy."

• • •

On the surface of it, *Suppliants* would seem to speak all too directly about Athenian politics. The *agōn* between Theseus and the Theban herald, for instance, hits all the familiar talking points of Athenian democratic discourse, trumpeting Athens's autonomy and popular sovereignty, its freedom of speech, full political participation, and equality before the law. Through such patriotic clichés, the play figures Athens as eternally and essentially democratic, even when it was ruled by a mythic king. At the same time, it links that democratic essence in a vague but deliberate way to Athens's imperial power, which is represented as beneficent protection of the weak and pious defense of Panhellenic law. This "political tragedy" would thus seem an enthusiastic expression of the self-congratulatory democratic and imperial ideologies of the City Dionysia: it presents itself as propaganda, and so it has often been read.

But this seemingly straightforward political content is immediately complicated by the play's formal structure, for these pro-democracy clichés are uttered by a king. Theseus not only speaks of the democracy but speaks for it: metonymically paired with the city throughout, this mythic king is both symbol and spokesman of the democratic polis.[8] At one level this is unsurprising, perhaps even inevitable. In tragedy, action is performed by agents who are necessarily singular and (for reasons we explored in the last chapter) almost always elite. The genre's structural division between the chorus—which is rarely civic in character and always constrained in its activity—and the elite/heroic protagonists makes it very hard for tragedy to represent collective political agency directly onstage.[9] *Suppliants*'s chorus of old Argive women does have a sort of political agency, as we shall see, but it is a far cry from the political sovereignty of the Athenian demos; and while this chorus, like all tragic choruses, was composed of citizens, its gender and ethnic difference masks that civic character. So although we hear much about the demos, we never see the Athenian people onstage, and they intervene in the plot (a plot that intimately affects them) only inasmuch as they are represented by their king.

In reality, though, classical Athens was a direct, not a representative democracy. The demos spoke for itself: it had no representative, much less an archaic king. The very democratic institutions that Theseus praises in his debate with the Theban herald—the annual alternation of offices, the right of all citizens to speak in the Assembly—militated against the kind of metonymic substitution that we see with Theseus and that governs the allegory of this drama. The paradox of the democratic king is not limited to this play, of course: the Athenians often projected democratic sensibilities back onto their early monarchs, and they were accustomed to seeing Athens ruled by a populist Theseus or Pelasgus on the tragic stage. By the same token, given the story of Phrynichus, we would not expect tragedy to offer a precise mimesis of contemporary realities. But *Suppliants* arouses such an expectation with its ubiquitous anachronisms. Theseus himself is an anachronism, an "optimistic rationalist" au fait with the latest sophistic debates (195–218), and the modernness of his character reinforces that of his political theory.[10] Thus a paradox that might otherwise pass unnoticed is forced to our attention by the mimetic compression between mythic and modern Athens and the anachronisms that draw the two into allegorical juxtaposition.

In this way, the play reveals the limits of the very allegory it establishes, reopening the gap between the tragic world and the world of the contemporary polis. Tragedy's representational strategies make it unable to represent the anti-representational logic of Athenian democracy. The result is an incoherence at the very place where the play seems to speak most unambiguously, for despite Theseus's inspiring democratic rhetoric, there is a marked confusion as to who actually governs this Athens. Theseus's openness to persuasion, his change of mind and decision to help the Argive suppliants may model proper democratic decision making, as some have argued; but it does so through a substitution that makes that decision his alone.[11] "I will do this," Theseus declares. "I will go and reclaim the bodies" (346–47). The approval of the demos seems to come as an afterthought.

δόξαι δὲ χρήιζω καὶ πόλει πάσηι τόδε,
δόξει δ' ἐμοῦ θέλοντος· ἀλλὰ τοῦ λόγου
προσδοὺς ἔχοιμ' ἂν δῆμον εὐμενέστερον.
καὶ γὰρ κατέστησ' αὐτὸν ἐς μοναρχίαν
ἐλευθερώσας τήνδ' ἰσόψηφον πόλιν.
λαβὼν δ' Ἄδραστον δεῖγμα τῶν ἐμῶν λόγων
ἐς πλῆθος ἀστῶν εἶμι· καὶ πείσας τάδε,

λεκτοὺς ἀθροίσας δεῦρ' Ἀθηναίων κόρους
ἥξω·

But I want the entire city to approve (*doxai*) this as well,
and it will approve (*doxei*), since I want it. But I may
    make the demos more agreeable
by giving them a share in the debate (*tou logou*).
For I established their sovereignty (*monarkhian*)
when I freed this city and made it egalitarian.
Taking Adrastus as evidence for my case,
I will go before the Assembly of citizens. And after per-
    suading (*peisas*) them
and gathering select Athenian young men,
I will return. (349–57)

Theseus at once insists upon the approval of the demos and takes it for granted. In the passage's faint allusion to the Athenian formula for democratic decrees ("it seems good [*dokei*] to the council and the demos"), the democratic vote seems to emerge as a product of the king's desire and its virtual embodiment. In the second line's echo of the first, the king's wish for democratic approval (in the complementary infinitive *doxai*) becomes fact (the confident future tense, *doxei*); the king's desire, meanwhile, moves from the main verb to a participle, but still determines the demos's *doxa*, both grammatically and politically.[12] The democratic practice of public debate (*tou logou*) seems to be introduced not to produce a decision but only to facilitate this convergence of demos and king. This debate, moreover, is a beneficence granted by the mythic monarch to his people, as is their sovereignty and equality; democracy itself is a royal largesse that ensures the king's continued rule under the demos's *monarkhia*. Theseus does not entertain the possibility that the people may resist his risky proposition. He assumes their approval in a self-assured participle (*peisas*, 355). That assumption turns out to be justified: the fifteen-line stasimon that follows presents the outcome of this vote as uncertain, but by the time it is over, Theseus has not only persuaded the demos but gathered his army and returned.[13] The brevity of the ode suggests the perfunctory nature of the demos's consent, and at the start of the next episode, Theseus again asserts that their decision follows automatically upon his own: "The city accepted this labor willingly and happily, since it saw that I was in favor" (*hōs thelonta m' ēistheto*, 393–94).

If the vote of the demos merely corroborates the will of its monarch, is democracy really the opposite of tyranny, as this *agōn* insistently proclaims?[14]

So *Suppliants*'s seemingly unambiguous political content is immediately complicated by its tragic form. The play appears to bring politics and tragedy together only to reveal the mimetic distortions that arise when tragedy tries to speak—even to "speak otherwise"—about politics. And yet perhaps these very distortions are themselves mimetic and point us toward a more subtle critique of political representation. Some have seen in the paradox of *Suppliants*'s democratic king the reflection of a tension within fifth-century Athens between the ideology of popular sovereignty and the de facto hegemony of the elite. Theseus is accordingly compared to Pericles, under whose leadership, Thucydides famously tells us (2.65.9), Athens was a democracy in name, but in fact the rule of the first man.[15] Looking beyond the jingoistic content of Theseus's political speech and action, this reading offers an immanent critique of the sort proposed by Jean-Pierre Vernant (1988), in which the internal ambiguities of the play's form encode the tensions of its historical moment. No longer a simple "encomium," this formally-riven play becomes an allegory for an ideologically-riven Athens.

But if the play's tension between tragic form and political content encodes the paradox of political representation within the democracy, it also reveals a contradiction within tragedy's mimetic representation of the political, for the same formal means by which *Suppliants* adumbrates the antagonisms of the real world prevent it from fully articulating those antagonisms within its own dramatic frame. Consider the treatment of class division. *Suppliants* refers with a certain obsessiveness to class difference within the polis: the language of class appears where we would not expect it and is only weakly integrated into or motivated by its context. In Adrastus's funeral oration, for instance, the virtues of the dead heroes are obtrusively class-coded. Capaneus was rich but not "haughty in his wealth" (*olbōi gauros*, 862); eschewing excess, he did not think himself superior to the poor man, but was satisfied with moderation (*metria d'exarkein*, 866). Eteoclus, meanwhile, was poor but respected; his poverty did not make him a slave to money nor a fan of demagogues (871–80). Likewise, the *hubris* of the victorious Thebans is compared to the excesses of the nouveaux riches (741–44; cf. 463–64). Tragic existence as a whole—the "struggle that is our life"—is imagined in its different effects on the rich and poor (549–57), and tragic pity analogized to the mutual regard of rich and poor (176–79). Life itself is economized as the one thing money cannot buy (775–77).

So the world is imagined, at the broadest and deepest level, as divided between rich and poor. Athens, though, is apparently free from such division. In his lecture to Adrastus, Theseus expounds on the political dangers of class difference: both the selfish, greedy rich and the resentful, easily manipulated poor threaten the order of the city, which is preserved only by the moderate middle class (237–45). Athens, as he presents it, has achieved this ideal socioeconomic balance by means of its democratic institutions: its *isonomia* (equality before the law) and *isēgoria* (equal right to speech) are mechanisms for eliminating the pernicious differences between "the weak" and "the fortunate" (433–41). As Athens's representative onstage, Theseus represents his city as it liked to represent itself, undivided by social or political difference.

This denial of difference cannot simply be put in quotation marks as part of Theseus's patriotic political rhetoric, though, because it is reproduced at the structural level in Theseus himself. A metonym that unifies the entire demos in the person of a single individual who is himself at once perfectly aristocratic and perfectly democratic, Theseus resolves in his own paradoxical person the social and economic differences that the play suggests are a feature of all human societies. The protagonist is a formal embodiment of the content of his own speech, and the play's structure is complicit with the Athenian king's misrepresentation of the realities of the fifth-century polis.

Instead of representing the serious internal antagonisms of contemporary Athens, Euripides' play converts them into a formal *agōn* between Theseus and a foreigner. The Theban herald counters Theseus's democratic slogans with the kind of critiques of democracy commonly heard from Athens's disgruntled elite: that the "mob" (*okhlos*, 411) is inconsistent, susceptible to the self-serving flattery of demagogues, too preoccupied with making a living to judge complex issues (410–22); that democracy undervalues good men and promotes the inferior (423–24). Like Theseus's speech, the herald's language is pointedly contemporary, deploying many of the buzzwords of late fifth-century anti-democratic discourse. Indigenous oligarchic critiques have been eliminated from *Suppliants*'s Athens and come to it only from without, in the mouth of this offensive foreigner.[16] The tragic *agōn*, which by its very form reduces complex issues to a simple binarism, is a blunt instrument for political discourse at the best of times. Here it both distorts and displaces the realities of Athenian political division, turning an internal political struggle into one between inimical polities and converting the heated ideological contest between democracy and oligarchy into a debate between democracy and tyranny, a debate of less pressing political consequence in the late fifth century and one with an undisputed winner. Finally, like most tragic *agones*, it fails to resolve anything: Theseus and the Theban herald agree to disagree (465–66), and their political debate has no direct effect on the plot that follows.[17]

Thus, if Theseus will not represent his Athens as divided, the play suggests that tragedy *cannot* represent that division. Theseus as a representative of democratic Athens becomes a figure who produces misrepresentations of the realities of the democratic polis. Those misrepresentations are political, and *Suppliants*'s ambiguities can be read as a mimesis of contemporary Athens's political tensions. But they are also aesthetic, for tragedy's generic commitment to the individual protagonist and the binary *agōn* make it unable to represent the actual divisions of the contemporary polis. This double misrepresentation—a distortion in both vehicle and tenor—marks the limits of tragic allegory, and casts a dubious light both on *Suppliants*'s claim to be a form of political discourse and on the allegorical assumptions of historicist readings of tragedy in general. The play's experiment in "political tragedy" exposes the inherent representational paradoxes of this hybrid genre and reveals a fundamental mimetic antinomy between the political and the tragic.

• • •

That latent antinomy becomes an audible antiphony in the second half of the play, as Theseus's ode to Athenian democracy is answered by the lugubrious refrain of the grieving Argive mothers. This antiphony amplifies many of the antitheses that characterize this play: male and female, public and private, reason and emotion, optimism and pessimism, speech and song.[18] It informs the overall structure of the play, which falls into two unequal halves, the first staging the political deliberations provoked by the mothers' supplication, culminating in Theseus's victory over the Thebans and recovery of the corpses of the Argive heroes; the second, enacting the responses to those deaths. It is replicated in a more acute form in the second half, in which those responses play out as a dissonant alternation between distinct discursive modalities: the political discourse of the actors and what Nicole Loraux has termed the "anti-politics" of lamentation. The tragic lament, Loraux proposes, subverts the city's glorification of patriotic self-sacrifice with its eternal grief and thus "lays claim to a logic different from the solely political logic of civic ideology." By privileging sound over sense, music over words, and emotion over cognition, tragedy's "mourning voice" solicits its audience not as members of the political community but as members of the human race, making the play always something more than just a political discourse.[19]

Loraux's humanist "anti-politics" complicates the historicist conception of tragedy as political allegory. Instead of "speaking otherwise" about the polis, tragedy speaks about something other than the polis—a domain of human experience in which the polis does not play a central role. At the same time, if tragedy's "mourning voice" speaks to the audience not as citizens but as human beings, it would seem to afford the genre different mimetic possibilities for representing its contemporary world and audience, re-presenting and giving mournful expression to the experiences of the Athenians beyond their identity as members of the demos.

The second half of *Suppliants* stages an extended *agōn* between political responses to the deaths of the Seven and the anti-politics of maternal lament. These laments are not *a*political. The mothers' grief appeals to political principles (377–80); it demands a political response and it gets one in Athens's war against Thebes. But that response, far from alleviating their suffering, only produces more suffering. The mothers' mourning seems impervious to political consolation or containment. To the herald's celebratory report of Theseus's victory and recovery of their sons' bodies, they sing: "Some things are good and some ill-fortuned: for the city and its generals, there is a double yield of good reputation and military honor; for me, though, it is bitter to see the limbs of my child, . . . the greatest sorrow of all" (778–85). Indifferent to Athens's political triumph, the mothers threaten to undermine the play's self-congratulatory narrative of heroic endeavor and Panhellenic generosity, calling into question the political successes of the first half of the play.[20]

If the lament in this play is anti-political, though, it is also in a strange way anti-, or at least sub-tragic. Lamentation is a generic marker of tragedy, and one of its most important formal resources. But the lament in this play has a peculiar quality, a kind of monotonous unloveliness. That is not a criticism, but an observation. Usually Euripides ornaments maternal grief in his highest lyric style: we saw examples in chapter 2 in the self-consciously aestheticized, densely metaphoric lamentation of *Hecuba* and *Trojan Women*. By comparison, the odes in *Sup-*

pliants are pared down, even prosaic. Consider the second stasimon (598–633), which is divided between two half-choruses, a technique unparalleled in Euripides. The line-by-line alternation of the two in the first two *strophai* (mostly in iambic meter) gives the ode almost the feel of verse stichomythia, as the two choruses exchange anxious questions and answers about the battle being waged offstage. Another choral intervention fails entirely to hit lyric velocity: after Theseus rejects Adrastus's appeal for help, at a point where we might normally have expected a stasimon, the chorus instead respond in nine lines of iambic trimeter: they essentially make a speech (262–70). This exceptional moment may show the chorus's deep involvement with the action, as commentators suggest, but it also tethers them tightly to that action. Even their odes stick unusually close to the plot, offering virtually no larger mythical or theological reflection on the drama.[21] When they fantasize about escape (as many tragic choruses do), they wish for wings to carry them not away from the action but closer to it, to the battlefield where they might witness the fate of their loved ones (617–23).

Likewise, the chorus's language in the odes is remarkably bare. The women use metaphor sparingly and avoid the colorful visual imagery typical of Euripides' lyric style; they do not call attention to their own artistry or indulge in the flights of aesthetic self-consciousness that so often characterize Euripides' "poetics of sorrow."[22] Instead, the mothers remain mired in their ritual action—the *goos* (wailing), the rending of skin, the tearing of hair—and weighed down by a melancholic materiality: again and again they return to the thought of their sons' lifeless bodies and their longing to touch, to embrace them, to enfold them in their arms (59–62, 69–70, 782–85, 794–97, 815–17, 1159). Their pain is measured in the physical heft of these bodies-become-ash, a literal and figurative "weight of pain" (818, 1123–30, 1158–89). Unable to sublimate their grief in the exquisite aesthetics of pathos, all these mothers can do is name it over and over again. The mothers' lament thus seems to stand apart from both politics and tragedy. In its dull intransigence, which resists either political consolation or aesthetic ornamentation, it gives mournful voice to the unending, unchanging Real of death.

Through its antithesis between an ostentatiously modern politics and a melancholy anti-politics, Euripides' "political tragedy" suggests that this hybrid, rather than effecting a mutually enriching synthesis between its two parts, is instead riven by the tension between them. On the one hand, the play is too political: its allegory collapses. On the other hand, it is too tragic: its suffering exceeds poetic expression.

Caught between the realities of contemporary politics and the Real of death, *Suppliants* is unable to represent either. Its second half dramatizes this tension in its *agōn* between the tragic and the political as two different modes of responding to the mothers' loss and attempting not only to represent it but to make it bearable, both for the chorus and for the audience.

In terms of plot alone, the last 400 lines of the play are unnecessary. The *muthos* is completed with Theseus's victory over Thebes: he has fulfilled his obligation to the supplicating mothers; Panhellenic law and divine right have been upheld and their transgressors chastised; the dramatic crisis of the suppliant plot has reached a satisfying resolution; and Athens has demonstrated the courageous benevolence that was the essential point of this myth. The following *kommos* (a traditional song of lament between actors and chorus) provides a measure of ritual and emotional closure, and the play could, in effect, have ended at line 836. What restarts it is not the grief of the mothers but the need of the city to make sense of their sons' death in civic terms and to appropriate the loss to its own civic ends. Theseus invites Adrastus to deliver a funeral oration over the bodies of the fallen heroes. The speech is an unmistakable allusion to the Athenian institution of the *epitaphios logos* delivered annually in commemoration of the war dead. Borrowing its rhetoric directly from the fifth-century oration and praising the Argive heroes for distinctly fifth-century virtues, the speech is one of the play's most egregious anachronisms, and all the more egregious for the fact that this very myth figured frequently in Athenian *epitaphioi logoi*. So obtrusive is Adrastus's speech that many take it as a deliberate parody of political rhetoric.[23]

If that's what it is, it seems designed expressly to show the failure of that rhetoric. Nicole Loraux and Helene Foley have discussed the Athenian *epitaphios logos* as a civic appropriation of the traditionally female role of lamentation, a means by which the city simultaneously contained the threatening excess of female grief and sought to make death meaningful—even desirable—by showering it in patriotic glory.[24] Adrastus's oration fails in both of these functions. It is presented as a moral education for the youth (842–43, 911–17), but the heroes it lauds have figured throughout the rest of the play as personifications of impious *hubris*. The eulogy opens with Capaneus, who swore that he would take Thebes with or without the gods' help and was accordingly struck by Zeus's lightning bolt as he scaled the walls; Adrastus alludes to the divine lightning bolt (860) before going on to praise Capaneus as a paragon of civic virtue. Morally empty as eulogy, the speech also fails as protreptic. The episode ends with Adrastus's despairing call for peace: "Oh long-suffering mortals, why do you possess spears and murder one another? Cease. Give up your toils (*ponōn*) and guard your cities in peace and quiet. Life is a small thing, and we should pass through it as easily as we can and without toil (*ponois*)" (949–54). This pacifist conclusion undercuts both the speech and the glorious *ponoi* that it celebrates, not to mention the heroic *ponos* of Theseus and Athens to recover the bodies afterwards. This *epitaphios logos* thus fails in its own terms. It also fails to staunch the mothers' lament or alleviate their grief. They respond in the fourth stasimon (955–79) with the same repetitive *goos* as has been their refrain from the start.[25]

Indeed, far from containing female grief, the *epitaphios* produces a dramatic new explosion of grief, as Evadne, the wife of Capaneus, appears suddenly atop the *skēnē* like a deranged deus ex machina. If the *epitaphios* is an overt, even exaggerated staging of the political, Evadne's suicide is an exaggerated staging of the tragic. It is tragedy doing tragedy, as it were.[26] Evadne appears in her wedding dress, and her song is full of the tragic tropes of marriage to death, as well as bacchic imagery (1001) and the only erotic language in the play (1019–30). Its poeticism—with intense visual imagery, metaphors, and compound adjectives—stands in sharp contrast with what I earlier termed the prosaic quality of the chorus's laments.[27] It was this sort of emotionally intense lyric monody that audiences expected from Euripides, to judge from Aristophanes' parody in *Frogs*, and this one plays it to the hilt. It is as if all the lyricism of the play is concentrated in this one song. Add to the poetry and music the effect of staging and costume, the desperately ironic exchange between Evadne and her father—in which she announces her suicide in terms that are crystal clear to the audience but "a malign enigma" (1064) to him—the drama of her climactic leap and the despairing cries of the chorus afterward (1072, 1073, 1077), and the episode becomes a paradigmatic, almost hyperbolic, example of tragic *thauma*.

As such, the scene constitutes a tragic riposte and reproach to the political rhetoric of the *epitaphios*. Evadne's deranged language of glory (*kleos*) and victory (*nikē*) is a tragic transmutation of the heroic values of the *epitaphios*, and her suicide a perverse enactment of its enticement to a glorious death.[28] If the *epitaphios logos* as a cultural institution was meant to contain female grief, the sudden eruption of Evadne's suicidal despair marks its failure, even as her indifference to the question of her husband's *hubris* makes a mockery of that speech's moral pedagogy: to her the thunder-struck Capaneus is simply her dear husband (1020). Arising out of the failure of the *epitaphios*'s political rhetoric, Evadne's leap stages a specifically tragic response to death. Intensely emotional, elevated in style and pathos, it is also purely negative. It suggests that the only response to death is death: the truth of the soldier's heroic sacrifice lies in the desperate self-immolation of his wife.

The nihilism of this gesture is elaborated in the speech of Evadne's father Iphis, with its chilling vision of returning to a dark and empty house to waste away from starvation (1095–96, 1104–6). This grim *rhēsis* is in fact the culmination of a strong strain of nihilism that runs throughout the play. Adrastus wishes he had died at Thebes (769, 821), or that he could die now (829–310). The chorus not only wish to die with their dead sons (796–97, cf. 86); more extremely, they wish to go back and undo their children's birth to preempt the pain of losing them (786–93, 822–23). Their death wish extends, retroactively, to the next generation. This counterfactual stillbirth, one of the most arresting themes of the play, offers a Euripidean twist on the Sophoclean mantra that "The best thing is not to be born; second best, to die as soon as possible," which Nietzsche saw as the essential wisdom of tragedy.[29] The theme is developed in Iphis's dark fantasy of living twice so that, learning from the suffering of his first life, he would not father children in his second (1080–93). His reproductive pessimism undercuts the political hope the play has vested in the youth, both in the youthful Theseus and in the future generation that is meant to profit from the political pedagogy of Adrastus's *epitaphios*, with its optimistic claims about the teachability of wisdom and its call to "teach your children well" (917). In Iphis's bleak vision, all age has to teach youth is that it should never have been born at all. Life, in his view, is a channel running straight to death (1111). Since we cannot extend its course, or divert it or reverse it, the best thing mortals can do, he concludes, is "when they are no longer of use on the earth, die and get out of the way of the young" (1112–13).

In Evadne's leap and Iphis's despair, tragedy would seem to offer a purely negative critique of the optimistic politics of the play's first half, "a heroism, born of grief, that can only destroy, and a passivity, born of despair, that can accomplish nothing at all."[30] Tragedy's anti-politics would seem to be solely that: the inverse of politics, its negative image, the death drive to its pleasure principle, thanatos to its eros. The play would seem to stage its contest of genres only to reach this dismal conclusion: neither tragedy nor politics can offer an adequate response to death, to make its sorrow meaningful to the audience, either as members of the polis or as members of the human race. With this speech, it seems we have reached an impasse not only between humanism and historicism, but between tragedy and politics, where this "political tragedy" self-destructs under the tension between its two constitutive parts. Unable to synthesize them, it dissolves into a perverse dialectic of despair and death, an allegory unable to say anything.

• • •

And yet out of the profundity of its despair, this speech points the way both toward a more positive conclusion and toward a possible synthesis between the tragic and the political. Iphis's grim final words—the old should just die and get out of the way of the young—literally call forth a procession of the young sons of the Seven carrying their fathers' ashes. Their *kommos* with the mothers, their grandmothers, concludes the dramatic action (although not, as we shall see, the play itself). This procession is strongly closural, unusually so for a Euripidean ending. Depicting the *ekphora*, the "carrying out" of the body for burial that was a central element of traditional funerary ritual, it not only offers ritual consolation to the mourning mothers but draws upon ritual experience to bring emotional closure for the audience, as well.[31] Dramatically, too, it offers structural and thematic closure. In its form it recalls the first *kommos*, which followed Theseus's victory and the return of the Argive bodies. As we saw, that *kommos* could—and in a sense should—have ended the play, but instead, it set in motion the series of responses, political and tragic, to loss that we have been tracing. That series, inaugurated with the first *kommos*, concludes with the second in a kind of ring composition. At the same time, the second *kommos* also introduces a new element: the sons of the dead, who enter as the final word of Iphis's speech—"the young" (*neois*, 1113)—is still resonating.

The parade of the young men, who have probably been onstage for most of the play but sing now for the first time, breaks the play's ritual paralysis and existential pessimism. As the chorus sing with their grandsons—addressing each other as mother and child (*māter*, 1123; *pai*, 1127)—these "childless mothers" (35) are no longer bereft. The rituals of Demeter, interrupted by their barren presence at the goddess's Eleusinian altar, can now resume, with new hope for the fertility those rituals were meant to secure. Sons bearing the ashes of their fathers, the boys undo the perversion of a mother burying her child (174–75) and restore the natural order of the generations. From its monotonous melancholia, *Suppliants* suddenly looks toward the future. That future will not be free of war: even as they mourn their fathers, the boys plan to avenge them, and it is clear that there will be more war, and more laments, in the next generation (1142–51). But at least there will be a next generation. The counterfactual infanticide fantasy of Iphis and the chorus is reversed, in a way striking to the eye, by the presence of these young men on the stage.

This closure also marks a new beginning. Out of its dialectic of politics and anti-politics, jingoism and despair, with this final procession *Suppliants* sublates itself in a stunning gesture of self-reflexivity and allegorizes the birth of a new political tragedy.[32] It does so by way of its most daring anachronism, the re-production of its own performance as a civic event. One of the civic rituals that preceded the dramatic competitions at the City Dionysia was a parade of boys whose fathers had died in war and who had been raised to adulthood by the city. *Suppliants*'s funerary parade of Argive orphans evokes the parade of Athenian orphans, who would have been sitting in the front row of the theater.[33] This startling reference to tragedy as a civic institution produces an extreme mimetic contraction, as the world of the play and the world of the performance become one. But whereas the play's previous mimetic compressions revealed the gap between the tragic and the political, as we have seen, here that gap disappears. Fully motivated by the *muthos* in its own dramatic terms and a fitting resolution to the ritual crisis that has structured it, this parade offers a spectacular new formal synthesis of the mythic and the modern: it infuses the traditional tragic form of the *kommos* with anachronistic self-reflexivity and melds the dramatic mimesis of funerary ritual with its own fifth-century praxis as civic ritual. As the play draws its civic context into its dramatic world, simultaneously presenting the tragic and re-presenting the civic, any distinction between the two dissolves. The allegory collapses in upon itself, its alterity lost: vehicle is tenor.

In this, the drama's ultimate mimetic conflation, *Suppliants* realizes new and expanded possibilities of representation, both aesthetic and political. The shared pathos of orphaned sons and bereaved mothers addresses the audience, as Loraux would have it, as members of the human race, who have themselves lost parents or beloved children and grieved for them. But in its evocation of the festival's parade of war orphans, this *kommos* also addresses the audience as members of the polis, arousing again the emotions they felt as they participated in that political ritual, perhaps only a few hours earlier. The tenor of the civic parade, if we can judge from fourth-century sources, was inspirational and patriotic, less a ritual of mourning than the hopeful display of a new generation of Athenian valor. As Aeschines describes it:

> The herald would come forward and present the orphans whose fathers had died in war, young men adorned in full battle-gear, and make this magnificent announcement, a superlative spur to valor: "These young men, whose fathers died bravely in war, have grown to manhood, raised by the demos, who now send them forth to go their own way, in full battle array, with best wishes for their success." And he would call them to take seats in the front row of the theater. (Aeschines 3.154; cf. Isocrates 8.82)

In *Suppliants*'s final *kommos*, this optimistic political ritual is superimposed on the tragic ritual of lament. The precise effect for an Athenian viewer is hard to gauge. Did the play's funerary procession cast a retrospective shadow over that patriotic ritual, a reminder of the death and loss entailed in Athens's militaristic ideology? Or did the real ritual lend its optimism to the *kommos*, helping it to produce a sense of closure and consolation for the mothers' loss? No doubt it worked differently on different members of the audience. For many, it probably did both at once.

But we don't need to specify the content of the Athenians' emotional response—they may have been unable to specify it themselves—in order to recognize that the form of that emotion, its affective substructure, is simultaneously tragic and political. The drama's formal synthesis gives form to an affective synthesis. The modern parade hails citizens as parents: as citizens of Athens, they are collective parents to the orphans the city has raised to adulthood. The mythic parade hails parents as citizens: at the end of the *kommos*, Theseus addresses the mothers as "women of the Argive race" (1165), a civic title they assume in the political exhortations with which they close the play (1232–34). Superimposing the two, this double parade, at once mythic and modern, tragic and civic, solicits its audience neither as members of the political community nor as members of the human race, but as both at once. It speaks to that part of their psyche where the two are indistinguishable, hailing it into being both anew and again through its own formal fusion.

It is here, in the psyche of the audience, that the play finally achieves its amalgamation of the political and the tragic and re-founds itself as allegory. "Speaking otherwise," it articulates the mothers' mourning through the Athenians' own emotions while watching the parade of orphans, and vice versa. As the sufferings of the tragic mothers blend with the Athenians' *oikēia kaka*, their own diverse feelings of pride and loss at the sight of their civic sons, the play once again breaks the Phrynichan law of mimetic distance, affectively, as well as formally, collapsing the mythic world of tragedy and the modern world of the polis. But the distance between self and other is bridged now not at the analytic level where allegory operates with its juxtaposition of different things, but at an affective level where those things don't feel different. If *Suppliants* is a "political tragedy," then, it is not because it spouts political slogans or dramatizes an encomiastic myth, but because its formal *psukhagōgia* leads the audience to a psychic space where the citizen and the human are one and the same.

And it is precisely through this psychic synthesis, the play suggests, that tragedy can have real political effect. Pointing to the orphans bearing the ashes of their fathers, Theseus calls on Adrastus to remember the service he and his city have done for the Argives:

> Adrastus and women of the Argive race,
> you see these boys bearing in their hands
> the bodies of their heroic fathers, which I recovered.
> The city and I grant them to these boys.
> You must preserve memory of these things and gratitude,
> seeing what you have gained thanks to me.
> And repeat to these children the same words:
> to honor this city, passing on always from one generation
> to the next the memory of what you have gained.
> Let Zeus be witness and all the gods in heaven,
> as you depart, of what benefits we judged you worthy.
>
> (1165–75)

This political alliance, an oath of eternal gratitude, evolves directly out of the tragic *kommos*; it is the immediate practical consequence of the mimetic procession, as Theseus bids the Argive mothers watch and remember. His brief speech transforms the burial urns, those props of grief, into symbols of the future alliance, and the intergenerational lamentation of the *kommos* into the trans-generational memory of *kharis* (favor, gratitude) between Argos and Athens. The visual spectacle of the parade will be a prompt to that memory and to the political alliance built on it; the boys themselves will be its future signatories. Theseus's promise of a more positive political future seems to emerge directly out of the dramatic *kommos*'s double ritual, the political effect of its affective synthesis of the political and the tragic.

That political future is then sealed by an ostentatiously tragic device.[34] As Theseus and Adrastus shake hands and say good bye, Athena appears and demands a formal oath of full and permanent alliance. Adrastus must swear that Argos will never attack Athens and will defend her if she is attacked. The appearance of the goddess is, like so many of Euripides' closing epiphanies, dramatically superfluous. The agreement between Theseus and Adrastus, with its language of eternal *kharis* and divine witnesses, in itself suggested a political alliance between the two states. The goddess solves no problems, but she does put a decidedly tragic stamp upon that alliance. Appearing on the *skēnē* where Evadne had delivered her tragic monody, the goddess echoes and inverts that scene of high tragedy.[35] The moment is both self-consciously theatrical and explicitly metatheatrical: it uses the theater's own *mēkhanai* to reach beyond the theater into the realm of political praxis. The oath Athena prescribes, with its marked political language and detailed ritual provisions, forges an ideal alliance: when the play was presented, the Athenians were at war with Argos, and although they would sign a treaty soon after, it would not be on such unilaterally favorable terms.[36] In this fantasy oath, the play breaks out of its own diegetic bounds: it crosses the bridge it had itself forged in the psychic synthesis of the final *kommos* and erupts into the real world, with real and positive political effects. Euripides does, then, ultimately affirm the role of tragedy in the city. He claims a political efficacy for the genre, not as a displaced form of political discourse—for the play has shown us the limitations of tragedy's political representation—but precisely as tragedy: as a civic institution and a "poetics of sorrow" and, above all, a vehicle of *psukhagōgia*. In this form, Euripides suggests, tragedy can do more than just represent politics; it can enact them.

In *Suppliants* (as in many of his other dramas), Euripides is using tragic form to think about tragic form and its relation to political contents; to explore its possibilities and its limitations as a mode of aesthetic and political representation. His appraisal, while highly critical, is not purely negative. The generic tension between the political and the tragic that structures this play shows that tragedy is not politics, but neither is it merely anti-politics. Instead, it is a strange hybrid of the two, what we might be tempted to call "political tragedy." *Suppliants* has warned us of the contradictions inherent in the phrase, but it has also proposed a new way of understanding it, one that challenges both historicist and humanist readings of the genre. Staging the birth of tragedy as a political institution, it suggests that tragedy produces political effect by way of its dramatic affect. Tragedy does something in the city because it does something to its audience, who are citizens as well as human beings. By means of its particular *psukhagōgia*, tragedy forges an affective and effective synthesis between aesthetic form and political praxis. As in *Suppliants*'s final *kommos,* so in the genre as a whole, the poetic and the political are inseparably fused, on the stage and in the soul of the viewer; and tragedy's political force lies in its allegorical power to speak both at once.

CHAPTER 5

Broken Plays for a Broken World

Suppliants suggests that tragedy, through its psychagogic effect on its audience, can have a real and material impact on the polis. If this is true, then we need to rethink the relationship between the dramatic text and its historical context. The assumption of historicist approaches to tragedy, as we saw in the last chapter, is that the plays reflect (albeit in the distorting mirror of allegory) their contemporary reality. Accordingly, one way in which scholars have tried to make sense of Euripides' chaotic aesthetics is by viewing it as a reflection of his historical moment. Athens was at war with Sparta from 431 on, and under the strain of that war and its economic hardship, the polis was riven by deep socioeconomic, cultural, and generational antagonisms that eventually led, at the end of the century, to civil war. On this reading, Euripides' fractured plots, veering action, and inconsistent tone all make perfect sense as the reflection of a society in which social norms were crumbling and traditional values could no longer be taken for granted. The plays become "seismographs," registering in their structure the turbulent history of Athens in the last third of the fifth century: broken plays for a broken world.[1]

Those who see Euripides' plays reflecting his age often adduce Thucydides and note the strong resemblance between the Athens he describes and the world depicted in Euripides' dramas. They quote from passages like Thucydides' description of the *stasis* (civil war) in Corcyra, a horrifying picture of social disintegration, political corruption, and the corrosion of moral values. This vivid passage is presented as a snapshot of contemporary reality that explains—or explains away— the oddities of Euripidean tragedy: the playwright was merely a faithful reporter, representing the world accurately in all its chaos. Consider this passage from William Arrowsmith's important article, "A Greek Theater of Ideas." After quoting extensively from Thucydides' Corcyrean narrative, he argues that Euripides' drama is antitraditional because tradition itself was broken:

> What Euripides reported, with great clarity and honesty, was the widening gulf between reality and tradition. . . . That gulf was the greatest and most evident reality of the last half of the fifth century, *the* dramatic subject *par excellence*, and it is my belief that the theater of Euripides, like Thucydides' history, is a radical and revolutionary attempt to record, analyze and assess that reality in relation to the new view of human nature which crisis revealed.

Euripides the reporter merely transcribed his contemporary reality, his disjointed aesthetics a faithful representation of the historical moment.[2]

Obviously one needs to be careful about taking Thucydides' history for reality itself: we will see that Thucydides' narratives are shaped by the very dramatic plotlines they are adduced to explain. But leaving that aside for the moment, we should resist the impulse to explain away the ambiguities of these plays by displacing them onto a putative reality. This approach shifts the burden of interpretation from the poetic text to the historical context, where poetic problems are solved in advance by appeal to the authority of Thucydides and the reality he is assumed to transcribe. But this hermeneutic shell game really explains nothing about either the text or the historical context; instead, it flattens historical reality, which is reified as an external referent, neither in need of nor subject to interpretation itself. It also flattens the play, which is reduced to mere reportage, an inert mirror on the world.

This chapter takes issue with this notion of tragedy as a reflection of its historical moment and argues for a more active understanding of tragic mimesis. It proposes that tragedy not only recreates its historical context but in fact *creates* it, producing the historical reality that it is usually thought to reenact. Euripides, as I hope to show, both anticipates this proposition and illustrates it. The argument will proceed in three stages. First, *Helen* will show how difficult it actually is to distinguish the literary text from its historical context and will suggest that, instead of drama fictionalizing history, history might be loosely based upon a play. Next, *Trojan Women* will allow us to elaborate on that insight, and its tragic story will expose the tragic structure of Thucydides' *History*. Finally, I turn to *Orestes*. With its broken plot and sudden *peri-*

peteia, this play's aesthetic form does more than simply mirror Athens's recent civil conflict; in the conflicting loyalties it generates, it reproduces the affective experience—"the structures of feeling"—of that crisis, forcing the audience to relive it urgently in the present moment. By rekindling the emotions of *stasis* and pushing them to the breaking point, with no hope of resolution, *Orestes* not only reflects the social turmoil of Athens's recent past but also stages a dress rehearsal for a tragic future soon to come. Through an analysis of that play, I hope to prove this chapter's central claim: that tragedy, far from passively reflecting contemporary reality, in fact anticipates and precipitates it by producing the affective and cognitive framework in which the future can unfold.[3]

This chapter thus elaborates on an anticipatory temporality of tragic politics suggested at the end of chapter 2 and chapter 3. In chapter 2, we saw that the ethical demands tragedy makes on its audience cannot be met within the Theater of Dionysus: if tragedy's beauty (or its ugliness) makes us just, that justice remains to come, and it is our responsibility to bring it into being. In chapter 3, I proposed that *Electra*'s utopianism lies not in its "realist" depiction of an egalitarian scenario, but in its staging of egalitarianism as an emergent possibility, not yet realized in the present time of the play's production. This chapter argues that tragedy can do more than just imagine such future possibilities. By representing—literally making present—the affective experience of emergent scenarios, it can make them real.

● ● ●

Euripides himself warns us to be suspicious of the notion that drama merely reflects its historical context. His *Helen*, a radical reimagination of the mythic history of the Trojan War, suggests that the play, far from being an imitation of the world, may in fact be its model. *Helen* tells a counterfactual history of the Trojan War. It seems that the Helen the Greeks thought they were fighting for in Troy for ten years wasn't actually the real Helen: the gods had made a decoy Helen, an image (*eidōlon*) fashioned out of cloud. That nebulous double went to Troy, while the woman herself sat out the war in Egypt. The play is set in Egypt and opens with Helen bemoaning her situation: separated from her husband Menelaus and blamed for the war fought for her double, she is trapped in this barbarian land where the king Theoclymenus is now pressuring her to marry him. Just at this moment, Menelaus and his men happen to arrive, shipwrecked by lucky coincidence on the Egyptian shore on their way home from their victory at Troy. Menelaus is understandably slow to believe that the woman he meets here is his wife: she looks like Helen, but that's impossible because he has Helen with him, having won her back in the war. But when what he thinks is Helen is revealed as a phantom—she disappears into the air, announcing that she was an *eidōlon* all along—he realizes that the woman before him is his real wife, and the couple are blissfully reunited. That leaves only the problem of how to escape from Egypt. Helen comes up with a plan: they will tell Theoclymenus that she has learned from the shipwrecked sailors that her husband is dead; they will stage a mock burial for him at sea and this will provide a means of escape. The scheme works: our heroes are saved and return safely to Greece in the end.

Structurally and thematically, *Helen* revolves around questions of illusion and reality: which is the real Helen and which the *eidōlon*? Scholars have connected this questioning of reality to the historical moment. In 415 BCE the Athenians had undertaken a huge naval expedition to Sicily, where they had expected to find rich natural resources and welcoming natives. Thucydides describes the triumphal mood in which the expedition sailed: "a marvel of daring and a dazzling spectacle," Athens's fleet was conspicuous equally for its military superiority over the enemy and for the exorbitant hopes that drove it (6.31.6). When it reached Sicily, however, the promised riches failed to materialize and the locals turned out to be resistant and well armed. The Athenians discovered that they had been pursuing an *eidōlon*, that what they thought was reality was actually just an illusion. *Helen* was produced in 412, just after the Athenians' final disastrous defeat in Sicily, and many have been tempted to view Euripides' tragic text as a staging of its traumatic historical context.[4]

And yet the play itself suggests that things are not so simple: in fact, *Helen* reverses and ultimately breaks down the opposition between fictional text and historical context. That opposition is here represented by the world of Egypt and the war in Troy. The scene in Egypt, for all that we see it onstage in front of us, is described throughout the first half of the play in terms that emphasize its fictionality. No one who sees Helen can believe it's really Helen. First Teucer, a forward scout for the shipwrecked Greeks, curses her for her uncanny resemblance to Helen; but he quickly apologizes: she can't be Helen because he watched with his own eyes as Menelaus captured Helen in Troy (71–83, 116–22). Then Menelaus sees her and is utterly flummoxed: she says she is Helen but how can she be, since the real Helen is back in the cave where he left her for safekeeping? The Helen we see onstage is repeatedly taken for a *mimēsis*, a fictional double for the real Helen. The play's theme of illusion and reality is developed as a self-conscious metatheatricality, as Euripides reminds us again and again that the world of the play is just a dramatic fiction.[5]

This fictional world is contrasted to the "real" world of Troy. The Trojan War—here, as often in tragedy—represents a hard reality that the characters seek to process and interpret: the "historical context," as it were, to the action within the play's fictional world. But in *Helen*, the historical fact of the Trojan War is represented in a distinctly counter-factual mode. If we believe the play's fiction, then the war, fought for an illusory Helen, becomes illusory itself (115–22): all those labors and lives were wasted, as one character notes, "for a cloud" (707). Troy's heroic truths become mere fictions, no more inherently credible than the Egyptian drama being enacted onstage. In fact, the Trojan War is transformed over the course of the drama into mere play-acting. The escape plot restages the war as part of an elaborate make-believe: when the ruse of the burial at sea is discovered, King Theoclymenus sends his navy after the fleeing Greeks and conflict ensues. The messenger describes this second battle for Helen in terms that explicitly compare it to the battle for Troy (1560, 1593–94; cf. 843–50, 1603). This second Trojan War is ostentatiously fictional: it is a fiction within a fiction. And yet this second Trojan War, unlike the first, is fought for the real Helen.

The play thus suggests that it is harder than we might have thought to differentiate historical fact from dramatic fiction. The historical fact of the Trojan War is shown to be no more substantial than the nebulous *eidōlon* for which it was apparently fought; the war gains meaning only when restaged as a theatrical fiction. Meanwhile, the dramatic world of Egypt becomes more and more real for us as the play progresses. The escape plot juxtaposes the acknowledged fiction of Menelaus's death to the "reality" that Menelaus is actually alive and well. As the disguised Menelaus reports the news of his own supposed death, we know that this bedraggled messenger is "really" Menelaus himself. The overt fiction of the escape plot turns the fictional world of Egypt and its implausible *eidōla* into reality.

In one final twist, that theatrical reality becomes our own reality. The play closes, as many of Euripides' plays do, with a deus ex machina—or *dei*, in fact: Helen's brothers Castor and Polydeuces, whose deification had already been presented as an improbable fiction (137–43) and who appear now by means of an overtly theatrical mechanism. These fictional gods tie the world of the play to our real, extra-dramatic world. The Euripidean deus ex machina often announces the establishment of cults or the founding of a particular site that was presumably familiar to the Athenian audience, thereby forging a historical link between the mythic world of the play and the contemporary world of the audience. So here the Dioscouroi announce the establishment of cult offerings to Helen and name an island off the coast of Attica "Helen Island" (1667–75), a name it still bore in the fifth century. In this way, the play's fiction becomes part of the reality that makes up the "real" fifth-century Athenian world. The play enters history, and it does so, moreover, precisely as fiction; for if, as some scholars believe, Euripides' aetiologies and the cults they founded were largely invented, then the gods' pronouncement here makes contemporary reality the historical legacy of the play's make-believe.[6]

But *Helen* does more than create a few cult offerings or lend an unimportant island its name. This play ends with a conventional choral tag, the same tag that we saw in *Alcestis* in the introduction (and will consider further in the conclusion): "Many are the shapes of the divinities; many things the gods accomplish against all hope. The expected (*ta dokēthenta*) is not accomplished; for the unexpected (*tōn adokētōn*) the god finds a way. That's how this affair has turned out." This final refrain sums up the play's insistent blurring of truth and illusion, of being and mere seeming (the literal meaning of *ta dokēthenta* and *tōn adokētōn*, from *dokein* "to seem"), and attributes the epistemological and ontological confusions of its Egyptian scenario to the vagaries of the divine. The refrain looks backward at the events we've just watched onstage, but it also looks forward beyond the bounds of the play; for if this is just the way the gods are, and the same gods govern us in the audience as govern Helen and Menelaus, then the illusions of the play become a condition of our own reality. Addressing the audience more or less directly to deliver the "take-home" message of the play, these lines mark the transition between the fictional world and the real.[7] But the message they deliver generalizes the play's uncertainties as a theology, a general law that governs our cosmos no less than the cosmos of the drama. They suggest that if the world is as unpredictable as the play, if historical fact is as hard to untangle from dramatic fiction as Troy is from Egypt, that is not because the play resembles the world, but because the world resembles the play.

Helen thus both reduces and reverses the distinction between tragic fiction and historical reality. Tragedy is not a mimesis of reality but its

model. It becomes more difficult now to see Euripides as merely reporting on the reality of his historical moment. *Helen* proposes that this
historical reality was already a kind of fiction: insubstantial in itself, it
becomes real only when tragedy rescripts it as a play within a play.
Moreover, this drama suggests that the cognitive frameworks that allow
us to perceive our reality *as* reality are derived from the play itself. The
theology of the last lines allows the audience to make sense not just of
the play but of their own world as well. Thus, if the Athenians discovered that they had been chasing a phantom in Sicily, that "the expected
is not accomplished; for the unexpected the god finds a way," they were
merely applying an insight gained from Euripides' drama. Far from the
play "reporting" on events in Sicily, Sicily becomes a real-life acting out
of the lessons of this tragedy: that truth and illusion are hard to distinguish, and human existence is full of unexpected *peripeteiai*. As a foot-
note to this point, Plutarch reports that some of the Athenian prisoners
of war in Sicily were saved by reciting songs from Euripides (apparently the Sicilians were mad for poetry), and when they returned to
Athens, they thanked the playwright for saving their lives.[8] This (no
doubt fictional) historical anecdote illustrates as well as Euripides himself ever could the way fiction shapes reality, as lines first uttered in a
play are re-performed on the historical stage, and the *eidōla* of Euripides descend from the *skēnē* to save the day.

With this in mind we can go back to the ubiquitous quotations from
Thucydides and reexamine the relation between dramatic text and historical context. Consider, as a very brief illustration, *Trojan Women*,
discussed in chapter 2. That play is often linked to the Melian episode
recounted in Book 5 of Thucydides' *History* (84–113). The Athenians
invited the small autonomous island of Melos to join their empire;
when the Melians declined, the Athenians killed all the Melian men
and enslaved the women. This episode, strategically insignificant in
itself, becomes for Thucydides a pivotal moment in the evolution of
the Athenian empire and the history of the Peloponnesian War. He re-
lates a dialogue between the Melians and the Athenians that displays
the cruel power politics behind Athens's so-called alliance. *Trojan
Women* was staged in the same year as the destruction of Melos, and
many scholars have read Euripides' play as a reflection of the ugly
truths about Athenian imperialism reported in Thucydides' Melian
Dialogue.[9]

Not only is that dialogue itself manifestly fictional, however
(Thucydides was not present at the negotiations, and there were no

transcripts of such discussions); it is also part of a larger narrative structure that sounds suspiciously like an Athenian tragedy—in fact, it sounds suspiciously like *Trojan Women*. As Francis Cornford demonstrated a century ago, Thucydides shapes his history of the Athenian empire as a drama of *hubris* and *atē* (delusion).[10] Starting with the noble ambitions of Pericles, the Athenians expand ever further; in their fear of losing what they have and their desire to acquire more, they are driven to acts of aggression that betray the fundamental principles of the democracy, enslaving free Greek states and slaughtering the innocent. Thucydides' *History* is unfinished, but there are clear hints throughout that this tale of imperial *hubris* will end with a drastic *peripeteia*: already in the incomplete Book 8 we can see the civil breakdown that presages Athens's eventual defeat. Episodes like the Melian Dialogue function as moments of *anagnōrisis* for the reader of this dramatic narrative, if not for the Athenian "characters" within it—a typically tragic irony.

Thucydides' narrative of the Athenian empire as the drama of an illustrious city's reversal from good fortune to bad through its own errors thus follows the ideal tragic plotline as Aristotle describes it in the *Poetics*. This shouldn't surprise us: long before Hayden White theorized the emplotment of historical narrative, Euripides' *Helen* suggested that fiction furnishes history's *muthoi*. Thus, if history is tragic, as Thucydides proposes it was in Melos, it is because that historical event has been understood—has been conceptualized as an event—by way of narrative patterns borrowed from the tragic stage.[11] A play like *Trojan Women* does not merely mirror the realities of Athens's ongoing war: it constructs those realities by providing the Athenians (of whom Thucydides is just one particularly articulate and authoritative example) with a means of comprehending the events unfolding around them.

Drama's mimesis thus has an active force: it not only reflects reality but produces it by supplying the narrative frameworks by which the Athenians interpreted their reality and thereby made it real. Tragedy's *mimēsis* of a *praxis* supplies the meaning of acts and the template for meaningful activity. In this sense, tragic mimesis is anticipatory or futural, "reflecting" a state of affairs that does not yet exist in the real world. This futurity is figured within *Trojan Women* itself in the formal tension between the raw misery of the immediate moment and a promised retribution. The divine prologue has assured us that justice will come in the end, but those living through the tragedy are not in a position to appreciate the elegant structure of its anticipated reversal:

Hecuba predicts that their suffering will make them the subject of song in generations to come (1242–45), but from her perspective in the desperate midst of things, all she can see is an undifferentiated eternity of woe: "what I suffer and have suffered and will suffer" (468). The play's tension between present and future, as we saw in chapter 2, gives it a monitory force for the Athenian audience: for them, as for the Greeks within the play, a *peripeteia* may be in store. Not just historiography, but history itself, this play proposes, will follow a tragic trajectory, for the end of the drama is still to come and it will be acted out, not onstage by the characters, but in the real world by the audience themselves. If Thucydides writes the sequel to *Trojan Women*, it is because he lived it.

• • •

The remainder of this chapter offers an extended illustration of tragedy's active, anticipatory mimesis and of the proposition that tragedy itself creates the historical context it seems merely to reflect. My example is *Orestes*, produced in 408 and paradigmatic of the structural oddities that typify Euripidean drama. The play begins six days after the murder of Clytemnestra: polluted by the matricide, Orestes is plagued by his mother's Furies. He and Electra are to be tried for their crime by the Argives. Their only hope of salvation is their uncle Menelaus, recently returned from Troy with Helen (the real one, not the *eidōlon*). They beg him to save them, but Menelaus proves weak and self-serving, unwilling to jeopardize his own political position to help them; their grandfather Tyndareus likewise leaves them to their fate, which is forthwith decided by the vote of the Argive assembly. With no allies or alternatives, it looks like they are done for: the brother and sister lament at length and prepare to die. Just at that moment, there enters Pylades, Orestes' bosom companion. Pylades hears about their desperate plight and resolves to commit suicide along with his friends. Orestes has the sword at his throat when Pylades has a sudden idea: before they die, they should get revenge on Menelaus by killing Helen. Orestes drops the sword, and the play suddenly starts anew as a revenge drama. Orestes and Pylades lure Helen into the palace and do battle against her servants in another parodic Trojan War; meanwhile, Electra seizes Hermione, Menelaus's daughter, as a hostage. The revenge plot culminates with Orestes, Pylades, and Electra on the walls of the now burning palace, holding Hermione at knifepoint, and Menelaus below, threatening war. But just in the nick of time Apollo—absent throughout the play—appears "ex machina" and fixes everything: he tells Orestes to release Hermione and marry her. Menelaus is to halt his army and make peace with Orestes. Pylades and Electra will wed. Everyone is miraculously reconciled.

As should be evident even from this bare plot summary, *Orestes'* action is violent and disjointed, broken between the supplication plot of the first half and the revenge plot of the second half. The mood veers between hope and despair, and the tone between high tragic lament and comic elements like Helen's Phrygian house slave, begging for his life in pidgin Greek. The play opens with the famous scene of Orestes' madness, and there is an air of hallucinatory madness to the entire play: here all the characters are weak or hateful; the gods absent or unjust; the ideals of Athenian society debased and perverted. So pervasive is the corruption that some scholars believe that this is in fact the point: the play is *about* corruption, and its fragmented form mirrors that central theme. So Peter Euben asserts that "Euripides' *Orestes* is about political corruption. That is the play's theme as well as the issue raised by the radical discontinuities that mark its plot and structure. In it, content and form conspire to provide an omnipresent atmosphere of political decay and disarray."[12]

The play's formal and thematic chaos is often explained by reference to the turmoil of the historical moment. Following the defeat in Sicily, with the war against Sparta going poorly, social tensions long simmering in Athens had come to a boil. In 411, a faction of disgruntled elites had tried to overthrow the democracy and establish an oligarchy. The democratic council was disbanded by force, democratic leaders arrested or assassinated. This internecine violence was soon quelled and the democracy restored. But the underlying social tensions that led to the coup of 411 were not fully resolved, and they erupted again in 404 in all-out civil war.

Scholarship on *Orestes* makes frequent reference to Thucydides' depiction of the civil conflict in Corcyra (3.82–83), which is assumed to have been colored by the historian's experience of *stasis* in Athens. Thucydides' clinical description of the breakdown of society during civil war is taken as a diagnosis of Euripides' text and an explanation of the disturbing tone and plot structure of the play, which becomes a field report from troubled times. "In short," writes Arrowsmith, "the world of the *Orestes* is indistinguishable from the culture in convulsion described by Thucydides; point for point, Euripides and Thucydides confirm each other. . . . I am tempted to see in this frightening play

Euripides' apocalyptic vision of the final destruction of Athens and Hellas."[13]

It is easy to imagine that Euripides looked at the world around him and translated its chaos to the stage. But Euripides, as we have seen, is no mere reporter, and his play does more than transcribe the history of civil war: it intervenes actively in it. Produced directly between the failed coup of 411 and the civil war of 404, *Orestes* reenacts the tensions of the former, and in so doing, it pre-enacts, as it were, and precipitates the latter. In its staging of a repetitive history of violence, the play mimetically reproduces the political tensions of the recent past and predicts their inevitable repetition. It also actively ensures that repetition by reigniting in its audience the conflicting loyalties that had divided the Athenians in 411. It leads us to sympathize with the elite protagonists and to hope for their salvation, even as it becomes clear that their salvation will mean catastrophe for the polis as a whole. Through its formal manipulation of sympathy, *Orestes* reawakens the feelings of the recent *stasis* and generates in its viewers the psychic conditions that would lead to civil war four years later.

In *Orestes*, then, tragedy not only provides a cognitive framework for understanding history, as we saw with *Helen* and *Trojan Women*. It also articulates what Raymond Williams calls a "structure of feeling," the lived experience of society as it takes shape in the present moment, with "all the known complexities, the experienced tensions, shifts, and uncertainties, the intricate forms of unevenness and confusion." Hovering "at the very edge of semantic availability," barely expressed or expressible, such embryonic sensibilities nonetheless "exert palpable pressures and set effective limits on experience and action." They are "social experiences in solution," not yet precipitated out in ideologies, institutions, or events. What suspends them there is aesthetic form, which, by giving expression to these latent experiences in the present, also facilitates their eventual emergence.[14] *Orestes* articulates the "structures of feeling" of Athens between the two *staseis*: it holds these feelings "in solution" within its dramatic structure, until they will precipitate, horrifically, in the crisis of 404.

The emotional trajectory of the play is set at the start by the desperate situation of the protagonists, Orestes and Electra, and their quest for survival, which dominates the action of the first half. If this play is to work for us as a drama—and not just as a grim dispatch from grim times—we must to some extent want this quest to succeed. Structurally, these protagonists, isolated onstage as the play opens, are presented as

the focus of our spectatorial attention and objects of attachment. We
don't have to "identify" with the characters; indeed, their mythic status
and unique situation bar full identification. We don't necessarily even
have to like them. But as spectators who have come to watch a play, we
have an inherent interest in its protagonists' continued existence.[15] That
dramatic attachment is reinforced by the myth. The frequent allusions
to Aeschylus's *Oresteia*, the canonical version of the story, remind us
that Orestes has to live long enough to undergo trial in Athens, and
can't die here in Argos as this play threatens. The audience know how
the myth has to end, and they want it to end that way, both as spectators and as Athenians, since Orestes' ultimate acquittal in a just and
lawful trial will be a credit to their city.

The play encourages more than just this minimal interest in the characters, though. In the pathetic opening scene, we see Orestes, wasted
by fever and tormented by the unseen demons of his dead mother. He
wakes from a peaceful sleep to madness and terror, a staging of subjective interiority nearly unparalleled in Greek tragedy. We see Electra,
herself hopeless and bereft, tenderly wipe the filthy hair from his brow
and the froth from his mouth: "a sweet servitude," she says, "to tend a
brother's limbs with a sister's hand" (221–22). The play thus opens by
showing not only the piteous suffering of these characters, but what
they mean to the one who loves them most. The chorus of Argive
women contribute to the sympathy: entering on tiptoe, they hush their
traditional entry song in order not to wake the sleeping Orestes (140–
207). The daring self-reflexivity of this parodos, which overtly acknowledges this formal element of tragedy and suborns it to the dramatic
scenario, enlists the genre itself in the attempt to alleviate Orestes'
suffering.[16]

The sympathy this first episode arouses is sustained throughout the
play in the theme of salvation, *sōtēria*. "I am searching for salvation
(*sōtērian*)," Orestes tells Menelaus, "which all men seek, and not only
me" (678–79).[17] His generalization is later affirmed by Helen's Phrygian
slave. This ludicrous foreigner begs for his life, saying, "Everywhere
sensible men find it sweeter to live than to die. . . . Every man, even if
he is a slave, takes joy in seeing the sunlight" (1509, 1523). This life in-
stinct is posited as a universal principle common to all human beings,
including, presumably, us in the audience. The desire for salvation thus
binds the audience to the protagonists. The theme is reinforced by the
structure of the play, which—up until its sudden *peripeteia* at 1098—be-
longs to the sub-genre of suppliant drama: the language and gestures

of supplication (e.g., 382–84) add religious weight to the protagonists' pleas. "Salvation" thus works at both a diegetic and extra-diegetic level to encourage the audience to sympathize with the characters and share in their quest for *sōtēria*.

The first half of the play stages the failure of that quest. That personal failure is represented as a broader societal failure, the breakdown of the fundamental values and institutions of contemporary Athens: law, kinship, democracy. This broad framing of the protagonists' plight also serves to strengthen our commitment to these characters. Those who reject their pleas for help are depicted in such negative terms that there is no competing claim on our sympathies: Aristotle notes with disapproval that Euripides makes Menelaus worse than he needed to be, and the same could be said of Tyndareus, the Argive assembly, even Apollo.[18] By the same token, by representing the protagonists as victims of a larger societal decay, the play not only makes it very hard to root against them (since to do so would mean siding against basic social values), but it also makes the endurance of those values—and indeed, of society itself—seem to depend upon Orestes' and Electra's individual fates.

The siblings first appeal for help to their grandfather, Tyndareus, but he rebuffs them harshly: Orestes murdered his daughter; Orestes should in turn be put to death, and he will exert his influence to see this done. Tyndareus's language throughout is legalistic: he appeals to precedent and insists on legal remedy as the alternative to endless blood feud. His speech evokes the *Oresteia*; but his ridiculous proposal that instead of killing Clytemnestra, Orestes should have taken her to court (496–503), and his cold insistence that justice demands his grandson's death, blur that trilogy's neat distinction between law and pre-law and make a mockery of its triumphant progression from blood vengeance to democratic justice.[19]

After their failure with their grandfather, Orestes and Electra turn to their uncle, Menelaus, their only "refuge of salvation," as they say (*kataphugē sōtērias,* 724; cf. 52, 68–70). They appeal to Menelaus on the grounds of *philia* (friendship, including kinship) and the established Greek principle of mutual aid between *philoi*.[20] That principle is strong generally in Greek culture and is evoked incessantly in *Orestes*. Menelaus can be expected to aid the siblings because he is their uncle and owes a debt of gratitude (*kharis*) to their father for the war he waged to recover Menelaus's wife (244). So Orestes begs him: "Give a share of your good fortune to your friends in their terrible misfortune. Don't just take what is good but also take a share of troubles in turn, paying back paternal favors to those you owe. For friends who are not friends in hard times are friends in name alone" (449–55; cf. 665–66). Menelaus acknowledges his obligation in principle and would like to fulfill it, he says, but he fears incurring war with Argos and the enmity of his father-in-law Tyndareus, by whose good graces he rules Sparta. He offers to try to restrain the rage of the Argive demos, though we later hear that he didn't even show up at the assembly. This niggardly satisfaction of the obligations of *philia* is, in Orestes' mind, no *philia* at all; Menelaus's offer is received as a betrayal not just of his brother and family but of the fundamental principles of friendship and reciprocal *kharis*.

Justice fails Orestes and Electra. *Philia* fails them. The god fails them. Having instigated the matricide, Apollo is not present to support Orestes through its dreadful aftermath, and the god's injustice is a repeated refrain right up until his unexpected appearance at the end.[21] Even the polis fails them. Orestes pleads his innocence before the Argive assembly, which the messenger describes in terms that evoke the democratic Ekklēsia of contemporary Athens (e.g., 46–50, 756, 884–85, 949). This assembly paints a dire picture of democratic politics. Orestes' speech and those of his supporters fall on deaf ears, as the unprincipled mob is swayed by speakers trying to curry favor with Tyndareus or with the powerful friends of Aegisthus.[22] In this debased democracy, "the evil man wins in the show of hands" (944). A decree is passed, a "bloody, inimical vote among the citizens" (974–75): Orestes and Electra are to die. Driven by corrupt rhetoric, sinister collusions, and a demos primed for blood, the unjust verdict of the democratic assembly only perpetuates the cycle of murder and violence.

And so our protagonists, betrayed by kin and city alike, prepare to kill themselves. We are at around line 1100 and it looks like the play is about to end: Orestes will not fulfill his mythic destiny, the court of the Areopagus will not be founded in Athens to conduct his trial, Aeschylus's *Eumenides* will be retroactively consigned to the ash heap of history. But just in the nick of time, the protagonists—and the myth and the play—are saved by the intervention of Pylades. This "dearest of men" (*tonde philtaton brotōn*, 725) redeems *philia*: himself both kin (he is Orestes' first cousin and intended brother-in-law) and "a *philos* better than a thousand kinsmen" (804–6), Pylades replaces those false *philoi* and treacherous kinsmen, Menelaus and Tyndareus. He also redeems the protagonists. Orestes literally has his sword to his throat when Pylades has his brilliant last-minute idea: before dying, they should get vengeance on Menelaus by killing Helen (1097–1102). Orestes stays his hand: the thought of vengeance against his enemy gives him a reason to live. And it gives him more than that: by killing Helen, the cause of all the Greeks' suffering at Troy, they will become heroes. So promises Pylades: "A cry will go up, and they will light fires to the gods praying for many blessings for you and me because we exacted blood from an evil woman. You will not be called a matricide after you kill her but, leaving that title behind, you will gain a better one: you will be called the killer of Helen, killer of many" (1137–42). Orestes, debilitated by disease and despair, will reclaim his status as hero and prove himself the true son of Agamemnon (1167–68) and rightful ruler of Argos. With Pylades' plan, our protagonists finally seem to find the salvation they have been seeking from the start.

Orestes and Electra are saved. The play itself is saved. It does not end in a triple suicide at line 1100. Instead, we get a sudden *peripeteia*, a reversal from despair to hope, from paralytic resignation to vigorous action.[23] *Orestes* essentially begins anew as a revenge drama. Even the pace changes, the extended debates of the first half yielding to increasingly frantic activity (unchecked by formal *stasima*) and a breathless assault of surprises as we accelerate toward the calamitous finale. This sharp *metabolē* (change) in the action and tone—one of the play's most surprising formal features—significantly complicates our sympathies for the protagonists.[24] For even as it satisfies our desire for the characters' survival, it sets the play on a disastrous new course in which the three friends are rapidly transformed from victims of a corrupt society into agents of sacrilege, bloodshed, and chaos. The attempted murder of Helen is figured as both a perverted sacrifice (1107, 1285, 1494) and, ironically, a perverted supplication (1408–15). That impiety is compounded by the kidnapping of Hermione, a virtual sister (1340; cf. 63–66, 109) and the one character in the play who is represented as wholly innocent. As Pylades and Orestes leap on the girl like bacchants (1493)—imagery used earlier of Orestes' tormenting Furies (319, 338, 411, 835)—their revenge comes to seem more a manifestation of Orestes' madness than its remedy. Meanwhile, the chorus and Electra, waiting outside, cheer them on with shocking bloodthirstiness: "Murder, slay, strike, kill!" (*phoneuete kainete theinet' ollute*, 1302–3).

Far from the remedy for a world gone mad, this catastrophic revenge plays out as an unwitting repetition of the crimes that caused its madness. *Orestes'* reversal is not accompanied by a recognition. In fact, it is marked by a striking moment of non-recognition. It isn't fair for Menelaus to prosper, Pylades tells Orestes, "but your father and you and your sister to die; and your mother . . . I pass over that: it is not fitting to speak about" (1144–45). In this apophasis, the matricide—the crime that haunts this play as much as it haunts its protagonist—is mentioned only to be silenced, its influence on the present action willfully forgotten. Through this non-recognition, history, as Hegel predicted, repeats itself.[25] The murder of Helen is staged as a repetition of the murder of Clytemnestra from Aeschylus's *Choephoroi*, but without the divine mandate of the latter—or its success, for Helen disappears in the middle of the murder.[26] We could thus add Marx's supplement to Hegel: here history repeats itself, the first time as tragedy, the second time as farce. "The first time as tragedy" quite literally: amid a chaos of literary allusions, the tragic tradition "weighs like a nightmare on the brain of the living."[27] "The second time as farce": a dark and futile farce that empties the actions it repeats of their meaning and value. So Orestes will prove himself his father's son by fighting a second Trojan War within the palace (1110–15, 1351–52, 1485, 1528); but this Trojan War will be a humiliating parody of the first, its bard a cowering Phrygian house slave.[28] "I will never tire of killing evil women," Orestes declares, his knife to his cousin's throat (1590); but with each iteration—Clytemnestra, Helen, Hermione—the woman's evil becomes less apparent and her killing less just.

So, too, the revenge plot repeats the fratricidal violence of this doomed house. Electra opens the play with a prologue laying out the mythic history of her family: "Strife introduced war (*polemon*) for Atreus against his brother Thyestes. But why should I recapitulate things unspoken/unspeakable?" (*ti t'arrhēt' anametrēsasthai me dei?* 13–14). In this artificial apophasis—artificial because fratricide, like matricide, haunts the action of this play—fraternal conflict is spoken only to be unspoken and declared unspeakable.[29] Willfully unrecognized, that past "war" between brothers is repeated in Menelaus's betrayal of his dead brother (241, 366, 745, 1228, 1463) and his nephew's "war" of retribution against him (*polemiōn timōrian*, 1160). The fraternal bond broken by Menelaus in the first half of the play seems to be resecured in the second half by Pylades, whose superlative friendship makes him "like a brother" to Orestes (882, 1015). But this new fraternity leads only to disaster, as Pylades incites Orestes to violence against his own kin and drives him on with delusions of heroic glory to set fire to his own house (1149–52). The spectacular final scene extends this kindred war to the city as a whole: the burning palace is represented as a besieged city, as Orestes threatens his enemy from the battlements while Menelaus musters an army of Argives below (1567–75, 1618–22). Orestes is determined now not only to survive but to seize control of Argos, and as the two exchange threats, we seem to be on the verge of civil war.

Orestes' fraternal violence would no doubt have resonated strongly with the Athenians, who figured themselves as brothers descended from the same divine parent.[30] The political resonances are sharpened by the play's specific language of fraternity. Traditionally, Pylades and Orestes are represented as *xenoi*, bound by the mutual obligations of inherited guest-friendship, *xenia*. That word does not occur in this play. Instead, we get a much more freighted word for their friendship: *hetaireia*. So Orestes exclaims after Pylades first declares his loyalty: "Have companions (*hetairous*), not just kin, since a man who melds to you in his ways, even if he comes from outside, is a better *philos* than a thousand kinsmen" (804–6).[31] In fifth-century Athens the word *hetaireia* denotes the exclusive gatherings where rich Athenians meet to drink, socialize, and talk politics. Part social club, part political action committee, *hetaireiai* figure prominently in Thucydides' account of the Corcyrean civil war: these alliances were formed, he says, not for lawful mutual support but to pursue power through revolution, and were sealed not by shared faith but by shared crime (3.82.6). In Athens, the *hetaireiai* were the crucible of the oligarchic movement that culminated in the coups of 411 and 404.[32]

What will an Athenian audience have made of Orestes' *hetaireia* and the calamitous scheme it hatches? A viewer with oligarchic sympathies may have observed that this alliance saves our elite protagonists, who have been abandoned by their other friends and by the polis. Indeed, one hardly needs to be an oligarch to feel that the protagonists had no alternative, for we have been shown at length the betrayal that led them to this point. Moreover, since this betrayal is represented as the breakdown of cherished Greek values and institutions, to the extent that the Athenian audience recognized their own polis in this Argos, they would have understood, perhaps even shared, the protagonists' desperation. Thus, some scholars read *Orestes* as a monitory tale: when the elite come to feel alienated within a corrupt democracy, they have no choice but to turn to one another for "salvation" and head down the path toward oligarchy.

And yet even those who shared the protagonists' despair could hardly help recoiling at the ruin wrought by their conspiracy. As we have seen, Euripides goes out of his way to emphasize the horror and madness of this revenge, which is staged less as a just retribution for, or rectification of, the protagonists' suffering than as a blind repetition of the crimes of the past. The sympathy evoked by Electra and Orestes' desperate situation and their doomed quest for salvation becomes much harder to sustain once that "salvation" is found to lie in the violent kidnapping of the innocent Hermione and to culminate in the conflagration of civil war. This elite *hetaireia* may save the protagonists, but at the cost of annihilating the entire polis.[33]

The tense stalemate of the final scene induces a kind of psychological stalemate for the audience, too, setting our sympathies against themselves. The play's structure, with its sudden *peripeteia* from supplication to revenge and the resulting clash between a desire for the protagonists' salvation and horror at the means and ends that salvation entails, allows for two different readings of the final scene, but for no synthesis or compromise between the two. The spectators are forced to choose between desperate, vengeful protagonists and a corrupt democratic city—an impossible choice, and one the play itself refuses to make. The pointed ambiguity of the end reproduces within the audience the madness of division they had so recently experienced in their own civil crisis, and it offers no hope of reconciliation. It reproduces that division, moreover, not only within the audience as a whole, but also within each individual audience member; for if we cheer for the protagonists' survival, as the play encourages us to do, then we become co-conspirators in their disastrous coup.

Arousing divided loyalties within the audience, individually and collectively, *Orestes* leads to an emotional and cognitive impasse that reproduces the tensions of Athens in 411. By the time this play was produced in 408, though, those political tensions had, at least superficially, been resolved. Civil war had been averted; the democracy had been restored and was apparently stronger than ever. And yet the problems underlying the coup of 411 persisted, and their historical necessity, unacknowledged in the wake of that first *stasis*, proved itself in the second. *Orestes* stages that historical repetition mimetically in its structure of nonrecognition and reiteration, as the unspeakable crimes of the past are replicated in the present. Those manic repetitions suggest the futility of any strategies of apophasis or denial the Athenians may have adopted after 411, and predict that the Athenians, like Orestes, will wake from blessed oblivion (*lēthē*, 213) to the madness of crimes remembered and soon to be repeated.

But the play does more than simply predict this future crisis: it precipitates it. By re-creating the tensions of the recent past but then intensifying them to the breaking point, with no hope of compromise, *Orestes* produces the psychic conditions—the "structures of feeling"—of civil war. The affective stalemate it generates is not a thing of the past, as the Athenians in 408 may have wanted to believe, but the lived experience of the present, urgent and excruciating. *Orestes* holds that experience "in solution," but also imagines its future precipitation in violent action. Forcing the audience to feel what it feels like to live in a city divided, the play not only shows history repeating itself, but enacts its future repetition in the present moment of the performance. Far from a passive mimesis of its historical context, then, *Orestes* creates that context: by articulating the unrecognized experience of the present, it produces the affective framework for future action. That terrible *praxis*, when it comes, will be a real-life acting out of the conflict first lived in the form of a tragic *mimēsis*.

The play does not end with this murderous stalemate, though, and there is a resolution of sorts in the eleventh-hour appearance of Apollo. I say "of sorts" because, like most Euripidean deus ex machinas, this one solves everything and nothing. Apollo simply commands that the conflict end: "Go now, each of you, where I command and reconcile your quarrels" (1678–79). Orestes is ordered to drop the sword from Hermione's throat and instead marry her, a union virtually performed onstage (1675). Menelaus is to go back to Sparta and allow Orestes to rule Argos: Apollo will reconcile the Argives to the idea of this polluted murderer on the throne by acknowledging that he himself commanded Clytemnestra's death (1663). Orestes will be tried in Athens and acquitted. Electra will marry Pylades and live happily ever after. And as for their murderous plot, it's all fine because it turns out they didn't kill Helen after all: instead, she was saved by Zeus and whisked up to join her brothers Castor and Polydeuces in the heavens. As Orestes says, "All is well in the end" (*eu teleitai*, 1670), and the play closes with a prayer to the "most beautiful goddess Peace" (1682–83).

This "happy ending" has, understandably, left many readers unsatisfied.[34] Apollo's breezy transformation of deadly enemies into allies and spouses seems to make a mockery of the play's fraught politics and to retroactively vitiate all its human dilemmas and decisions, stripping them of consequences and meaning. Through a blithe textual apophasis, everyone agrees simply not to recall the crimes of the past.[35] The whole thing feels too facile, too artificial, to be believable. Even Orestes wonders whether to believe it. "Oh prophetic Loxias," he cries, in response to the god's speech. "You were not after all a prophet of false oracles, but you were true. And yet I was afraid that I had imagined I heard your voice, when I was really hearing one of my avengers" (1666–69). Even as he affirms his restored faith in Apollo, he admits the possibility that the god's command was never anything more than a hallucination, a symptom of his madness. Perhaps it is just a hallucination now. But he quickly sets aside that fear: "But all is well in the end, and I will obey your commands" (1670).

This mad, hallucinatory exodos seems manifestly implausible, and its implausibility seems only to reemphasize the impossibility of resolution. One can imagine Athenians in the audience drawing this pessimistic conclusion: barring divine intervention of the most improbable sort, the history of civil conflict will repeat itself ad infinitum. And yet precisely in its improbability, this resolution anticipates the highly implausible resolution of Athens's own political crisis. The civil war ended in 403 with a reconciliation agreement in which the Athenians swore simply to forget their former enmities: to drop the sword from the neck of their victims, as it were, and relinquish past grudges. In this oath of amnesty (*a-mnēsteia*, "not remembering"), the Athenians swore literally not to remember the crimes of the past (*mē mnēsikakēsō*). This artificial amnesia constituted a sort of collective apophasis, a willful refusal to recall crimes they could not forget in the hope that they might not be repeated. *Orestes'* repetitions have taught us to be skeptical of such a hope.

And yet, amazingly, it seems to have worked. Even Athenians at the time were amazed: contemporary authors emphasize the surprising success of the amnesty agreement, which they represent as universally upheld and unprecedented in human history. Isocrates recounts, in a speech delivered the following year, that before the amnesty, the Athenians were locked in bitter war; but after taking the oath, "We have lived so harmoniously that it was as if no disaster had ever befallen us" (*hōsper oudemias hēmin sumphoras gegenēmenēs*, 18.46). During the *stasis*, everyone considered the Athenians to be the most unfortunate (*dustukhestatous*) of people; but now, he concludes, "We seem to be the wisest and most blessed (*eudaimonestatoi*) of the Greeks" (18.46).[36]

This narrative of the amnesty's immediate and universal effect is no doubt itself the product of a certain willful amnesia, but what's important is less the historical veracity of contemporary accounts like Isocrates' than their structure of astonishing *metabolē*: they present the reconciliation as a miracle. Like Apollo's command, the amnesty agree-ment blithely reconciled the demos and the oligarchic *hetaireiai*, resolv-ing in one wave of the hand the bitter hostilities between fellow citizens and setting behind them the catastrophic violence they had wrought. Transforming non-recognition into a fruitful non-remembering, the Athenians declare an arbitrary end to the repetition of past crimes: the madness of the past will simply be forgotten "as if no disaster had ever befallen us." Thus the Athenians will stage for an admiring Greek audi-ence a surprising *peripeteia* from enmity to friendship and from bad fortune (*dustukhia*) to good (*eudaimonia*). For them, as for the charac-ters in Euripides' play, and no less miraculously, "All is well in the end" (*eu teleitai*).

The improbability of *Orestes*' "ex machina" conclusion may indicate political despair, then, as critics have argued. And yet, in its very im-probability, it set the stage for the Athenians' wondrous resolution of their own insoluble problems. Euripides showed the Athenians what it meant—literally how it felt—to live with the internal division of civil war. He also enabled them to imagine the miraculous possibility of rec-onciliation. Miracles happen: they happen onstage, and they can in real life as well. The act of collective make-believe that sustained the am-nesty was rehearsed first in the Theater of Dionysus before being en-acted in real life. And so we might modify Marx's modification of Hegel: all world-historical events happen twice—the first time as trag-edy, the second time as history.

• • •

The last play Euripides wrote in Athens, *Orestes* is often read as a symp-tom of the impending "death" of tragedy, a demise apparently caused by its diseased relation to its epoch.[37] Standing too close to the sick world it depicts, the genre is infected by history. It is subsumed by its own historical context; losing the distance it required to reflect criti-cally on that context, all it can do is mimetically reproduce its chaos, over and over, in its form and themes. Alternatively, tragedy remains free of contamination but as a result becomes detached from history and the polis: it proves inadequate to the traumas of its moment and, unable to remedy the sickness of the polis, withdraws—as Euripides himself did—exhausted into its own world of intertextual allusion and impotent despair. Too close to its context or too far from it, with *Orestes* tragedy seems to many finally to have lost the vital link to its historical

moment that, as Vernant argues, was the genre's life blood and the condition of its very existence.[38]

But I hope to have shown that in *Orestes*, tragedy is very much alive.
It is neither swallowed by history nor alienated from it, but instead is
actively engaged with and in it: reflecting its historical moment, in all
its chaos, but also shaping it. *Helen* and *Trojan Women* propose, and
Orestes illustrates, the active force of tragedy's mimesis: that far from
merely recreating a historical reality that exists prior and exterior to it,
tragedy *creates* that reality by producing the cognitive and affective conditions necessary for its realization. Its plotlines furnish the meaning of
history's narrative arc, providing a structure for understanding and re-
cording historical experience. But they also articulate that experience
itself—not after the fact as an object of mimetic re-presentation, but in
the lived moment of the performance. Through its own formal structure—its peripeties of action and of sympathy—tragedy sustains the
structures of feeling that will determine history's mad repetitions and
its miraculous reversals. Euripides' plays cannot be explained away,
then, on appeal to historical context. Instead, that context is immanent
within them, as their dramatic form gives form in turn to the outside
world and reality is conjured for the audience, with a wave of his hand,
by the play's mechanical god.

Content of the Form

We end at the end. Five Euripidean tragedies end with the same generic closing tag:[1]

> πολλαὶ μορφαὶ τῶν δαιμονίων,
> πολλὰ δ' ἀέλπτως κραίνουσι θεοί·
> καὶ τὰ δοκηθέντ' οὐκ ἐτελέσθη,
> τῶν δ' ἀδοκήτων πόρον ηὗρε θεός.
> τοιόνδ' ἀπέβη τόδε πρᾶγμα.

> Many are the shapes of the divinities;
> many things the gods accomplish against all hope.
> The expected is not accomplished;
> for the unexpected the god finds a way.
> That's how this affair has turned out.

These lines promise, or pretend, to sum up the baffling action of the play we have just watched. The lines are generic in every sense of the word: in content, they are so general that they can be applied to almost any play Euripides wrote, not just to the five they actually do close; in form, the choral anapests are tragedy's generic way of marking the end of a play. The lines have long been scorned as a later interpolation or as an empty gesture, a device used to conclude the play but devoid of particular meaning in themselves.[2] It's true that, as a synopsis of their plays, these lines are singularly unsatisfying. On the one hand, they seem to say, "That's it. That's all, folks." By pointing to the gods' mysterious ways, they offer an explanation of sorts for the play's action and thus grant some impression of closure: "That's how this affair has turned out." On the other hand, though, that explanation doesn't really explain anything; instead its taut paradoxes defer explanation and displace the play's uncertainties onto the larger world, our world. Instead of making sense of the play, they make nonsense of the cosmos. The lines promise a summation that they don't in fact deliver, leaving the audience with a sense that "That's not quite it."

This tension between "That's it"—the show's over—and "That's not it" captures the characteristic riddling quality of Euripides' dramatic form. The lines seem to offer an alignment between form and meaning: five lines that, by summing up the play's meaning, grant it a formal ending and retroactively fix its dramatic shape. And yet it seems that formal closure can be achieved only by an evacuation of meaning in a generic platitude, a kind of resigned shrug: Isn't life strange? Alternatively, if we take seriously the lines' philosophy, they preclude the very closure they seem to offer: the gods will always take new shapes and accomplish unexpected things, and so we can never say once and for all, "That's how this affair has turned out."[3] Either there is a surplus of form, a formal gesture of closure that gives up on meaning, or a surplus of meaning, a lingering perplexity that undoes the formal closure.

Euripides' imperfect alignment of form and meaning—not a schism or antithesis, more the disconcerting awareness of their non-identity—forces form itself onto center stage. It makes us aware of a play's form, granting it density and texture. Even at its emptiest (as this generic closing tag suggests), form is always full, replete with meaning. We have seen Euripides exploring that meaning, thinking in form about tragic form and its fullness and emptiness. The plays have shown us form as generative and enabling, producing, for example, an aspiration to justice (in *Hecuba* and *Trojan Women*), or a renewed attachment to the polis (in *Ion*), or even history itself (in *Suppliants* and *Orestes*). In the last cases, the text's aesthetic form generates its own social context, making possible new contents and opening new avenues of thought and action. We have also seen the constraints and oppressions of form, both dramatic and social. In *Electra*, empty forms encrusted with outdated content constrained human behavior and foreclosed radical social possibilities. Form functioned there as a deadweight upon the play's own imagination. That this critique is articulated by way of the genre's formal mechanisms points to the equivocal nature of formal structure, which is always at once constraining and enabling: *Electra*'s analysis of the stale conventionality of the recognition scene is performed through an exuberantly creative reworking of that very convention.

In *Electra*, as in all the plays we have examined, tragic form is both an object of thought and its vehicle. Euripides, like any playwright, thinks in plot structure as much as in words, images, or themes: to that extent, Aristotle may be right to prioritize *muthos* over *lexis* (language) and *dianoia* (thought expressed in speech). The arrangement of the action is a means of arousing emotion, as Aristotle stresses, but also of articulating ideas. Consider the *anagnōrisis*, which Aristotle lists as one of the genre's greatest resources for producing pity and fear. Its delay in *Ion* suggested the contingency of Athens's founding myths, while in *Electra* its near-parodic demystification enacted the misrecognitions that sustain heroic and social identity; *Alcestis*'s asymmetrical recognition scene between Admetus and his silent wife presented a disturbing exception to the universal law of mortality; in *Orestes* a *peripeteia* unaccompanied by *anagnōrisis* turned the action into the historical repetition of a criminal past. Through its deployment of such structural elements, tragedy becomes enacted philosophy. It has no philosophical metalanguage: there is no privileged authorial voice in tragedy, and those moments where we might seem to get a higher-level commentary on the action (like the closing lines) prove illusory. Instead, the commentary is immanent in the action and the varied generic devices for its elaboration: *anagnōrisis* and *peripeteia*, stichomythia, *kommos* and *agōn*, poetic imagery or anachronistic rhetoric, characterization, the prologue and the epilogue, even the closing choral anapests. These formal elements are, in Adorno's phrase, "knowledge in the form of a nonconceptual object."[4]

That form is an essential part of the content is true of all art—indeed, it is one definition of art. But this general feature is insistently foregrounded in Euripides through his novel enactment of the genre's formal possibilities. Aristotle's organic model of tragedy—in which a well-structured *muthos* can be compared to the human body in its intelligibility and internal coherence (*Poetics* 1450b34–51a6)—is only one way of parsing tragic structure, of course, and may well have been idiosyncratic. But if Aristotle's aesthetic of unity naturalizes tragic form, Euripides denaturalizes it. We saw this in particular in chapter 2 in *Hecuba* and *Trojan Women*. Presenting an appeal for justice through the beauty of their lyrics, these plays raise insistent questions about the relation between aesthetics and ethics. Does beauty make us just? The plays' most provocative answer to this question comes by way of their own formal "ugliness": the asyndeton between the prologue and the body of the play in *Trojan Women*, the broken-backed action of *Hecuba*, the ragged and aporetic endings of both plays. This pointed refusal of wholeness and coherence challenges not only the aesthetics of unity but also its ethics, forcing us to contemplate the iniquities entailed by formal symmetry and the injustices concealed behind the smooth surface of Aristotle's "whole and complete action" (*Poetics* 1450b24). Advertising rather than concealing their own aesthetic choices, Euripides' plays reveal the active force of aesthetic form—whether "beautiful" or "ugly"—and insist that we ask what form means and what it does.

Means *and does*. One of my aims in this book has been to investigate how tragic form acts upon its audience, how it affects or moves them: the process the Greeks termed *psukhagōgia*. This process is partly cognitive. Tragedy asks its audience to think, and Euripidean tragedy does so more than most, if we are to trust the poet's phantom in Aristophanes' *Frogs*. This Euripides—an avant-garde intellectual, contemporary of the Sophists and deeply engaged with their philosophy, claims to benefit the polis by teaching his audience to think. The ghost has often been taken at his word: Euripides the "wise poet" is either credited with "the instruction of the Athenians" or, alternatively, condemned for killing tragedy with his philosophizing.[5] Our closing anapests could be taken as evidence for either position, their traditional wisdom read as a homily on the nature of the gods, or their sophisticated (even sophistic) paradoxes as provocation to radical epistemological and ontological questioning.

But the "wise poet" was also the master of pathos, the "most tragic" of the tragedians (as Aristotle grudgingly concedes, *Poetics* 1453a29–30) in producing the tragic emotions; and his plays not only ask their audience to think but also force them to feel. The closing choral tag may provoke emotion along with intellectual reflection: either reassurance from its familiar theology or unease at its philosophy of uncertainty, or perhaps a mixture of the two. These feelings aren't preclusive of, nor necessarily antithetical to, reason, as Plato feared. Indeed, they can't be fully separated out from reason: we may be able to distinguish the cognitive and affective heuristically (though even that, with difficulty), but within the theatrical experience they are usually indistinguishable.[6]

Take the bedeviled question of catharsis. Scholars debate whether tragic catharsis—as imagined by Aristotle or identified in actual plays—should be understood as intellectual clarification or as emotional release. Charles Segal argues for the latter, and juxtaposes to the shared release of emotion with which so many tragedies end "the 'anti-closural' elements that emerge when we reflect more intellectually and abstractly on the work, reviewing its meaning in our minds as a total design."[7] Segal is surely right that our emotional and intellectual responses to a play can operate independently and complicate or at times even contradict one another. But as often, I think, the effect of tragedy (both in its ultimate moment of "catharsis" and throughout) is to fuse the two. If one feels discomfort at the cavalier resolution of a Euripidean deus ex machina, it is partly from an intellectual judgment that it doesn't fully resolve the problems it pretends to resolve. Drama makes us experience the thought as felt. Indeed, this is one of its most salient (and advantageous) differences from other discourses: its ability to animate thought with affect—to make us *feel* the consequences or contradictions of our beliefs—even as it heightens our feelings and, in this way, exposes them to intellectual examination. Affect and cognition work together in tragedy's *psukhagōgia*, and it is through their synthesis that the genre has its impact on the citizen and in the city.

This psychagogic force is complex not only because of the labile relation between reason and affect, but also because of the ambiguity of those affects themselves. Aristotle, of course, identified pity and fear as tragedy's characteristic emotions, and we have seen many examples of these in Euripides' plays. But we have also seen sensations more fleeting and contradictory: the conflicted happiness of the "happy ending" in *Ion* or *Alcestis*, the skeptical credulity of *Electra*'s recognition scene, the clashing loyalties generated by *Orestes' peripeteia*, or the sheer bafflement (relief? despair? wonder? irritation? all of these at once?) of its miraculous resolution. Because drama arouses these sensations without necessarily defining them or requiring the audience to define them, their contradictions needn't be resolved or rationalized.[8] The final *kommos* of *Suppliants*, for example, elicits a dense melange of human sorrow and civic pride, without differentiating these sensations or examining their incompatibilities; by arousing multiple sensations simultaneously—and arousing them *as simultaneous*—the play's *psukhagōgia* acts on a part of the viewer's *psukhē* where the human and the civic are felt as one. Interpellating its audience in this way as citizens and human beings at once, it humanizes the civic and politicizes the human. This capacity to hold together diverse, potentially contradictory affects without requiring resolution or even recognition of their contradictions makes tragedy a particularly suitable medium for articulating the imaginary relations (themselves structured by social antagonisms and so inevitably contradictory) that constitute ideology. Thus, it makes no sense to ask whether tragedy reaffirms civic ideology or subverts it:

arousing inseparable feelings of commitment and alienation, it works on its audience at a psychic level where the two are not mutually exclusive.

The ideological force of tragedy's *psukhagōgia* is particularly apparent in *Ion*. That play, as I argued in chapter 1, dramatizes the very process of ideological attachment, as the plot's endless deferrals engender a commitment to civic beliefs that those same deferrals have shown to be arbitrary and contingent, a passionate attachment that persists despite that critique and is even (in accordance with the non-exclusionary logic of affect) strengthened by it. Ideology is not a determinate content—a set of doctrines or fixed ideas—that the play's structure contains. Instead, it is an affective form conjured into being by the play's aesthetic form, its lucky coincidences and chance encounters, its formal repetitions, the tempo of its long-awaited reunion between mother and son. *Muthos*, Aristotle's analytic taxonomies notwithstanding, is not just a structured structure, but also a structuring structure: dramatic form does not merely "contain" ideological content but produces it, generating through its *psukhagōgia* new sentiments, new frameworks for thought and for action, the barely recognized "structures of feeling" that constitute ideology. A play like *Ion* does not just depict ideology, then; through its formal effects, it makes its audience experience it, right there in the real time of the performance. The dramatic experience is, quite literally, ideology at work.

Nor does that experience end with the end of the play. Our final choral tag, even as it declares the play over—"That's how this affair has turned out"—generalizes its uncertainties beyond the Theater of Dionysus: the structure of the play, its variety and surprise, is the structure of the world. The ideological affect forged in the course of the drama is carried out into the polis, where it provides the raw material for politics: the impulse behind decisions, the provocation to action. Tragedy can only supply the provocation; it cannot itself perform the action. Plato may compare lawmakers to tragedians (*Laws* 817a-d), but tragedy does not make the law—a limitation Euripides' drama acknowledges and explores. *Hecuba* and *Trojan Women* stage the crucial gap between tragic emotion and political action: in both plays, tragic suffering arouses pity, but that pity does not translate into action. In fact, it risks preempting action if, by crying sympathetic tears, we feel we have done enough. These plays suggest that justice, if it is to come, will come not in the theater but beyond it; and it is the responsibility of the viewers in their role as citizens to bring it about. *Electra* likewise dramatizes tragedy's political limitation: it shows how radical political impulses can be smothered by the weight of generic convention and the empty social forms it perpetuates. Tragedy, as we saw in *Suppliants*, is not politics: its strategies of aesthetic representation are fundamentally at odds with the democracy's logic of political (non-)representation. When it tries to speak politically, it fails both as politics and as tragedy. It loses the autonomy that, as Adorno argues, allows art to articulate its social conditions by aesthetically transforming them.

Instead, as *Suppliants* suggests, it is by asserting that autonomy that tragedy becomes political: not by ventriloquizing political discourse but through its own discursive specificity as a poetic genre, mimetic mode, civic institution, and psychagogic force. In that play's self-referential final procession, tragedy intervenes in politics by means of the affective synthesis it produces in the souls of its audience, with real and (in the projected peace treaty) material effect for the city. *Orestes* pushed that same claim further: it let us see how Euripides' aesthetic form—his structuring of the traditional *muthos*, his arousal and reversal of sympathies—provides the affective scaffolding for the civil war to come. The play's structure holds "in solution" (in Raymond Williams's words) the barely articulated thoughts, feelings, experiences, and beliefs that will precipitate out in real political action. Plays like *Suppliants* and *Orestes*, I have argued, do not merely reflect their historical context but actively produce it. They make history happen. Tragedy is not just a *mimēsis* of a political *praxis*; through its mimesis—its aesthetic formation and transformation of reality—it is itself a political praxis.

That tragic *praxis* operates within a temporality of emergence, as *Electra* showed. In that play, the "utopian tendency" of Athenian democracy—the full extension of its egalitarian principles—was encoded as a potentiality, a *dunamis* (in Aristotle's terminology), that is denied the *energeia* of tragic *enargeia*. The play is radical in its formal realism, but even more so in its enactment of the tension between the congealed forms of the past and the emerging forms of the future. Showing how the former can block the latter, it stages "realistically" the dynamics of its present moment. At the same time, it contributes to their transformation, for if the play leaves its audience feeling frustrated by that formal blockage and uncomfortable with the compromises it has forced upon them, that frustration might precipitate real political change. (Or it might simply resolve into political resignation: the emergent is, by definition, unpredictable from the perspective of the present, and tragedy's political impact can thus never be more than potential.) By reconfiguring the audience's imaginary relations to their real conditions of existence, tragedy can precipitate a shift in those conditions. The latent structures of feeling that tragedy brings to the surface, the fleeting and disorganized experiences that it grants visibility or duration or urgency, supply the structures of *praxis* within which future political transformation can play out.[9]

I can't say whether Euripides' aesthetic allows more space for the emergent than Sophoclean or Aeschylean tragedy, or any other classical genre. Certainly many readers have felt a kind of fin-de-siècle untimeliness in Euripidean drama and sensed tectonic historical shifts at work behind his plays' surprising aesthetic form.[10] As we saw in the last chapter, Euripides is often associated with—when he is not blamed for—the death of both tragedy and Athenian democracy. This sense of an ending is explained not only as a crisis of context—the broken relation of his plays to their broken historical moment that we traced in the last chapter—but also as an immanent crisis of form: the impression the plays leave that the inherited forms of the genre are no longer equal to the traumatic realities of the present moment. Either there is a deficiency of form—*agones* that decide nothing, recognitions based on nothing, divine resolutions that resolve nothing—or its surplus: self-referentiality, obsessive intertextual allusion, art for art's sake; aesthetic experimentation proliferates as a kind of autoimmune response of an organism in crisis. Either way, tragic form and historical content (if they were ever really aligned) seem to have come apart.

Within that fatal rupture scholars have identified the seeds of future forms, both aesthetic and political. Is there any other classical author whose formal peculiarities are so often explained by reference to genres that did not yet exist? Euripides' tragedy is said to anticipate Middle Comedy or New Comedy, tragicomedy, melodrama, romance—as if his aesthetic were so disturbing it could only be explained through a literary-historical *Nachträglichkeit* or deferred action. Even as his plays have been read as barometers of their historical moment, Euripides' style has been felt to belong as much to the future as to his present. The popularity of his plays and their frequent revival throughout the fourth century are often cited, alongside the tradition of their cool reception during his own lifetime.[11] And it is not just his aesthetics: scholars have also seen in his plays the seeds of fourth-century political developments—particularly a shift of energy away from the polis, toward the domestic and the individual, on one side, and Panhellenic cosmopolitanism, on the other side.[12] Euripides' paradoxical position within the narrative of Athenian cultural and political history at the end of the fifth century thus reiterates the logic of his own final anapests, with their simultaneous closure and non-closure. Euripides marks both the end of Athens—that's it: that's how the fifth century turned out—and its continuity in new and unexpected shapes.

Obviously, there are many reasons to be leery of this obituary for fifth-century Athens with its organic, teleological model of cultural evolution, its idealization of Greece's vital prime (an idealization enabled precisely by its death), and its melodramatic double suicide of democracy and tragedy. Likewise, one might well question the narrative of continuity that obscures real social differences behind the unchanged name of "tragedy" or "democracy."[13] But I share the sensation that some kind of historical transformation is being played out within Euripides' aesthetic form. Perhaps not a "revolution"—whether the end of the fifth century should be considered a revolution, cultural or political, is much debated[14]—but a certain shift of sensibility that gives fourth-century Athens a different tenor from the fifth-century city, despite the apparent continuity of its external cultural and political forms.

In fact, one way to conceptualize that difference would be precisely as a new attitude toward those traditional forms: a reconfiguration of the relation between form and content and the emergence of a new "formalism."[15] In politics, there is a transformation from the "rational disorganization" (in Sheldon Wolin's phrase) of the fifth-century radical democracy to the more constitutional regime of the fourth century.[16] Laws were regularized, codified, and archived; dēmokratia came to be understood as a fixed distribution of powers and offices rather than the spontaneous will of the demos enacted immediately through the speech and action of individual citizens. Drama, too, became more formalized, both as an institution (culminating in the 330s, when Lycurgus erected statues of the three canonical fifth-century tragedians and authorized official copies of their plays), and as a mode of mimesis (with the standardization of plot, character, setting, and social world in Menander, for example).[17] Meanwhile, Plato formalized Being itself, investing Form with a new ontological substance. This new sensibility would reach its acme in Aristotle, for whom all realms of human knowledge and experience, regardless of their specific content, could be analyzed through taxonomic organization, and to whom, of course, we owe the first formalist analysis of tragedy. This new formalism (if such it was) should not be imagined as the sclerosis of content, but instead as a new way of articulating content—or a way of articulating new content—and of conceptualizing its relation to the formal structures of that articulation. That new conceptualization bespeaks less a naive faith in formal structures than an awareness that form and content are not organically fused or necessarily identical, a new self-consciousness about the substantiveness of form and its capacity to shape—to deform as well as form, repress as well as express—content.

Euripides' plays may not be directly responsible for this new order of things, but they do seem to me to crystallize the possibility of such a transformation within their novel aesthetics. Euripides' meditations on form and its relation to content, the non-congruity of the two that we feel in his closing anapests and throughout his plays, register this larger historical shift and, I would suggest, facilitate it. We have seen how his formal innovations denaturalize aesthetic form, rendering it perceptible—*aesthetic* in the root sense of the word. They allow us to see that form is not inert or neutral: it has both a substance and a politics of its own. If in the process his plays arouse a certain unease, a troubling sense that form and meaning are not fully commensurate, that they do not completely exhaust or organically express one another, that their relation is susceptible to or even in need of realignment—if, in other words, they reveal the *dis*content, as well as the content, of form—then perhaps they also produced the psychic conditions in their dramatic present for the aesthetic and political transformations that would come to characterize their future.

Notes

Preface

1. Jameson 1981: 74–102, 1988: 137–52. All translations are my own.
2. Halliwell 1987: 94.
3. Like Aristotle, I devote relatively little attention to *opsis*, staging and spectacle (on which, see Hourmouziades 1965; Taplin 1978), or to music/meter (West 1982: 77–137; Csapo 1999–2000; Hall 2006: 288–320; de Poli 2011). The plays we have were originally performed as part of a tetralogy consisting of three tragedies and a satyr play. Its position in its tetralogy and relation to the other plays no doubt shaped the perception of a play's form, but this aspect cannot be reconstructed with confidence, given that no complete Euripidean trilogies have survived.
4. See, e.g., Rooney 2000: "The very articulation of form is part of the *task* of reading; form emerges from reading's work, and it advances by means of the reader's polemic" (37).
5. On the composition of the fifth-century audience, see Csapo and Slater 1995: 286–305; Goldhill 1997: 57–66; Roselli 2011. I am not convinced by Sommerstein 1997's argument that theater audiences were more elite, and thus "right-wing," than the demos as a whole; see Revermann 2006; Roselli 2011: 63–117. Women may or may not have attended the plays (the debate is ongoing); at least some other Greeks certainly did. But the primary notional audience was, I take it, male Athenian citizens.
6. As argued, for instance, by Goldhill 1987, 1997; Longo 1990; Ober and Strauss 1990; Winkler 1990: 37–42; and widely (but not universally) presupposed. I address this debate in the introduction.

Introduction: The Politics of Form

1. Mendelsohn 2002: 50–134; Tzanetou 2011, 2012: 73–104. Heath 1989: 5–9 discusses the search for thematic unity as a response to the perceived formal disunity of Greek tragedy (his test case is Euripides' *Suppliant Women*).
2. See Mastronarde 1999–2000, 2010: 58–62 on these generic labels. Michelini 1987: 3–51 and Mastronarde 2010: 1–25 provide helpful surveys of the reception history; see also Michelini 1997. Among the many treatments of various aspects of Euripides' tragic form, see especially: Strohm 1957; Spira 1960;

Schwinge 1968; Burnett 1971; Jens 1971; Erbse 1984; Hose 1990–91; de Jong 1991; Lloyd 1992; Csapo 1999–2000; Dubischar 2001.

3. Arrowsmith 1963: 37 (original emphasis).

4. Goldhill 1987 (the quotation is on p. 68). See, further, Goldhill 2000a, 2000b. On the civic administration of the festival, see Wilson 2000, 2011. Carter 2007: 21–63 surveys the major Anglophone literature on the politics of Greek tragedy; additionally, see Rösler 1980; Kuch 1983a; Meier 1993; Hose 1995; Saïd 1998.

5. "Reflect and reflect on" is Euben's formulation (1986: 223). Goldhill 2000a: 35 explicitly situates this approach (which he notes had by then become "the mainstream of critical opinion on the politics of tragedy") as a reaction to New Criticism. The watershed collection *Nothing to Do with Dionysus?* (Winkler and Zeitlin 1990), in which Goldhill's Great Dionysia article was reprinted, likewise presents its contextualization of drama as a turning away from "the familiar premises of formalist criticism, that 'the text is the thing!' and the only thing" (4). Study of the texts themselves is only begrudgingly included in its (prescient) list of directions for future tragedy scholarship (10).

6. This debate between historicizing and aestheticizing approaches to tragedy has deep historical roots (traced by Goldhill 2012: 137–65; Billings 2014; and Leonard [in press, 2015] among others). New Critical readings of tragedy perpetuate the universalizing tradition of German Idealism going back to Kant; the twentieth-century "re-politicization" of tragedy (Goldhill 2012: 154–58) develops a Hegelian strand within that tradition (see Leonard 2005). The latter line of influence also leads directly to the modern critics who provide my theoretical framework here, especially Adorno and Jameson. I am conscious of this broader critical genealogy, even though my primary points of reference are more proximate.

7. See, for instance, the essays in Wolfson and Brown 2000; Rasmussen 2002. Critiques of historicism in tragedy studies have generally come from a historicist perspective, focusing, for example, on whether tragedy addresses specifically Athenian or more broadly Greek issues (Rhodes 2003; Carter 2004, 2011; Roselli 2011). For smart theoretical critiques, see Goff 1995a; Gellrich 1995. Others have denied the political nature of tragedy altogether, stressing instead its pleasure (Griffin 1998, with the critique of Goldhill 2000a: 37–41; Heath 1987, with the clarifications of Heath 2006); and current tragedy studies seem caught at an impasse between hedonic formalism and ideological functionalism.

8. Adorno 1991a, 1997: 4–15. This hermeneutic has been developed in literary studies most famously by Fredric Jameson, esp. Jameson 1981. See also Balibar and Macherey 1981.

9. Adorno 1997: 6: "This, not the insertion of objective elements, defines the relation of art to society." Cf. 225–30.

10. Art is ideological "behind the author's back": Adorno 1991a: 43.

11. Vernant 1988b: 24–25; cf. 1988a: 32–34. Other works that explicitly analyze the politics of tragic form include Zeitlin 1990a; Rose 1992: 185–330; Griffith 1995; Hall 1997, 2006: 288–320; Goldhill 2012: 13–133.

12. And it is not just tragedy, as the superb analyses of Homer, Pindar, and

Plato in Rose 1992 attest. The politics of genre has been studied as a marked instance of the politics of form: see esp. Williams 1977: 180–85; Jameson 1981: 103–50; Derrida 1992b; as well as Frye 1973; and within classical studies, Depew and Obbink 2000.

13. See especially Plato *Laws* 652a–671a, 797a–802e, 810b–813a, 814e–817e; *Republic* 376d–403c, 595a–608b; Aristotle *Politics* 1339a11–1340b19; Anderson 1966.

14. *Laws* 700a–701b; Aristophanes *Frogs* 1281–82, 1301–3. On the New Music, see Csapo 2004. His list of Plato's complaints about the New Music (Csapo 2004: 236) could serve as an introduction to Euripidean style.

15. Wallace 2004.

16. See Wardy 1996: 35–51. Theophrastus (frs. 87–88) believed that a certain harmony could cure sciatica. *Psukhagōgia* was associated with seductive pleasure and deceptive persuasion: Demosthenes 44.63.7, 59.55.8; Isocrates 2.49.6, 9.10.9; Aeschines 2.4.6; Lycurgus 1.3. In Plato's *Phaedrus* (261a8, 271c10), it is a virtual definition of rhetoric (cf. Plutarch *Pericles* 15): see Asmis 1986. It is a quality of visual art at Xenophon *Memorabilia* 3.10.6 and of tragedy at Timocles fr. 6 K-A; Plato *Minos* 321a4–5; and Aristotle *Poetics* 1450a33, 1450b17. On the association with magic and/or charlatanism, see Euripides fr. 379a Kannicht. *Psukhagōgia* was also the term for raising the souls of the dead: Aeschylus wrote a play entitled *Psukhagōgoi*, now lost.

17. Plato is not referring explicitly to poetry here, but *eidōla* and *phantasmata* are both connected with mimetic art elsewhere (e.g., *Republic* 598b1–8); and as Peponi 2012: 135–40 shows, poetry is also linked to the appetitive part of the soul throughout *Republic* 10. On the psychology of aesthetic perception in Plato, see especially Halliwell 2002: 72–97.

18. Halliwell 2002: 177–206. Woodruff 2008 offers a modern theory of the intellectual and ethical value of tragic emotion.

19. *Poetics* 1450b7. And although the *Poetics* generally avoids any mention of the political (Hall 1996), the long discussion of the ethical impact of music in *Politics* 8 shows that for Aristotle, as for Plato, how poetry led the soul, and where, was a matter of profound political importance.

20. I am alluding, of course, to Althusser's classic definition of ideology: Althusser 1971: 162.

21. Porter 2010: 124.

22. Thus, although in his defamiliarization of generic conventions, Euripides resembles the Russian Formalists (Porter's model for this making-visible of form: 2010: 124; cf. 75–81), defamiliarization is not an end in itself for him, as it is, e.g., for Shklovsky (1965b: 35, 1965a: 12; cf. Jameson 1972: 75–91). In this sense, Euripides' *Verfremdungseffekt* is more Brechtian than Shklovskian: see Jameson 1972: 58–59. Euripides' "alienation-effect" and the comparison to Brecht and/or Russian Formalism has become something of a trope: Willetts 1973: 206; Walsh 1977: 289; Goldhill 1986a: 252; Michelini 1987: 54 n.9; Segal 1993: 85; Hose 2008: 241. On Euripides' self-referentiality, see Segal 1982: 215–71; Goldhill 1986a: 244–64; Bierl 1991: 137–218; Dobrov 2001: esp. 70–85; Torrance 2013.

23. Loraux 2002b: 18.

24. No one, to my mind, has adequately explained why it was felt that this play belonged in the fourth slot. For various attempts and discussion, see Dale 1954: xviii–xxii; Sutton 1980: 180–90; Marshall 2000; Parker 2007: xix–xxiii. Burnett 1971: 22–46 reads the play as a compound of tragedy and satyr play; Segal 1993: 37–50, 85–86 and Seidensticker 1982: 129–52 as "tragicomedy." Riemer 1989: 1–5 surveys the scholarly consternation surrounding the play's generic designation.

25. The phrase comes from Heath 1987, the principal modern proponent of this approach. See also Stanford 1983.

26. Griffith 2002: 203: "The world of the satyr-play . . . is much more self-consciously 'fantastic' than that of tragedy. . . . Escapist fantasies and the gratification of desires play a much larger role in the motivations of the characters and twists of the plot than they do in the more political and serious medium of tragedy." Cf. Sutton 1980: 171–73. On *Alcestis* as "fairy tale," see Lesky 1925; Parker 2007: xi–xv; and Von Fritz 1956: 64–65, who sees it as a realist rebuke to the fairy tale's idealism; in a similar vein, Smith 1960; Kullmann 1967; Seidensticker 1982: 129–52 (contra, Rivier 1972).

27. Political readings of the play have mainly focused on its gender politics (Rabinowitz 1993: 67–99; O'Higgins 1993; Segal 1993: 73–86; Wohl 1998: 121–75). Closer to my interests here is the argument of Gregory 1991: 19–49. She too stresses the universal law of death and the tension between that law and the play's plot, but she reaches conclusions opposite to my own. Working primarily on the level of thematics (Gregory 1991: 11), she sees this egalitarian principle strongly affirmed at the end; I hope to show that it is significantly complicated by the play's formal structure.

28. Or perhaps better, both satyric and sympotic: given the satyrs' constant inebriation, there is a good deal of overlap between the two. I argue for a sympotic Heracles at Wohl 1998: 148–51. Admetus also had a strong connection to sympotic literature beyond the play. There was a fifth-century sympotic song known as "Admetus's song" (*Carmina convivalia* 897 PMG) that celebrated precisely the values of friendship and reciprocity that are so profitable to the hero of this play: Scodel 1979. Garner 1988: 67–70 finds in *Alcestis* echoes of epinician, another Archaic aristocratic genre.

29. On *xenia* in general: Herman 1987; in *Alcestis*: Schein 1988; Stanton 1990; Goldfarb 1992; Wohl 1998: 164–70; Pedilla 2000.

30. Following the manuscripts' punctuation of the passage. Cf. 857, 860: *gennaios*. Heracles' reciprocal favor to his *xenos* is likewise proof of his own *eugeneia*: 1120, 1136. Smith 1960: 134–36 discusses the theme of "good breeding" and the ironic light it sheds on Admetus.

31. "Euripides' *Alcestis* presents its audience with a curious problem. Why is a blatant coward rewarded?" (Nielsen 1976: 92). Most critics have shared this negative opinion of Admetus (e.g., Von Fritz 1956); his primary defender is Burnett 1965, 1971: 22–46; cf. Buxton 2003: 181–84. Admetus's "late learning" that a life thus gained is not worth living (935–60) gives a fingerhold to spectators who want to see him as meriting reward for his moral growth: Golden 1970–71; but contra, Segal 1993: 51–72, who sees his development curtailed by

the return of Alcestis. Seidensticker 1982: 140–52 stresses the ambiguity of the character produced by the generic doubleness of this tragicomedy.

32. Gregory 1991: 43 argues that the necessity of death is reinforced at the end, since Alcestis's return implies Admetus's death. That conclusion may be logical, but it is not mentioned amid the final scene's celebration.

33. A sardonic or ironic ending: Von Fritz 1956: 63–67; Smith 1960: 141–45; Seidensticker 1982: 149–52; Riemer 1989: 93–103; Segal 1993: 81–82, 85–86. See also Lloyd 1985 on the tension between "happy and unhappy elements" in the play.

34. Griffith 2002: 235. See further Griffith's nuanced discussion of tragedy's negotiation of class relations and ideologies (Griffith 1995: 107–24).

35. *Alcestis*'s closing gesture recalls Attic comedy, which often concludes by inviting the audience to join the characters in revelry. I discuss the formulaic closing tag in the conclusion. This is one of only three Euripidean tragedies not to end with an *aition* connecting the action on stage to the audience's present (Dunn 1996: 48), thus reinforcing the distant "fairy-tale" quality of the action.

36. Adorno 1991a: 46.

Chapter 1. Dramatic Means and Ideological Ends

1. Brooks 1984: 23; cf. 93–94. On endings and literary form, see Brooks 1984: esp. 90–112; cf. Kermode 1967, Smith 1968.

2. Brooks 1984: 52: "If the motor of narrative is desire, totalizing, building ever-larger units of meaning, the ultimate determinants of meaning lie *at the end*, and narrative desire is ultimately, inexorably, desire *for* the end."

3. See Halliwell 1998: 82–108 and Wohl 2014 on the probable in Aristotle and Euripides.

4. Oedipus is not ultimately banished, as the oracle of Apollo seems to demand, and his fate is left open. Burian 2009 contrasts the play's formal closure with its conceptual non-closure. On the *OT*'s problematic ending, see further Pucci 1992: 169–73; and on the force of telos in the play, Pucci 1992: 16–29.

5. On Euripides' proleptic prologues, see Schmidt 1971: 34–44; Erbse 1984: 73–82; Goward 2004: 125–26; Mastronarde 2010: 107–10, 175, 180–81.

6. Mastronarde 2010: 63–87 (the quotation is on p. 72). He adopts the terminology from Manfred Pfister (Pfister 1988: 240–45).

7. So Dunn 2007: 100–102, who connects the license of Euripides' plots to *parrhēsia*, democratic freedom of speech. See also Arrowsmith 1963. Mastronarde himself resists a political interpretation of Euripides' structural openness, linking it instead to religious experience (Mastronarde 2010: 87), and his detailed study relegates politics to a praeteritio in the conclusion (Mastronarde 2010: 307–8).

8. Wright 2005: 373–80. The word appears, by his count, fifty-two times in *Ion*; the plays with the next most occurrences of the word are *Helen* and *Phoenissae*, with forty-seven instances each. But Euripides uses the term more in each of his plays than does either Sophocles or Aeschylus. See, further, Giannopoulou 1999–2000, as well as Romilly 1986: 31–35 on the working of *tukhē* in Euripidean plots.

9. Owen 1939: xxii; Wassermann 1940; Grégoire 1950a: 164–72; Goossens 1962: 478–506; Swift 2008: 80–100. A sophisticated version of this approach is offered by those who see the play as supporting Athenian ideology indirectly by resolving its inherent contradictions or unifying its disparate strands (Dougherty 1996; Lape 2010: 95–136). For a recent defense of tragedy as socially affirmative, see Allan and Kelley 2013. Saïd 1998: 282–84 critiques both affirmative and subversive readings.

10. See esp. Saxonhouse 1986; Hoffer 1996.

11. Thus, as Žižek frequently notes, the psychic master trope of ideology is disavowal: "I know very well but still . . ." (Žižek 1989: 11–53). A toxic form of ideological disavowal is studied by Berlant 2011.

12. Conacher 1967 labels it "Romantic Tragedy" (along with *Helen* and *Iphigeneia among the Taurians*); cf. Grégoire 1950a: 172–73; Wolff 1965: 169; Whitman 1974: 69; Rivier 1975: 109–14; Meltzer 2006: 181. Pedrick 2007 terms it a "romance of belonging," an allusion to Freud's "family romance"; cf. Lape 2010: 95. The label of "romance"—or, even more so, "comedy" (Knox 1979: 257–70; Gellie 1984) or "tragicomedy" (Kitto 1973: 311–29; Troiano 1985: 49–51)—is sometimes used to deny the play "tragic" substance (e.g., Rivier 1975: 129–48). Obviously, I do not believe an experimental form is incompatible with serious thought (cf. Seidensticker 1982: 211–14); nor would I subscribe to Conacher 1959's antithesis between the "propagandic superstructure" of *Ion* (i.e., its "national-dynastic" themes, 22) and its "theatrical meaning" ("structural virtuosity," 20). On the contrary, I am proposing that the play's political force arises precisely from its structural virtuosity.

13. On the ideology of autochthony, see especially Loraux 1993; in *Ion*: Mastronarde 1975; Walsh 1978; Saxonhouse 1986; Loraux 1993: 184–236; Lape 2010: 95–136. Autochthony functions here, as elsewhere in Athenian literature, as an ideologeme, a fragment of ideology that is susceptible both to full conceptualization and to narrativization (Jameson 1981: 87–88).

14. For *Ion*'s Ionian ideology, see Dougherty 1996: 252–54; Zacharia 2003: 48–55. Zeitlin's characteristically rich and insightful reading of the play (Zeitlin 1996a) examines its multiple revelations of identity as part of the tragic project of constructing a self in its mythic, social, and psychological dimensions. I am very much sympathetic to her focus on the "mysteries" of tragic subjectivity (cf. Wohl 1998), although my concerns here are different.

15. Mastronarde 2010: 184 calls it "a veritable orgy of imperialistic genealogy"; cf. Dunn 2000: 23–27. Xuthus and Creusa's children will be Dorus and Achaeus, founders of Doris and Achaia in the Peloponnese (1590–94), an aetiological wish-fulfillment fantasy that makes Sparta a lesser limb of the Athenian family tree.

16. Wassermann 1940; Spira 1960: 33–82; Wolff 1965: 177–78; Erbse 1984: 73–82; Neitzel 1988; Arnott 1996: 111; Giannopoulou 1999–2000.

17. Loraux 1993: 198: "To assign the prologue of a tragedy to Hermes is to place the play explicitly under the sign of ambiguity." For "deceptive plot prolepsis," see Segal 1992: 87–92; Goward 2004: 39–52, 149–65; cf. Arnott 1973 on other Euripidean "red herrings."

18. I am here summarizing the argument of Saxonhouse 1986. See also Walsh 1978; Rabinowitz 1993: 189–222; Hoffer 1996.

19. The sensitive reading of Pedrick 2007 stresses this desire for belonging and shows how it shapes both characters, as well as the play's thematics and structure.

20. χρόνον γὰρ ὅν μ' ἐχρῆν ἐν ἀγκάλαις /μητρὸς τρυφῆσαι καί τι τερφθῆναι βίου / ἀπεστερήθην φιλτάτης μητρὸς τροφῆς (1375–77): the multiple alliterations (khron, khrēn, tros, truph, terph, tros, troph) give this trimeter passage the quality of a lullaby.

21. Solmsen 1934: 391–406. See, further, Strohm 1957: 64–92. In Helen and Iphigeneia among the Taurians the anagnōrisis is likewise delayed (although not as long as in Ion), and movement toward it constitutes the play's dramatic suspense. But in those plays, the recognition, when it finally comes, does not bring resolution, but creates new quandaries that set the plot in motion again. In Ion, the anagnōrisis is a lusis; in Helen and IT, it is a desis masquerading as a lusis.

22. On Euripides' use of stichomythia, see Seidensticker 1971: 209–19; Rutherford 2012: 173–79; and the exhaustive study of Schwinge 1968. This play contains the longest stichomythia in extant tragedy, at 255–368, as well as the second longest at 934–1028.

23. Seidensticker 1971: 213; Lee 1997: 186 ad 237–400.

24. Knox 1979: 260.

25. On the play's chthonic imagery, see Mastronarde 1975; Rosivach 1977; Goff 1988. On its many repetitions, thematic and structural, see Wolff 1965: 170–73; Loraux 1993: 193–95; Zeitlin 1996a: 293–313; Lee 1997: 25–26; Pedrick 2007: 79–101; Zacharia 2003: 66–70, 76–102; and on the narrative force of repetition more broadly, Brooks 1984: 90–142. In addition to the double anagnōriseis and double murder attempts, there are also double monodies, double stichomythiai, double ekphraseis. These repetitions both defer and build toward the final anagnōrisis, which will transform repetition-as-delay into repetition-as-closure.

26. Kermode 1967: 45–46 and Smith 1968: 1–37 view endings as an apperception of the structure of the work; Brooks 1984: 23, 92–96, 108 proposes that the anticipation of that moment is the condition of the possibility of meaning in narrative.

27. Self-recognition being the grounding gesture of ideology: Althusser 1971: 172–73.

28. Note that Ion's speech against democratic politics is not answered. If, as Barker 2011 and Burian 2011 propose, the tragic agōn enacts the Athenian ideal of parrhēsia, then this agōn manqué eliminates democratic politics (ironically, given that parrhēsia is the one benefit of Athenian political life that Ion is eager to claim, 672). Many see Ion's diatribe as an expression of the alienated quietism that was one reaction of late fifth-century elites to the democracy: see Carter 1986 (and 155–62 on this scene).

29. Creusa's sympathetic characterization is tied to her elite status. Her "innate nobility" is immediately visible in her appearance and is what first draws Ion to her (237–46). Likewise, her noble lineage magnifies the trauma of her

apparent barrenness (306–7, 619–20; cf. 468–71). Throughout the play, *eutukhia* and *eudaimonia* are strongly associated both with *euteknia* and *eupaidia* ("good offspring," 307, 567, 658, 775) and with *eugeneia* (264). The first stasimon yokes all these terms, hymning the good fortune of good children in a good house (468–91), a collocation that anticipates the play's resolution. On *eugeneia* in *Ion*, see esp. Walsh 1978.

30. Compare the argument of Dougherty 1996 that the play synthesizes the competing ideologies of autochthony and empire to produce "the synoptic illusion of an Athens in which the contradictions of contemporary politics can be reconciled" (Dougherty 1996: 264; cf. Walsh 1978). Reading the play allegorically, she sees this ideological synthesis operating through the play's mythic content (the union of autochthonous Creusa with Ionian Apollo) rather than its dramatic structure. The latter, I am proposing, does not synthesize so much as subsume particular ideological positions.

31. On the sightseeing motif in Euripides, see Zeitlin 1994: 147–48, 1995; Zacharia 2003: 14 n.46. The parodos of *Iphigeneia at Aulis* provides the closest parallel. For these two touristic choruses, see further Hose 1990–91, vol. 1: 136–39, 153–55.

32. The irony of the opening is well analyzed by Seidensticker 1982: 222–25. The prologue's yoking of Ion's familiar Ionian genealogy to his Apolline paternity is significant if the latter is Euripides' innovation (Owen 1939: ix–xvii; Grégoire 1950a: 159–61; Cole 1997). Other versions of the myth make him Xuthus's son (e.g., Herodotus 7.94, 8.44; Euripides fr. 481.8–10 Kannicht). Euripides may have been developing a current legend (Conacher 1959: 24–25; Swift 2008: 17), elaborating on the name *Patrōos*, Apollo's cult title in his role as joint ancestor of the Athenians and Ionians (Dougherty 1996: 261; Zacharia 2003: 44 n.1). Nonetheless, Ion's divine paternity, for all that he accepts it, eludes definitive proof: Loraux 1993: 209–13; Zeitlin 1996a: esp. 285–95, 320–26; Meltzer 2006: 177–87; Lape 2010: 127–36.

33. On these reiterations and the discrepancies between them, see especially Pedrick 2007: 79–101. See also Dunn 1990: 30–33; Rabinowitz 1993: 195–201; and Fletcher 2009 on Creusa as "weaver" of her own story.

34. Wassermann 1940: 591; Wolff 1965: 180–81. Cf. Burnett 1962: 95–96 on the ode's imagery: "The poetry celebrates what the speaker reviles" (95; cf. Barlow 1971: 49–50; Thornburn 2000: 40–42). Larue 1963 catalogues the hymnic elements in the ode, and Swift 2010: 90–101 discusses the use of paianic language here and throughout the play. On the communicative function of female lyric in Euripides more generally, see Chong-Gossard 2008.

35. The first episode frames the play as a trial of Apollo's injustice (*adikia*, 253–55, 357–58, 384–89, 436–51), and scholars have rushed to the prosecution (Conacher 1959; Troiano 1985; Hartigan 1991: 69–88) or the defense (Wassermann 1940; Burnett 1962, 1971: 126–29; Müller 1975; Lloyd 1986b; Farrington 1991). See the balanced assessment of Lee 1997: 32–33 and discussion by Meltzer 2006: 146–87.

36. Williams 1977: 128–35; see also Žižek 1989: 83–84. I return to Williams's "structures of feeling" in chapter 5.

Chapter 2. Beautiful Tears

1. "Songs of sorrow" is Segal's phrase (Segal 1993: 227–36). He emphasizes the recuperative force of tragedy's aestheticized lament (Segal 1993: 1–33; cf. Pucci 1977, 1980: 21–58). For a more critical view, see Eagleton 2003: 23–40.

2. Scarry 1999: 97. This articulation of aesthetics to ethics and politics has a long modern history, of course. See, e.g., Eagleton 1990.

3. Aristotle *Rhetoric* 1385b13; Konstan 2001: esp. 27–48, 2006: 201–18. On pity in Aristotle, see especially Halliwell 1998: 168–84, 2002: 207–33.

4. See, e.g., Isocrates 4.168; Andocides 4.23; Lada 1996: 92–98; Sternberg 2006: 2–3; Dué 2006: 163–64. The politics of pity and compassion are much debated; by way of example, see Nussbaum 2001: 297–454; Berlant 2004.

5. I use *pathos* here in a lay sense to denote suffering that evokes pity, rather than in the narrower sense of Aristotle, for whom pathos is "a corrupting or painful action, like visible deaths and physical pain and woundings and the like" (*Poetics* 1452b11–13). I follow his insight, however, that pathos is a resource for structuring action so as to heighten pity and fear (see Halliwell 1987: 119–20; Belfiore 1992: 134–41). Romilly 1980 examines the central role of pathos and pity in Euripides, and Romilly 1986: 73–115 surveys the playwright's diverse techniques for augmenting them.

6. This aesthetic may be more modern than ancient if Heath 1989: 38–55 is right that Aristotle's understanding of unity was more "centrifugal" than usually assumed. Cf. Heath 1987: 98–111. On Aristotelian unity, see also Halliwell 1998: 96–108.

7. This point is well made by Williams 1966: 46–54. There is no tragic equivalent, for example, to the wretchedness of the Megarian farmer in Aristophanes' *Acharnians*, already poor and forced by war to sell his daughters. Entrenched poverty, on the few occasions it is depicted on the tragic stage, is not the object of pity, as we shall see in chapter 3. By reserving pity primarily for royalty enslaved through war, tragedy also reinforces the distinction between natural and conventional slavery (Hall 1997: 111). Kuch 1978b treats slavery in relation to class in the Trojan plays.

8. See Barlow 1986: 184 ad 511; Segal 1993: 29–33; Croally 1994: 235–48; Visvardi 2011: 283–86; and see Torrance 2013: 218–45 on the play's larger "metapoetic agenda."

9. The ship is a metaphor for metaphor ("carrying across"): the vehicle is a vehicle. Hecuba comments self-consciously on this self-conscious image: "I myself have never yet been aboard a ship, but I have seen them in paintings and know from hearing about them" (686–87). She calls attention to her own metaphorical language, even as she uses it to describe her inability to describe: like sailors slackening the sail, "I slacken my mouth (*pareis' ekhō stoma*) . . . and am voiceless, submerged by a wave from the gods" (688–96). On the play's exceptionally dense metaphoric language, see Barlow 1971: 28–32, 51–52, 114–19.

10. Cf. 1310–11, 1325–26, and the similar effect in the stichomythia at 721–25. Barlow 1986: 188 ad 577–607 observes that "Words are made to seem in danger of breaking down altogether, so great is their grief." See also Chong-

Gossard 2008: 98–100 on the pathetic force of the epirrhematic amoibaion (235–92).

11. Barlow 1986: 198–201 provides an excellent analysis of the ode's style; see also Burnett 1977. Whether Zeus is watching the suffering of humans is also questioned at *Hecuba* 488–91.

12. And contributes to it, persuasion being closely linked to both desire and magic in Greek thought. The locus classicus is Gorgias's *Encomium of Helen*, on which this *agōn* can be read as an extended commentary. The framing of the scene between the impassive Ganymede of the second stasimon and the impassive Zeus of the third implicates the *agōn*'s much-noted rhetorical artistry in the play's critique of impassive spectatorship. With its verbal virtuosity and inconclusive verdict, does the *agōn* satisfy our aesthetic desire at the cost of justice? If so, we are no different than Menelaus.

13. Havelock 1968: 126–27; Scodel 1980: 98–100; Meridor 1984: 211–12, 2000: 26–27; Dubischar 2001: 342–57; contra, Lloyd 1984: 304, 1992: 110–12. Audiences would also know from *Odyssey* 4 that Helen, Menelaus, and their marriage all survive the war.

14. I return to the relation of *Trojan Women* to Melos in chapter 5. The play is, unsurprisingly, often read as a critique of Athenian imperialism: see esp. Rosenbloom 2006. Contra, Roisman 1997.

15. Munteanu 2012: 138–237 looks at the emotional responses of internal spectators as models for the audience. Goldhill 2012: 37–55 pursues the political implications of this modeling. On the role of Talthybius, see further Gilmartin 1970; Dyson and Lee 2000; Goff 2009: 47–49.

16. Segal 1996: 165 (= Segal 1993: 26); cf. Johnson and Clapp 2005; Dué 2006: 163–67; and, more broadly, Boltanski 1999: 50–55; Woodruff 2008: 145–64. Visvardi 2011: 272–73 stresses the political (specifically, Panhellenic) nature of this universal pity in both *Trojan Women* and *Hecuba*. The politics of tragedy's humanism is discussed further in chapter 4, below.

17. This is Rousseau's objection to theatrical pity: Rousseau 1960: 25, discussed by Halliwell 2002: 214. Likewise, Brecht: see Lada 1996. Plutarch reports that the tyrant Alexander of Pherae left the theater in the middle of a performance of *Trojan Women* so as not to be seen "weeping at the suffering of Hecuba and Andromache." But apparently this dramatic experience did not curb his legendary cruelty (Plutarch *Pelopidas* 29.5).

18. Lee 1976: 66 ad 1–152: "The language and content of this opening are not arresting and the use of a formal prologue is a convention which leaves much to be desired." Cf. Mastronarde 2010: 77.

19. Dunn 1996: 101–14. Cf. Meridor 1984; Mastronarde 2010: 78, 179–80.

20. In light of this ethical imperative, Lee's reminders of the prologue's prophecy throughout his commentary seem motivated by a worry that we will forget (Lee 1976: xv–xviii and passim; e.g., 161 ad 511–67, 182 ad 612–13, 253 ad 1102–4). He posits that the play deals with two tragedies, the Trojans' and the Greeks', and imagines that we leave the theater with Athena's threat of shipwreck "ringing in our ears" (xviii). Cf. O'Neill 1941: 316–20; Burnett 1977; Erbse 1984: 60–72. Others see the prologue's reassurances drowned out by the mournful din of the action: Poole 1976; Scodel 1980: 67, 132–37; Meridor 1984:

209–11; Gregory 1991: 175–76. See the helpful discussion of Goff 2009: 36–42. The reaction of the original audience would no doubt have been influenced by the previous two plays of the trilogy, on which, see Scodel 1980.

21. Michelini 1987: 179. Heath 2003 provides a history of the complaint about the play's double plot. Matthiessen 2010: 13–16 stresses the discrepancies between the two plots, while Steidle 1968: 44–50; Collard 1991: 21–23; Zeitlin 1996b and Mastronarde 2010: 71–73 stress their connections. Unity has often been found in the character of Hecuba, whose moral decline has long preoccupied the scholarship (see, e.g., Kirkwood 1947; Conacher 1967: 146–65; Nussbaum 1986: 397–421). The ambiguity of Hecuba's moral agency is well discussed by Rabinowitz 1993: 103–24; Mossman 1995: 164–203; Foley 2001: 283–86.

22. On the simile: O'Sullivan 2008: 188–95. In a related image, Hecuba wishes she had a voice in her arms and hands and hair and feet "by the art of Daedalus or one of the gods," so that she could supplicate Agamemnon with her entire body (836–40). In a sense, the play fulfills her wish: through its artistry it turns her body into a voice calling for pity and justice. Cf. Thévenet 2009: 320–35 on Hecuba's self-presentation as an allegory of suffering.

23. See esp. Polyxena's speech of self-sacrifice (342–78): Why should I live? I whose father was king of all the Phrygians am now a slave. "To live without honor (mē kalōs) is the greatest ordeal" (378). The chorus respond by praising the "conspicuous stamp of good parentage" and "the title of nobility" (eugeneias onoma, 379–81). The report of Polyxena's nobility at the moment of her death is Hecuba's only consolation for her loss (591–602). Roselli 2007 argues for a complex negotiation of class relations around Euripides' virgin sacrifices, as elites identified with the girls' nobility and non-elites with their subordinate status as young women. Leaving aside the question of whether an Athenian laborer would have recognized himself in an aristocratic maiden, Hecuba poses a more problematic example than Heracleidai (Roselli's focus), since the political value of the girl's act is so unclear.

24. Thalmann 1993: 136–48 analyzes the parallels between the two scenes; cf. Scodel 1996. Steiner 2001: 44–56 argues that statues in tragedy can stand in for theatrical mimesis.

25. 107–8, 117–40, 189, 195–96, 218–21, 254–59. Note especially the gratuitous presence of the sons of Theseus (122–29). Hecuba's equally gratuitous diatribe against the "ungrateful race of demagogues" generalizes Odysseus's betrayal to democratic politics as a whole (254–57): Michelini 1987: 142–44; Gregory 2002. The debate is also a perversion of Homeric heroic ideals, as King 1985 argues (cf. Barker 2009: 330–35; contra, Adkins 1966: 195–200).

26. Michelini 1987: 165: "The appeal to shameful pleasures is very satisfyingly blended with high moral tone: what audience could fail to indulge themselves?" On the eroticism of the scene, see Michelini 1987: 158–70; Rabinowitz 1993: 54–62; Segal 1993: 172–73; Thalmann 1993: 143–44; Scodel 1996: 121–26; contra, Mossman 1995: 142–63. On its aestheticism: Pucci 1977: 180–81; Segal 1996: 174–79, 235–36; Dué 2006: 126–30.

27. Fletcher 2012: 226–28; see also Barker 2009: 342–45. Zeitlin 1996b: 186–91 tracks the theme of vision in the play; cf. Nussbaum 1986: 410–14.

28. Likewise, in the first stasimon's anxious travelogue (444–83), the sacred and beautiful landscape of Greece is suffused with the chorus's poeticized grief. Sung while the sacrifice is being performed offstage, the ode's aesthetic pleasure sublimates the erotic pleasure of the sacrifice, and implicates the Athenians through their love for their own beautiful city (466–74). Meanwhile Hecuba lies on the ground in a faint. On the first stasimon, see Rosivach 1975; Mossman 1995: 78–82 (and cf. the similarly aestheticized geography of Greece in *Trojan Women*'s parodos, 197–234). On the third stasimon, Mossman 1995: 87–92. Needless to say, I disagree with those critics who find the beauty of the odes (here and in *Trojan Women*) an escape from and consolation for the horror of the action.

29. Diggle prints Kayser's σῶν in 805, but ἴσον is the reading of all the manuscripts and preferred by Collard 1991; Gregory 1999; and Matthiessen 2010 ad loc. On the problematic status of *nomos* in *Hecuba*, see Kirkwood 1947; Nussbaum 1986: 397–421; Gregory 1991: 98–102; Segal 1993: 191–213; Fletcher 2012.

30. On the aesthetics of retributive justice, see Burnett 1998: 2–3; Miller 2006; Wohl 2010: 309–16.

31. Meridor 1978; Burnett 1998: 165–72 (cf. Burnett 1994); Kovacs 1987: 107–12; Mitchell-Boyask 1993. Gellie 1980 deems the play "a success story" (41) and un-tragic. Most critics are less sanguine: e.g., Reckford 1985, 1991; Segal 1993: 191–226; Barker 2009: 354–62. This sense of dramatic closure is seemingly reinforced by the play's frequent allusions to the *Oresteia*, with its paradigmatic progression from revenge to justice. But the echoes of Agamemnon's death in the offstage cries of Polymestor as he is blinded (1035–37; cf. *Agamemnon* 1343–46) undermine the justice of the revenge, and the parting predictions seem to refer the case on appeal to Aeschylus. On *Hecuba*'s reworking of the *Oresteia*, see esp. Thalmann 1993.

32. He is further implicated by his sexual relationship with Cassandra. Hecuba reminds him of his "intimate nights" and "loving embraces" with her daughter (824–30). Many readers have expressed revulsion that she should so prostitute her child. Moreover, it doesn't work: the shame of seeming to act for the sake of his concubine prevents him from helping avenge Polydorus (855–56), just as it invalidated his objection to the sacrifice of Polyxena (121–29). For Agamemnon, no less than for his brother Menelaus in *Trojan Women*, eros impedes the execution of justice.

33. *Kharis* has been an extremely compromised term throughout this play. It is associated with the Greeks' gift of Polyxena to Achilles' ghost (137, 320, 384) and Polymestor's murder of Polydorus (1175, 1201, 1211, 1243); with corrupt demagogic rhetoric (254, 257, 276); as well as with Agamemnon's sexual relationship with Cassandra (830, 832). See Zeitlin 1996b: 203–8.

34. Zeitlin 1996b: 191–200.

35. The women's involvement is stressed at 880–82, 1052, 1060–65, 1095–96, 1120, as well as in the report of the act itself (1151–72). The chorus do not participate, but they sing of Dikē as it is taking place (1024–33), and are contemplating going to Hecuba's aid when she appears onstage (1042–43).

36. The play is equivocal as to whether Achilles actually demands her sacri-

fice: see Gregory 1999: xxiv–ix. Hecuba presents Polyxena's death as a perversion of retributive justice: if the Greeks want to kill their killers in return (262), they should kill *her*, since she bore Paris (383–88); or better yet, Helen, who wronged the Greeks (*adikousa*) by leading them to Troy (265–70). The third stasimon ends with the chorus blaming Helen for their misery (943–52). This leads directly into the entrance of Polymestor, suggesting that he, like Helen, will be another object of the victims' misdirected anger. The inadequacy of Helen as a scapegoat is also a theme in *Trojan Women*: Poole 1976: 273–74; Gregory 1991: 174–75; Goff 2009: 69.

37. Polyxena's name evokes the *xenia* central to the second half of the play; Polydorus's, the gift (*dōron*) of his sister to Achilles. Meanwhile, Polymestor (*mēstor*: planner, counselor) suggests the many plans of Hecuba. Mossman 1995: 60 points out that Hecuba could have remained onstage during the second stasimon, as she does (in a faint) during the first: "It begins to seem as if the poet wished to emphasize the very feature which has caused critics so much distress, namely the bipartite structure of the play." Unifying the two parts would have been all the easier if, as seems to be the case, the Polymestor plotline was a Euripidean invention: see Gregory 1999: xvii–xxiii. The omission of Hecuba's revenge from the ghost's proleptic prologue is one among many signs of the deliberate non-integration of the two stories.

38. See n. 22 of the introduction.

39. Derrida 1992a: 27.

Chapter 3. Recognition and Realism

1. Hall 1997: 125–26 (original emphasis). Contrast Griffith 1995: esp. 72–81, for whom tragedy's diverse focalization reinforces existing social hierarchies, onstage and off. Rose 1992: 33–42 provides an excellent theoretical discussion of "the utopian impulse" in Marxist literary criticism; cf. 260–65 on that impulse in the *Oresteia*.

2. Roselli 2005 examines the class and literary politics of the comic Euripides. For a lucid explication of class ideology in fifth-century Athens and its implications for tragedy, see Roselli 2007: 90–106.

3. See especially Gellie 1981. "Unglamorous" is Arnott 1981's term; Conacher 1967: 207 speaks of a "realistic and faintly sleazy social climate." Goff 1999–2000 offers a perceptive survey of the scholarship.

4. E.g., Adkins 1960: 195–96; Arnott 1981: 181.

5. Griffith 1995 offers a nuanced argument for this position. See also Griffith 1998, 2011.

6. The hypothesis calls him "a Mycenean *autourgos*," that is, a free man who works his own land. That he works his land himself and apparently has no slaves puts him at the bottom of the social ladder. See Basta Donzelli 1978: 227–69 and Roy 1996: 104–10 on the fifth-century realities of the setting.

7. Cropp 1988: 113 ad 191.

8. *Polupēna pharea dunai khrusea te kharisin prosthēmat' aglaias.* Both *polupēna* and *prosthēmata* are *hapakes* that take humble words (the woof of a weaving, *pēnē*, or the prosaic *prosthēkē*, appendage) and turn them into unique coinages.

Such unique vocabulary, as well as the gleam of gold; the vocabulary of charm, pleasure, and delight; and the interwoven word order are all markers of tragedy's highest aesthetic. Add to this the echoes (in language, theme, and meter) of the Archaic partheneion, which ennobles this rustic chorus both by literary allusion and by attaching it to a venerable (and elite) choral tradition. According to Plutarch (*Lysander* 15.3), this song, performed at a symposium in 404 BCE, persuaded the Spartan generals not to raze Athens. Wrapping agrarian simplicity in tragedy's sophisticated aesthetics, the ode seems perfectly calibrated to elicit Spartan sentimentality about Athens and its literary culture.

9. Mastronarde 2010: 221 sees this uniform language as a "distinctive antirealism." Contrast Hall 1997: 123: "Tragic language is a democratic property owned collectively by all who use it."

10. The comic aspect of the play's realism is discussed most fully by Michelini 1987: 181–206; see also Knox 1979: 251–54. On comedy in Euripides more generally, see Knox 1979: 250–74; Gregory 1999–2000; Allan 2001: 183–85; and especially Seidensticker 1982: 18–20, 89–248, who assumes throughout that the introduction of elements of everyday life into the mythic world of tragedy produces a comic effect (he does not discuss *Electra*).

11. Hammond 1984: 380–81; Cropp 1988: 103 ad 55; Luschnig 1995: 86–120; Raeburn 2000: 151–54.

12. Diggle brackets 373–79, but the passage is convincingly defended by Denniston 1939 ad loc.; Cropp 1988 ad loc.; and Goldhill 1986b.

13. *Doxasma* is an uncommon word, used elsewhere in classical Greek only by Thucydides, Heraclitus, and (most often) Plato. Interestingly, the only other occurrence in Euripides (fr. 495.42 Kannicht) also contrasts *kena doxasmata* with true *eugeneia*.

14. Goldhill 1986b notes that Orestes himself exemplifies this disconnect between high birth and moral worth; cf. Hartigan 1991: 110. Others question the sincerity of the sentiments: O'Brien 1964: 33–34; Vellacott 1975: 49–51; Tarkow 1981: 149–50; Schottlaender 1982: 492. Likewise, as Denniston 1939: 93 ad 367–72 remarks, "The general identification of nobility of birth and nobility of character . . . is not here denied by Orestes. You cannot conceive of a 'confusion' (ταραγμός) unless you conceive of an order which the confusion disturbs."

15. The play's date is uncertain, but it is assumed to have been produced in the late 410s. Goff 1999–2000: 104 suggests that the mere presence of the lower-class Farmer on the tragic stage indicates the pressure social inequality exerted on the Athenian imagination. On *Electra*'s vocabulary of class, see Denniston 1939: 80–82 ad 253.

16. Bloch 1977. Bloch is countering an argument of Georg Lukács that lies behind Hall's "what Marxists call art's 'utopian tendency'" (Hall 1997: 125). I return to Lukács's position at the end of this chapter.

17. Goldhill 1986a: 252. We might also note that setting the action outside the polis, with a chorus that professes ignorance of civic affairs (297–99), limits from the start the political significance of this realist scenario. On this displacement from and of the political, see Ormand 2009.

18. Aeschylus's *anagnōrisis* was popular throughout the fifth century (Aristophanes *Clouds* 534–36; Prag 1985: 51–57) and into the fourth century (Taplin

2007: 49–56). The Euripidean scene is no longer athetized on the basis of this allusion (Bond 1974; Davies 1998), but its purpose and tone—parody? homage? critique?—are much debated. See the discussion in Halporn 1983: 114–18. On this recognition scene, see further Pucci 1967; Schwinge 1968: 252–61, 295–317; Basta Donzelli 1978: 102–35; Solmsen 1982: 38–47; Goldhill 1986a: 247–51, 2008: 56–59; Kucharski 2004; Thévenet 2009: 142–56; Zeitlin 2012: 369–74; and on the Euripidean *anagnōrisis* more broadly, Solmsen 1934; Goward 2004: 131–47.

19. Goldhill 1986a: 249: "a literary, theatrical theme, a game complete with rules and conventions." Cf. Torrance 2011: 181–82. The play's allusions to the *Oresteia* are enumerated by Hammond 1984.

20. See Kurke 1999: 53–57 (on *kibdēlos*) and 320–24 (on *kharaktēr*). It is noteworthy that Orestes is compared to a silver coin. Silver was a democratic metal (Kurke 1999: 318–19), as opposed to "barbarian" gold. In *Electra*, gold is associated particularly with the "tyrannical fantasy" of the golden lamb (705, 719, 726). Identifying Orestes as a genuine silver coin paves the way for his later coronation as a populist king.

21. Judgment of both main characters has generally been harsh. Critics have found Electra whiny and snobbish; Orestes, weak and unheroic. Steidle 1968: 63–91 and Lloyd 1986a defend them.

22. On the scar and its Odyssean precedent, see Tarkow 1981 and Goff 1991, for both of whom the allusion highlights Orestes' failure to live up to this heroic model. Other Odyssean parallels are listed by Zeitlin 2012: 373–74. Aristotle deems recognition via tokens to be the "least artistic" type of *anagnōrisis*, and particularly those where the tokens are introduced deliberately to prove the character's identity, rather than naturally in the course of the plot. His example of this distinction is the double recognition of Odysseus's scar, naturally by Eurycleia and as proof by Eumaios, in the *Odyssey* (*Poetics* 1454b20–30). Although he does not discuss this recognition scene, it would seem a conspicuous example of what he calls "fabricated" tokens (*Poetics* 1455a20), and all the more so in that it wasn't Euripides himself who fabricated them.

23. This is the "legitimation of the arbitrary" that Pierre Bourdieu identifies as one of the primary mechanisms of the reproduction of elite domination: Bourdieu 1990: 112–34.

24. This ode's narrative of cosmic justice is anticipated at the very moment of Orestes' recognition: the chorus hail him as "shining, long-awaited day" and predict a victory brought by the gods (585–95). On the relevance of the ode to the action, see Kubo 1967: 19–20; Mulryne 1977: 31–34; Rosivach 1978.

25. See Cropp 1988: 154 ad 774–858 for the specifics of this "ugly event"; cf. Arnott 1981: 186–88. For Burnett 1998: 233–35, by contrast, the killing is a legitimate heroic revenge; cf. Lloyd 1986a: 15–16. Zeitlin 1970 discusses the theme of corrupted sacrifice in the play.

26. Arnott 1981: 186–88 and Swift 2010: 156–70 examine the epinician language in this scene and its tension with the action. On tragedy's use of epinician more generally, see Swift 2010: 104–71.

27. The messenger's speech is itself marked as a formal element of the genre by Electra's metatheatrical question "Where are the messengers?" (759), right at

the moment in the plot when we would expect a messenger. "They will come," the chorus respond (760), and immediately the messenger appears. See Winnington-Ingram 1969: 131–32; Arnott 1973: 50–53.

28. Likewise, the realist scenario becomes a backdrop for the mythic action (1139–40). The countryside itself is suborned to the heroic plot: in the first stasimon, "rustic" Pan is an adjunct to the Gorgon-slaying Perseus (458–62); in the second stasimon, he conveys the golden lamb (703–6).

29. And even their belief is empty: as the Paidagogos notes, slaves tend to be well-disposed to whoever is in power (632). Likewise, Castor won't reproach Apollo because "he is my lord" (1245). Compare Lacan's suggestion that the job of the tragic chorus is to feel in place of the audience: Lacan 1992: 252, quoted by Žižek 1989: 34–35.

30. The justice and justification of the act are debated at length in the *agōn*. The ethical questions raised there no doubt shaped the way the audience interpreted the *praxis*, but they have curiously little impact on the *prattontes*. Electra is shown to be motivated less by ethical considerations than by an intense and personal hatred. She exhibits no moral qualms before the murder. Orestes does, but his hesitation, as Lloyd notes, is separated from the discussion of Clytemnestra's character (material that was combined in Aeschylus): the effect "is to detach the agon from any practical consequences, since Orestes has already decided to kill Clytaemestra before she arrives" (Lloyd 1992: 59). This is in keeping with Romilly's thesis that Euripides shifts focus away from the *praxis* itself to the pathos it entails (Romilly 1980: 9–50).

31. The oracle has barely been mentioned up to this point (87, 399–400). See Hartigan 1991: 107–27 on the ambiguities of Apollo's command.

32. O'Brien 1964 examines the symbol of the Gorgon's head. The imagery and mood of the first stasimon are well analyzed by King 1980; Morwood 1981; Csapo 2009. On the ode's (ironic) heroic models for Orestes, see Mulryne 1977: 36–38, 40–43; Walsh 1977: 282–89; Torrance 2013: 75–82.

33. The ordering and distribution of the lines at 1292–1305 is disputed, and it is not clear who asks to approach the god at 1292–93. Diggle gives the lines to the chorus, but Castor's surprising absolution of Orestes comes across more forcefully if Orestes speaks them: see Basta Donzelli 1978: 210–12. In Attic law, a murderer was not allowed to come into contact with the relatives of his victim.

34. As Roberts 1987: 60 comments, this is "surely the emptiest, if truest, of all gnomic endings."

35. Dunn 1996: 16 notes that the sixty-five lines of anapests following the god's speech are a "departure from the usual pattern" of tragic closure and mark the failure of this ending. Most critics feel a lack of resolution in this exodos: e. g., Michelini 1987: 226; Dunn 1996: 139. Thury 1985 is the rare exception; cf. Spira 1960: 100–112.

36. Cropp 1988: 187–88 ad 1286: "a final loose end neatly tied up—though he is not being asked whether he wants this transportation and ought not to be impressed with the grant of wealth (cf. 426–31)." See also Goff 1999–2000: 105.

37. Lukács 1977: 47–48.

38. Lukács 1977: 48. Hall 1997, presumably building on Lukács, stresses the

futurity of tragedy's utopianism. This futurity may also explain why *Electra's* realist scenario "recalls" New Comedy, a genre that did not yet exist. The ideas it contains had not yet found their formal expression, either in Athenian drama or in Athenian democracy. I return to the relation between tragic form and emergent social forms in the conclusion.

39. Adorno 1991b.

Chapter 4. The Politics of Political Allegory

1. By contrast, *Heracleidai*, Euripides' other "political play," is also set in Attica and is strongly Athenocentric in plot and themes, but it avoids overt anachronism. Its Athens is ruled by two kings (34–37, 114–15) who make decisions on its behalf without consultation with the people. We hear of "tight knots" (*puknas sustaseis*, 415) forming to judge those decisions, and of the threat of "internal war" (*oikeios polemos*, 419) and "conflict with the citizens" (*politais mē diablēthēsomai*, 422). These terms evoke political relations but not democracy per se, much less Athens's particular brand of democracy. Cf. the "law" against the assassination of Eurystheus, described in democratic language (*dokei*) but attributed variously to the polis (1019) and to the "leaders of this country" (*tois tēsde khōras prostataisin*, 964). The classic study of tragic anachronism is Easterling 1985; cf. 1997a.

2. Travis 1999 argues for the allegorical nature of Greek drama. For a definition of the trope, see Fletcher 1964: 7–8: he distinguishes allegory from mimesis (e.g., 107, 150–51, 248–49), but I take the former as a particular elaboration of the latter. For tragedy as *allotrion pathos*, cf. Gorgias fr. 11.9 DK; Plato *Republic* 604e5–6, 606b1. On the temporal and spatial distance at the heart of tragedy, see (respectively) Vernant 1988a and Zeitlin 1990b; and on Phrynichus's *Sack of Miletus*, Rosenbloom 1993.

3. In Sourvinou-Inwood's much-cited model of "distancing and zooming," for instance, the notional camera moves along an assumed allegorical continuum (Sourvinou-Inwood 2003: 15–66, applied to *Suppliants* by Grethlein 2003: e.g., 109–99). The same allegorical assumption underlies Hose 1995, for example, and the essays in Pelling 1997a; see esp. Pelling 1997b: 228–34, where *Suppliants* illustrates the historiographical issues. A previous generation of scholars read *Suppliants* (and all tragedy) as a more precise allegory for specific contemporary events: see, e.g., Delebecque 1951: 9–56; Goossens 1962: 417–66; and the critique of Zuntz 1955: 58–63, 78–81; 1958. See further the discussion of Kuch 1983b: 30–39.

4. Bowie 1997: 45–56 (the quotation is on p. 51). *Suppliants* is usually dated to the late 420s, partly on the basis of these presumed historical references: Collard 1975, vol. 1: 8–14; Morwood 2007: 26–30.

5. Compare Adorno 1992's critique of "committed" art: it sells short both politics and art. "Autonomous" art, through its formal transformation of reality, *does* what committed art only talks about (90; cf. Adorno 1997: 225–61). Tragedy could hardly be considered "autonomous," but *Suppliants* supports Adorno's general point that art is most political when it proclaims its commitments least, and vice versa.

6. E.g., Michelini 1991, 1994 (on political, including class, ideology); Mendelsohn 2002 (on gender and political ideologies); Goff 1995b and Tzanetou 2011 (on imperial ideology).

7. See Spivak 1994: 70–75 on the distinction between political representation (*Vertretung*) and mimetic re-presentation (*Darstellung*), and the political consequences of conflating the two.

8. This is stressed by Kuch 2005. Mills 1997: 97–104 notes the contradiction between the Theseus myth and the Athenian democratic ideal but explains it away by reference to tragic convention (101).

9. Contrast contemporary comedy, where the chorus frequently represents the citizen body or some portion thereof. Gould disputes the long-standing equation of the tragic chorus with the Athenian demos (Gould 1996, with the response of Goldhill 1996), but Griffith 1995: 119–22 shows how the chorus could indirectly represent the demos's perspective. See, further, Mastronarde 1999; Murnaghan 2011.

10. "Optimistic rationalist" is Mastronarde's apposite term: 1986: 202–4. See also Assaël 2001: 123–28.

11. Kuch 2005: 7–8. On Theseus's change of heart, see, e.g., Lloyd 1992: 79; Mills 1997: 106–17. Hesk 2011: 127–36 reads the play as a meditation on *euboulia* (good counsel).

12. I have offered a strong translation of *doxei d'emou thelontos* (350), which could simply mean "and I will support its decision." The weaker translation does not make as good sense of the adversative *alla* or the explanatory *gar*, and the stronger seems justified by the overall logic of the passage, but my point does not depend on it. The same goes for *hōs thelonta m' eïstheto* (394), quoted below, which could mean "since it saw that I was willing."

13. Collard 1975, vol. 2: 201 ad loc. The chorus smooth over the inconsistencies of this political situation by shifting the responsibility for their salvation from Theseus (367, 369–43) to the city itself (373–80). Compare Aeschylus's *Suppliants*, where King Pelasgus insists that the decision whether to help the suppliants must be the demos's (368–75, 397–401); he speaks to persuade them, but their vote, described in detail in anachronistically democratic language, is decisive (515–23, 600–624). Likewise, the active agency of the suppliant chorus in Aeschylus's play is, in Euripides, usurped by Theseus and his mother: Hose 1990–91, vol. 2: 225–59. Bernek 2004: 265–307 reads Euripides' *Suppliants* against Aeschylus's, as well as other suppliant dramas.

14. This question is also raised by an odd verbal repetition (noted by Michelini 1994: 240). In his criticism of tyranny (447–49), Theseus alludes to the tyrant Thrasybulus's advice for tyrannical success: to eliminate prominent citizens as if mowing down the tallest stalks of grain (Herodotus 5.92ζ2). Later, in the messenger's narrative of the battle at Thebes, Theseus himself is described as mowing off the heads of his enemies and breaking them from the stalk (717).

15. Goossens 1932, 1962: 440–46; Fitton 1961: 433; Collard 1975, vol. 2: 198 ad 350–51; Vellacott 1975: 28; Podlecki 1975: 22–27; Michelini 1994: 233–36; Kuch 2005: 15; Carter 2007: 118.

16. Morwood 2007: 176 ad 409–25 suggests that "By putting such antidemocratic sentiments into the mouth of this unappealing character, Euripides

may be offering us a satire on upper-class responses to democracy." This displacement distorts the political realities not just of Athens but also of Thebes, which was, in fact, an oligarchy at this time, not a tyranny. Similarly, political opposition to Theseus's "international" politics, his reluctance to aid the suppliants, is displaced onto sexual difference by being attributed to the Argive mothers (263–70) and Aithra (294–331).

17. Indeed, it is so irrelevant that the *agōn* needs an unusual second set of speeches to debate the actual issue of the return of the bodies: Lloyd 1992: 79–80. Burian 1985: 139–41 sees the failure of the *agōn* as its point: discourse fails to serve the common good; cf. Smith 1967: 161; Gamble 1970: 399–400. On the formal structure of Euripides' *agones* in general, see Strohm 1957: 3–49; Lloyd 1992; Dubischar 2001.

18. Mastronarde 2010: 80–83 stresses the structuring force of antithesis in *Suppliants*. A previous generation of scholars labeled the same phenomenon formal incoherence. The play's antitheses have been variously defined: real vs. ideal (Fitton 1961: 442–45; Grethlein 2003: 152–55, 167–68, 188–89); Athenian vs. Argive (Shaw 1982); intellect vs. emotion (Burian 1985a); male vs. female (Mendelsohn 2002: 135–223). Gamble 1970 views the play as "an extended δισσὸς λόγος" (404) whose oppositions are designed to display the ambiguity of human existence. Grethlein 2003: 123–88 traces the dichotomy between panegyric and tragic discourse, stressing the polyphony of the latter in contrast to the former (cf. Michelini 1994).

19. Loraux 2002a (the quotation is on p. 87). Loraux situates her study explicitly in opposition to historicizing readings of tragedy (2002a: 14–25) and as a return to Nietzsche, a figure marginalized by historicists (including Loraux herself: see Leonard 2012). Honig 2013, in her reading of Sophocles' *Antigone*, critiques what she terms "mortalist humanism," which she associates particularly with Loraux (Honig 2013: 24–26, 142–47). Drawing on Rancière, she argues that Antigone "works the interval" between civic politics and universal lament (144–50). I am proposing that *Suppliants* as a whole does something similar, and that it locates the political force of tragedy as a genre precisely within this "interval."

20. Burian 1985: 149; Michelini 1991: 29–30. Foley 2001: 19–55 stresses the tension between the politics of tragic lament and those of the city; she reads *Suppliants* as a (failed) attempt to suppress maternal mourning (2001: 36–44).

21. Only twice, for instance, do they link this episode to the story of Oedipus (833–36, 1078–79). Their only other mythical reference is at 628–31, a prayer to Zeus with an allusion to Inachus and Io (this may be a literary allusion as well: cf. Aeschylus *Suppliants* 531–37). Also largely absent from their odes is the typical tragic language of fate, necessity, and divine will. When they use this language in the second stasimon, it is to refer only to the outcome of the battle, not to some larger metaphysical or theological superstructure.

22. The title of Segal 1993 (which does not discuss *Suppliants*). I notice only two strong similes in all the chorus's odes: lines 80–82 compare their eternally flowing tears to a stream flowing down a rock face (perhaps a weak allusion to Niobe); at 961–62 they compare themselves in their grief to a cloud, wandering adrift. Significantly, the only references to *Suppliants* in Barlow 1971's study of

Euripidean imagery come from the messenger speech. The lower poetic register of this chorus may be partly explained by the fact that it is Greek, not barbarian (as in *Hecuba* and *Trojan Women*).

23. E.g., Mendelsohn 2002: 187–96. Other ironic readings include Fitton 1961: 437–40; Smith 1967: 162–64; Loraux 1986: 108. Contra, Zuntz 1955: 13–16; Collard 1972; Bernek 2004: 294–99. Of course, the similarity is not exact: for instance, Adrastus's speech praises individuals, whereas in the Athenian *epitaphios*, praise was usually (if not always: Hesk 2013: 52–60) collective. Perhaps this is another example of tragedy's failure to represent collective political agency that we saw in reference to Theseus: see Loraux 1986: 107.

24. Loraux 1986: 45–49, 1998: 15–17, 19–26; Foley 2001: 22–26, 43–44.

25. Grethlein 2003: 177–88 details the speech's failure as consolation, exhortation, and *didaxis*. See also Burian 1985: 147–50.

26. Mastronarde 2010: 82–83 notes the extraordinary "causal and thematic isolation" of this scene; cf. Michelini 1991: 29: it is "as though a miniature personal tragedy had been encapsulated in the more social and public body of *Suppliants*."

27. Note, for instance, the use of *diphruein* with a cognate accusative (990–91); the metaphoric use of *purgoō* (998); the epicizing compound adjectives (*ōkuthoai*, 993; *khalkeoteukheos*, 999); the fire imagery and play of light and dark (990–93, 1002, 1019, 1025); the allusion to the hymeneal (1025); and the "extreme example of 'pathetic' paregmenon" (Collard 1975, vol. 2: 367 ad loc.) of *thanatos sunthnēiskein thnēiskousi* (1006–7). See also Collard 1975, vol. 2: 359 on the meter and the effect of the tension between the controlled strophic form and the emotional content. This poeticism continues in the trimeter exchange between Evadne and Iphis: e.g., in the ironic *pēdēsasa* (1039) and the bird simile at 1045–47.

28. Smith 1967: 164–65; Foley 2001: 42; Mendelsohn 2002: 202–8. See also Chong-Gossard 2008: 213–27.

29. Sophocles *Oedipus at Colonus* 1224–28. This theme of perverted fertility is underscored by allusions to the myth and ritual of Demeter: see Krummen 1993: 203–8; Rehm 1994: 110–21; Mendelsohn 2002: 135–48; Kavoulaki 2008; Vinh 2011: 333–37; and on the politics of this ritual framework, Goff 1995b.

30. Burian 1985: 152. Even the pacifist message that many readers see in the play is predominantly negative. Both Adrastus (949–52) and the herald (481–85) attribute pacifism to the fear of death, while Aithra sees *hēsukhia* (inactivity) as the shameful inverse of the *ponoi* (labors) through which the polis thrives and grows (323–25). The contrast between *hēsukhia* and *ponos* resonates strongly with Athenian imperialist discourse: see Michelini 1994: 226–28, 231; Mendelsohn 2002: 172–74, 195–96.

31. Jouan 1997: 225–32; Toher 2001; Kavoulaki 2008: 312–13. Segal 1996 stresses tragedy's use of ritual, and particularly ritual lament, to produce closure through the shared release of emotion; this communal experience is for him the essence of tragic catharsis.

32. Wilson and Taplin 1993 make a similar argument for the final procession of the *Oresteia*, to which this procession is sometimes compared. I owe the reference to Kavoulaki 2008: 313.

33. Rehm 1988: 290 n.103; Rehm 1994: 118–19. On the parade, see Goldhill 1987: 63–64.

34. Criticized as such already in antiquity: Plato *Cratylus* 426d; Antiphanes fr. 189.13–17 K-A; Aristotle *Poetics* 1454a37–b8. On Euripides' use of the *mēkhanē*, see Hourmouziades 1965: 146–69; Mastronarde 1990.

35. On the staging, see Collard 1975, vol. 1: 15–16; Mastronarde 1990: 263–64; Morwood 2007: 235 ad loc.

36. *Inscriptiones Graecae* I³ 86; Thucydides 5.47; Zuntz 1955: 71–78; Collard 1975, vol. 1: 10–11. The bridge to the real world is secured by the detailed *aitia* surrounding the oath. Dunn 2000: 4–5 compares these to metaphors that assert the identity of mythic past and civic present. That *Suppliants*'s aetiologies (like many of Euripides' closing aetiologies) were likely apocryphal exposes the fictionality of this identity (Dunn 2000: 12–15; cf. Scullion 1999–2000: 219–20; contra, Seaford 2009: 223–24) and reinforces the sense that this historical treaty is the product of the tragedy itself.

Chapter 5. Broken Plays for a Broken World

1. "Seismographs": Hose 2008: 241. The appeal to historical context as an answer to puzzles of form is ubiquitous in Euripides scholarship. See, by way of example, Reckford 1985, 1991 (on *Hecuba*); Euben 1986 (on *Orestes*); in addition to Arrowsmith 1963, discussed below.

2. Arrowsmith 1963: 38; cf. 51. Compare Dunn 1996: 156 on *Helen*: "By closely observing his chaotic world, by honestly *reporting* how it resists the search for order, Euripides shows . . ." (emphasis added). Arrowsmith does go on to complicate this journalistic metaphor: "The task imposed upon the new theater was not merely that of being truthful, of reporting the true dimensions and causes of the crisis, but of coping imaginatively and intellectually with a change in man's very condition" (38). These appeals to Thucydides reflect a desire not only to render Euripides transparent but also to make him political. So Euben 1986: 226: "I quote his [Thucydides'] examples at length because they resonate with, and add political dimension to, the corruption in the *Orestes*." As I argue throughout this book, Euripides does not need Thucydides to lend a political dimension to his plays: that dimension inheres in their dramatic form.

3. Two recent papers argue along similar lines. Dunn 2012 proposes that Euripides' *Bacchae* and Sophocles' *Oedipus at Colonus*, through their innovative use of metatheater, created a new metaphysical way of knowing that anticipated Plato. Rosenbloom 2012, in the same volume, argues that *Orestes* (and Aristophanes' *Frogs*) perpetuated a pervasive narrative about the degeneration of democratic leadership and in this way contributed to the rise of the oligarchs at the end of the century. While the former understands tragedy's intervention rather more abstractly than I, and the latter more specifically, both argue, as I do, for drama's capacity (as Dunn puts it, quoting Badiou), to "change the world."

4. Friedman 2007: 198: "The *Helen* seems to confirm Thucydides' interpretation of the effect of this loss on the Athenians." Cf. Grégoire 1950b: 9–24; Kan-

nicht 1969, vol. 1: 55–57; Meltzer 1994: 238, 254–55; Dunn 1996: 155–57; Steiner 2001: 292–93; Wright 2005: 47. Arguing against "l'interprétation historique," Zuntz 1958.

5. The play's metatheatricality and thematics of illusion are both widely discussed: see, e.g., Burnett 1971: 84–85; Segal 1971; Downing 1990; Pucci 1997; Wright 2005: 278–337; Allan 2008: 47–49. I examine the blurred lines between historical events and fictional probabilities in *Helen* (and Aristotle) in Wohl 2014.

6. Scullion 1999–2000: 220–21 argues that the cult of *Helen* is an invention. He is generally skeptical of the historical referentiality of Euripidean *aitia*, which he sees as "a reflex of the play's themes rather than of cultic practice" (229). Contra, Seaford 2009. On the likely fictionality of *Helen*'s closing *aitia*, see also Allan 2008: 14–16, 339–40 ad 1642–79, and 343 ad 1670–75; Wright 2005: 357–62; and on the "avant-garde conventionality" of the end and its relation to the play as a whole, Dunn 1996: 135–42.

7. Roberts 1987: 57–64.

8. Plutarch *Nicias* 29. Compare the similar story about the parodos of *Electra* (Plutarch *Lysander* 15.3; cf. above, chapter 3, n.8). These anecdotes probably have less to do with historical fact than with Plutarch's nostalgia for classical culture and for tragedy as its acme, combined with the tradition (already established in Aristophanes) of Euripides' mass appeal.

9. Carter 2007 notes the "obvious correspondence" (132) with Melos: "It is hard to see how the play at its original performance could not have put some members of the audience in mind of recent events at Melos" (133); cf. Barlow 1986: 26–27; Croally 1994: 231–34; Garvie 2001. As van Erp Taalman Kip 1987 shows, the chronology makes it unlikely that *Trojan Women* was composed as a direct response to the destruction of Melos: the Melians surrendered in the winter of 416–15, after being under seige since the summer. The play was produced in March 415, but would have already been at least partly drafted by the previous summer, when plays were selected for spring production. For discussion, see Roisman 1997; Kuch 1998; Green 1999; Sidwell 2001; and the helpful synopsis of Goff 2009: 27–35.

10. Cornford 1965: 79–250, and esp. 174–87, on the Melian Dialogue. Cornford's model of tragedy is Aeschylean, but he concludes his discussion of Melos by quoting from *Trojan Women* (187). Goff 2009: 28 further notes that the Melian Dialogue, in contrast to Thucydides' other speeches, is set up like a play script: "The Thucydidean narrative has chosen to recast whatever was said at Melos in terms of the period's most compelling art form, tragedy" (29).

11. White 1978: esp. 81–100; cf. 1973: 1–42 (and 191–229 on the tragic emplotment of history). That this tragic pattern was not unique to Thucydides is suggested by an early fourth-century speech attributed to Andocides, which denounces Alcibiades for taking a Melian concubine after having caused the enslavement of her people: "When you watch such things in tragedies, you consider them terrible; but when you see them happening in the city, you think nothing of them" (4.22–23).

12. Euben 1986: 222. Cf. Reinhardt 2003 [1960]; Lanza 1961; Arrowsmith

1963: 45–47; Ebener 1966; Wolff 1968: 142; Burkert 1974; Schein 1975; Longo 1975. Porter 1994: 1–44 surveys the extensive scholarship on the play.

13. Arrowsmith 1963: 47. Reference to the Corcyrean *stasis* is virtually obligatory in scholarship on the *Orestes*: see especially Wolff 1968: 146; Parry 1969: 350; Rawson 1972: 161; Longo 1975: 266, 269–70, 274–75, 279–81; Euben 1986: 223–27, 247; Dunn 1996: 174; Pelling 2000: 184–85; and the extended treatment of Porter 1994: 327–32.

14. Williams 1977: 128–35. The quotations are on pp. 129, 132–34. Adorno also uses the language of precipitation and crystallization for the relation of art to materiality: see, e.g., Adorno 1991a: 42. Compare, too, Marx's metaphor of ideas and ideologies as "sublimates" of material reality: Marx and Engels 1976: 36 (cited by Hall 2006: 4, 393).

15. Woodruff 2008: 103–5 proposes that in order to care about a character, the audience must be able to imagine that he or she has a past and hopes for the future, and loves and is loved. Orestes and Electra meet these minimum conditions. Hose 1994 contains an interesting discussion of identification in the play, drawing on Jauss's taxonomy of aesthetic identification.

16. Generally, characters do not notice the music of the choral odes: Electra's reference to the *aulos* that accompanies the chorus (145–47) is a remarkable transgression of that dramatic convention. Such allusions to the machinery of stagecraft are more characteristic of Attic comedy.

17. Cf. 127, 657, 678, 724, 778, 1173, 1188, 1203, 1343, 1348, 1637. *Orestes* contains nearly twice as many occurrences of the word *sōtēria* as any other Euripidean play. See Wolff 1968: 136–38 and Parry 1969 on the theme.

18. Aristotle *Poetics* 1454a28–29. See Cilliers 1991; Hose 1994 for assessments. Aristophanes of Byzantium in his hypothesis deems all the characters "base" (*phauloi*) except Pylades, an arguable exemption.

19. The play as a whole reiterates this confusion: in the *agones* with Tyndareus and Menelaus and the vote of the Argive assembly, it restages Orestes' trial from the end of *Eumenides*; but these quasi-legal procedures result in Orestes' condemnation and exacerbate, rather than end, the violence. Classical Athenian law had a relatively straightforward procedure for dealing with a situation like Orestes': it allowed the murderer to go into exile. By ignoring this possibility, *Orestes* forces Tyndareus (and his agents at the Argive assembly) to argue a position that would have seemed harsh by Athenian standards.

20. I discuss the theme of *philia* in *Orestes* in Wohl 2011, with further bibliography on *philia* in Greek culture. On *philia* in *Orestes*, see also Greenberg 1962; Rawson 1972: 157–62; Longo 1975; and (on marriage and kinship bonds, in particular) Griffith 2009, 2011: 201–7. Belfiore 1992: 70–82 stresses the importance of *philia* to Aristotle's understanding of tragic structure and emotions.

21. E.g., 28, 121, 163–65, 191–94, 285–87, 417, 591–98, 955–56. See Mastronarde 2010: 192–95. Burnett 1971: 205–22 defends Apollo against these charges.

22. Among these is an anonymous rhetor described as a "loudmouth, forceful and brash . . . who trusts in the roar of the crowd (*thoruboi*) and in uneducated free speech" (*amathei parrhēsiai*, 903–5), a caricature drawn from contemporary critiques of democracy. This jaundiced representation of Athenian democratic

practice is much discussed: see, e.g., Romilly 1972; Euben 1986: 236–37; Hall 1993: 265–68; Saïd 2003: 197–99; Burian 2011: 113–14; Barker 2011; Rosenbloom 2012: 421–29; Allan and Kelley 2013: 110–12.

23. Reinhardt 2003: 40. It is unclear whether this moment would count as a *peripeteia* in the strict Aristotelian sense of a "specific kind of discontinuous action that occurs when the action of an agent is prevented from achieving its intended result and instead arrives at an opposite actual result" (Belfiore 1992: 143). Lacking the pointed irony of the paradigmatic *peripeteia* of Sophocles' *Oedipus Tyrannus*, it is more a sharp right turn in the action than its inversion. Scholars who view the attempted murder of Helen as the play's central action see no discontinuity here: Vellacott 1975: 53–81; Willink 1986: xxviii–xxxviii.

24. The reversal of sympathy is stressed by Conacher 1967: 217, 222–24; Schein 1975. Contra, West 1987: 33, who believes that the imperative of self-preservation would have justified the plan for Greek audiences; cf. Steidle 1968: 108–9; Erbse 1975: 445. The question is discussed by Hose 1994: 242–45.

25. Hegel 2011: 445–47, as elaborated by Žižek 1989: 58–62: it is the initial misrecognition of historical necessity as merely contingent that propels its repetition and constitutes its necessity.

26. Greenberg 1962: 160. See also Wolff 1968: 132–34; Burnett 1971: 209–12; Rawson 1972: 155–56; Burkert 1974: 103–4; Zeitlin 1980: 58–59; Euben 1986: 233–37; Nisetich 1986: 52; Gärtner 2005. Likewise, the violence against Hermione echoes the sacrifice of Iphigeneia: Komorowska 2000.

27. Marx 1979: 103. On the play's uncontrolled intertextuality, see especially Zeitlin 1980. On its use of myth, Fuqua 1976: 63–95, 1978; Wright 2006.

28. Burnett 1971: 191–92, 1974: 104–6; Zeitlin 1980: 60–62; Euben 1986: 331–33. See Seidensticker 1982: 101–14 on the farcical nature of the Phrygian's monody; cf. Wolff 1968: 139–42; Dunn 1996: 177–79; and below on the "comic" resolution.

29. This entire prologue is marked by apophasis (27, 28, 37), and the play as a whole structured by simultaneous acknowledgment and denial. Electra does later recapitulate the ancestral fratricide (996–1011), and the chorus likewise ensure that the unspeakable crimes of matricide (819–43) and fratricide (807–18) do not go unspoken; but as Schein 1975: 51 notes, this mythic background has little bearing on the action of the characters.

30. Loraux 2002b: esp. 197–213 explores the intimate connection between fraternity and *stasis* in Greek thought. The sister was excluded from Athens's fraternal polity (as Derrida 1997 stresses), and Electra's strong bond with her brother and active participation in his plot are striking.

31. Likewise, when things look bleakest, Pylades cries, "Why should I live without your *hetaireia*?" (1072, cf. 1079). The bond between Pylades, Orestes, and Electra also takes on conspiratorial overtones when Pylades calls on Zeus and Dikē to grant them success: "For three friends, one struggle, one justice!" (1244). Cf. 1192: "For we're all one in this friendship," and 1618–20, where Orestes calls to Pylades and Electra to help him burn down the palace. See Griffith 1995: 90–95 on the *xenia/hetaireia* of Pylades and Orestes in the *Oresteia* (with 68–72 on the politics of these terms).

32. Thucydides 3.82.4–6, 8.48.3–4, 8.65.2. See Calhoun 1964: 4–9 for the ter-

minology and Calhoun 1964: 97–147; Connor 1971: 25–32 on the political activities of the *hetaireiai*. The political implicatons of *Orestes' hetaireia* are noted by Rawson 1972: 160–62; Burkert 1974: 107–8; Hall 1993: 269–71; Hose 1995: 131–32; Wright 2008: 103–6; Rosenbloom 2012: 417–19. The elite status of these mythical princes would have been obvious to an Athenian audience; it becomes marked at 772–73, where they debate the virtues of democratic deliberation.

33. Pelling 2000: 185–87 offers a brief but nuanced argument along these lines, imagining how the Athenians' diverse recent experiences shaped their reception of the play.

34. E.g., Arrowsmith 1963: 45–46; Wolff 1968: 148; Burkert 1974: 100; Euben 1986: 242–45; Hartigan 1991: 154–56; Dunn 1996: 170–73; Mastronarde 2010: 194–95; contra, Steidle 1968: 100–117; and see the balanced treatment of Porter 1994: 251–89.

35. Even in antiquity, *Orestes'* sudden reversal from bad fortune to good struck readers as un-tragic. Aristophanes of Byzantium in his hypothesis comments: "The drama has a rather comic reversal." Cf. Aristotle *Poetics* 1453a35–39: plays in which enemies "become friends in the end and no one is killed by anyone" give a pleasure more appropriate to comedy than to tragedy. On the "comic" nature of the ending, see Dunn 1989, 1996: 158–79; Hall 1993: 277.

36. The Aristotelian *Constitution of the Athenians* reports the exception that proves the rule: a nameless individual who broke the amnesty was summarily executed as an example. "After his death no one ever afterwards broke the amnesty, but the Athenians seem to have dealt with their past misfortunes, individually and collectively, in the most excellent and most statesmanlike manner of any people" (40.2). Cf. Xenophon *Hellenica* 2.4.43. On the amnesty as a willful act of civic amnesia, see Loraux 2002b: esp. 145–69. I owe the connection between *Orestes'* deus ex machina and the amnesty to a suggestion from Kurt Raaflaub.

37. For *Orestes* as the "death of tragedy," see Wolff 1968: 149; Burkert 1974: 105–9; Kuch 1978a: 191; Zeitlin 1980: 70–71; Euben 1986: 244–51; Dunn 1996: 158; see also the survey of the trope in Wright 2006: 33–34. One hears a similar claim with other plays (e.g., Gellie 1981: 9 on *Electra*; Dunn 1996: 157 on *Helen*), but the rhetoric gets particularly apocalyptic with *Orestes*. I return to the "death of tragedy" and Euripides' responsibility for it in the conclusion.

38. Vernant 1988b, 1988a: 29–30. Tragedy's unique historical moment is preserved—if not created—by the determination that both tragedy and democracy died in 403. The narrative becomes significantly more complicated and less convincing when one considers tragedy's (and democracy's) fourth-century "afterlife": see Easterling 1993; Hall 2007; Csapo et al. 2014; Hanink 2014: 191–220; and, critiquing a similar narrative about comedy, Csapo 2000.

Conclusion: Content of the Form

1. *Alcestis, Andromache, Helen, Bacchae,* and with slight variation, *Medea*.

2. Dunn 1996: 25: "The closing anapests should be read less for significant content than as a gesture or ritual of closure." See the excellent discussion of Roberts 1987.

3. Roberts 1987: 60.

4. Adorno 1992: 92.

5. The latter is, of course, Nietzsche's view. The former is the title of Gregory 1991. "Euripides: *Poiētēs Sophos*" is an article by Winnington-Ingram (1969).

6. A point well made by Taplin 1983: "Tragedy is essentially *the emotional experience of its audience*. Whatever it tells us about the world is conveyed by means of these emotions" (10, original emphasis); cf. Stanford 1983: 104–5, 164–68; and Heath 1987: 37–89, who, however, insists that tragedy's intellectual and moral content is subordinate to its primary emotive purpose. In *Frogs*, Aristophanes imagines tragedy's moral pedagogy working in part through the emotions it arouses, like the longing for war and desire for victory (*ēros*, 1022; *epithumia*, 1026), or the sense of moral shame (*aiskhunē*, 1051).

7. Segal 1996; the quotation is on p. 163. For good discussions of this perplexing term in Aristotle, see Belfiore 1992: 255–360; Halliwell 1998: 184–201, 350–56. There is also a physical dimension to this response (as Segal 1996: 164–66 emphasizes). Aristotle (*Poetics* 1453b5) and Gorgias (*Encomium of Helen* 9) speak of shuddering and tears, and *psukhagōgia* implies movement within, if not also of, the body.

8. Affects don't always rise to the level of conscious articulation, but they are accessible to articulation: indeed, drama can help to articulate them. For this reason, we cannot call them "unconscious" in a strict (psychoanalytic) sense. They are rather pre-conscious, and whether or not they enter consciousness, in what form and under what conditions, is a political question. My thinking on affect has been shaped especially by Ahmed 2004a, 2004b; Ngai 2004; Berlant 2011.

9. For Adorno, as Kaufman stresses, aesthetic form makes historical change itself possible: "Aesthetic experiment helps construct and make available the intellectual-emotional apparatus for accessing, and to that extent helps make available the social material of, the new" (Kaufman 2004: 363; cf. 2000: 711).

10. This untimeliness is the reverse face of the timeliness that we examined in the last chapter: Euripides is a man of his time inasmuch as it was a time out of whack. Thus *Orestes*, Euripides' last Athenian tragedy and his most popular in fourth-century revival, is at once posthumous and premature in relation to the history of the genre, even as it is the most faithful image of its historical moment.

11. On Euripides' fourth-century reception, see especially Kuch 1978a, 1993; Xanthakis-Karamanos 1980: 28–34; Revermann 1999–2000; Taplin 2007: 108–219; Hanink 2008, 2010, 2014: 31–53, 83–89, 134–51, 166–83. It is telling that the only complete extant fourth-century tragedy, *Rhesus*, was falsely attributed to Euripides even in antiquity and preserved with his manuscripts.

12. Kuch 1978a: 200–201, 1993: 551–53; Xanthakis-Karamanos 1980: 3–6; Michelini 1999–2000: 55–56. On Euripides' Panhellenism, see Rosenbloom 2012: 366–81.

13. On the changing content of the genre "tragedy," see, e.g., Williams 1966: 15–45; Most 2000. On the construction of the synchronized "golden age" of Athenian democracy and of tragedy, see Hanink 2014: 25–125.

14. Eder 1995; Osborne 2007.

15. For Raymond Williams, these are precisely the conditions of both revolution and true tragedy. Revolution occurs when structures of feeling are out of synch with social structures (Williams 1966: 75–76); tragedy, meanwhile, arises at moments of social disruption, out of the tension between "received beliefs, embodied in institutions and responses, and newly and vividly experienced contradictions and possibilities" (Williams 1966: 54; cf. 1977: 189–91: the same conditions foster new aesthetic forms). For Williams, revolution, as the violent forging of new order out of the experience of disorder, is quintessentially tragic: see Leonard [in press, 2015], chapter 1.

16. Wolin 1994. Reacting against those (like Ostwald 1986) who see constitutionalism as democracy's "proper" form, Wolin views form itself as repressive, hierarchal, and antithetical to the radical essence of democracy.

17. For the canonization, see Plutarch *Lives of the Ten Orators* 841f; Webster 1954; Easterling 1993, 1997b; Wilson 1996; Hanink 2014. For standardization in Menander, see Petrides 2010.

Adkins, A.W.H. 1960. *Merit and Responsibility: A Study in Greek Values.* Oxford: Clarendon Press.

———. 1966. "Basic Greek Values in Euripides' *Hecuba* and *Hercules Furens.*" *Classical Quarterly* 16: 193–219.

Adorno, T. W. 1991a [1957]. "On Lyric Poetry and Society." Trans. S. W. Nicholsen. In *Notes to Literature.* Vol. 1. Ed. R. Tiedemann. New York: Columbia University Press, 37–54.

———. 1991b [1958]. "Extorted Reconciliation: On Georg Lukács' *Realism in Our Time.*" Trans. S. W. Nicholsen. In *Notes to Literature.* Vol. 1. Ed. R. Tiedemann. New York: Columbia University Press, 216–40.

———. 1992 [1962]. "Commitment." Trans. S. W. Nicholsen. In *Notes to Literature.* Vol. 2. Ed. R. Tiedemann. New York: Columbia University Press, 76–94.

———. 1997 [1970]. *Aesthetic Theory.* Ed. and trans. R. Hullot-Kentor. Minneapolis: University of Minnesota Press.

Ahmed, S. 2004a. *The Cultural Politics of Emotion.* New York: Routledge.

———. 2004b. "Affective Economies." *Social Text* 79: 117–39.

Allan, W., ed. 2001. *Euripides: The Children of Heracles.* Warminster: Aris & Phillips.

———., ed. 2008. *Euripides: Helen.* Cambridge: Cambridge University Press.

Allan, W., and A. Kelley. 2013. "Listening to Many Voices: Athenian Tragedy as Popular Art." In *The Author's Voice in Classical and Late Antiquity.* Ed. A. Marmodoro and J. Hill. Oxford: Oxford University Press, 77–122.

Althusser, L. 1971. "Ideology and Ideological State Apparatuses (Notes Towards an Investigation)." Trans. B. Brewster. In *Lenin and Philosophy and Other Essays.* New York: Monthly Review Press, 127–86.

Anderson, W. D. 1966. *Ethos and Education in Greek Music: The Evidence of Poetry and Philosophy.* Cambridge, Mass.: Harvard University Press.

Arnott, W. G. 1973. "Euripides and the Unexpected." *Greece and Rome* 20: 49–64.

———. 1981. "Double the Vision: A Reading of Euripides' 'Electra.'" *Greece and Rome* 28: 179–92.

———. 1996. "Realism in the *Ion*: Response to Lee." In *Tragedy and the Tragic: Greek Theatre and Beyond.* Ed. M. S. Silk. Oxford: Oxford University Press, 110–18.

Arrowsmith, W. 1963. "A Greek Theater of Ideas." *Arion* 2: 32–56.

Asmis, E. 1986. "*Psychagogia* in Plato's *Phaedrus*." *Illinois Classical Studies* 11: 153–72.

Assaël, J. 2001. *Euripide, philosophe et poète tragique*. Louvain: Peeters.

Balibar, E., and P. Macherey. 1981. "On Literature as an Ideological Form." Trans. I. McLeod, J. Whitehead, and A. Wordsworth. In *Untying the Text: A Poststructuralist Reader*. Ed. R. Young. London: Routledge and Kegan Paul, 79–99.

Barker, E.T.E. 2009. *Entering the Agon: Dissent and Authority in Homer, Historiography and Tragedy*. Oxford: Oxford University Press.

———. 2011. "'Possessing an Unbridled Tongue': Frank Speech and Speaking Back in Euripides' *Orestes*." In *Why Athens?: A Reappraisal of Tragic Politics*. Ed. D. M. Carter. Oxford: Oxford University Press, 145–62.

Barlow, S. A. 1971. *The Imagery of Euripides: A Study in the Dramatic Use of Pictorial Language*. London: Methuen.

———., ed. 1986. *Euripides: Trojan Women*. Warminster: Aris & Phillips.

Basta Donzelli, G. 1978. *Studio sull' Elettra di Euripide*. Catania: Università di Catania.

Belfiore, E. S. 1992. *Tragic Pleasures: Aristotle on Plot and Emotion*. Princeton: Princeton University Press.

Berlant, L. G. 2004. *Compassion: The Culture and Politics of an Emotion*. New York: Routledge.

———. 2011. *Cruel Optimism*. Durham: Duke University Press.

Bernek, R. 2004. *Dramaturgie und Ideologie: der politische Mythos in den Hikesiedramen des Aischylos, Sophokles und Euripides*. Munich: K. G. Saur.

Bierl, A. 1991. *Dionysos und die griechische Tragödie: politische und metatheatralische Aspekte im Text*. Tubingen: Gunter Narr.

Billings, J. 2014. *Genealogy of the Tragic: Greek Tragedy and German Philosophy*. Princeton: Princeton University Press.

Bloch, E. 1977 [1938]. "Discussing Expressionism." Trans. R. Livingstone. In *Aesthetics and Politics*. By E. Bloch, T. W. Adorno, W. Benjamin, B. Brecht, and G. Lukács. London: Verso, 16–27.

Boltanski, L. 1999. *Distant Suffering: Morality, Media, and Politics*. Cambridge: Cambridge University Press.

Bond, G. W. 1974. "Euripides' Parody of Aeschylus." *Hermathena* 118: 1–14.

Bourdieu, P. 1990. *The Logic of Practice*. Trans. R. Nice. Stanford: Stanford University Press.

Bowie, A. M. 1997. "Tragic Filters for History: Euripides' *Supplices* and Sophocles' *Philoctetes*." In *Greek Tragedy and the Historian*. Ed. C.B.R. Pelling. Oxford: Oxford University Press, 39–62.

Brooks, P. 1984. *Reading for the Plot: Design and Intention in Narrative*. Cambridge, Mass.: Harvard University Press.

Burian, P. 1985. "*Logos* and *Pathos*: The Politics of the *Suppliant Women*." In *Directions in Euripidean Criticism*. Ed. P. Burian. Durham: Duke University Press, 129–55.

———. 2009. "Inconclusive Conclusion: The Ending(s) of *Oedipus Tyrannus*." In

Sophocles and the Greek Tragic Tradition. Ed. S. Goldhill and E. Hall. Cambridge: Cambridge University Press, 99–118.

———. 2011. "Athenian Tragedy as Democratic Discourse." In *Why Athens?: A Reappraisal of Tragic Politics.* Ed. D. M. Carter. Oxford: Oxford University Press, 95–117.

Burkert, W. 1974. "Die Absurdität der Gewalt und das Ende der Tragödie: Euripides *Orestes.*" *Antike und Abendland* 20: 97–109.

Burnett, A. P. 1962. "Human Resistance and Divine Persuasion in Euripides' *Ion.*" *Classical Philology* 57: 89–103.

———. 1965. "The Virtues of Admetus." *Classical Philology* 60: 240–55.

———. 1971. *Catastrophe Survived: Euripides' Plays of Mixed Reversal.* Oxford: Clarendon Press.

———. 1977. "*Trojan Women* and the Ganymede Ode." *Yale Classical Studies* 25: 291–316.

———. 1994. "Hekabe the Dog." *Arethusa* 27: 151–64.

———. 1998. *Revenge in Attic and Later Tragedy.* Berkeley: University of California Press.

Buxton, R. 2003. "Euripides' *Alkestis*: Five Aspects of an Interpretation." In *Oxford Readings in Euripides.* Ed. J. Mossman. Oxford: Oxford University Press, 170–86.

Calhoun, G. M. 1964. *Athenian Clubs in Politics and Litigation.* Rome: Bretschneider.

Carter, D. M. 2004. "Was Attic Tragedy Democratic?" *Polis* 21: 4–25.

———. 2007. *The Politics of Greek Tragedy.* Exeter: Bristol Phoenix Press.

———., ed. 2011. *Why Athens?: A Reappraisal of Tragic Politics.* Oxford: Oxford University Press.

Carter, L. B. 1986. *The Quiet Athenian.* Oxford: Clarendon Press.

Chong-Gossard, J.H.K.O. 2008. *Gender and Communication in Euripides' Plays: Between Song and Silence.* Leiden: Brill.

Cilliers, L. 1991. "Menelaus' 'Unnecessary Baseness of Character' in Euripides' *Orestes.*" *Acta Classica* 34: 21–31.

Cole, A. T. 1997. "The *Ion* of Euripides and Its Audience(s)." In *Poet, Public, and Performance in Ancient Greece.* Ed. L. Edmunds and R. W. Wallace. Baltimore: Johns Hopkins University Press, 87–96.

Collard, C. 1972. "The Funeral Oration in Euripides' *Supplices.*" *Bulletin of the Institute of Classical Studies* 19: 39–53.

———., ed. 1975. *Euripides Supplices.* Groningen: Bouma's Boekhuis.

———., ed. 1991. *Euripides Hecuba.* Warminster: Aris & Phillips.

Conacher, D. J. 1959. "The Paradox of Euripides' *Ion.*" *Transactions of the American Philological Association* 90: 20–39.

———. 1967. *Euripidean Drama: Myth, Theme and Structure.* Toronto: University of Toronto Press.

Connor, W. R. 1971. *The New Politicians of Fifth-Century Athens.* Princeton: Princeton University Press.

Cornford, F. M. 1965 [1907]. *Thucydides Mythistoricus.* London: Routledge and Kegan Paul.

Croally, N. T. 1994. *Euripidean Polemic: The Trojan Women and the Function of Tragedy*. Cambridge: Cambridge University Press.

Cropp, M., ed. 1988. *Euripides Electra*. Warminster: Aris & Phillips.

Csapo, E. 1999–2000. "Later Euripidean Music." In *Euripides and Tragic Theatre in the Late Fifth Century*. Ed. M. Cropp, K. Lee, and D. Sansone. *Illinois Classical Studies* 24–25: 399–426.

———. 2000. "From Aristophanes to Menander? Genre Transformation in Greek Comedy." In *Matrices of Genre: Authors, Canons, and Society*. Ed. M. Depew and D. Obbink. Cambridge, Mass.: Harvard University Press, 115–33.

———. 2004. "The Politics of the New Music." In *Music and the Muses: The Culture of Mousike in the Classical Athenian City*. Ed. P. Murray and P. Wilson. Oxford: Oxford University Press, 207–48.

———. 2009. "New Music's Gallery of Images: The 'Dithyrambic' First Stasimon of Euripides' *Electra*." In *The Play of Texts and Fragments: Essays in Honour of Martin Cropp*. Ed. J.R.C. Cousland and J. R. Hume. Leiden: Brill, 95–109.

Csapo, E., and W. J. Slater. 1995. *The Context of Ancient Drama*. Ann Arbor: University of Michigan Press.

Csapo, E., H. R. Goette, J. R. Green, and P. Wilson, eds. 2014. *Greek Theatre in the Fourth Century B.C.* Berlin: De Gruyter.

Dale, A. M., ed. 1954. *Euripides Alcestis*. Oxford: Clarendon Press.

Davies, M. 1998. "Euripides' *Electra*: The Recognition Scene Again." *Classical Quarterly* 48: 389–403.

de Poli, M. 2011. *Le monodie di Euripide: note di critica testuale e analisi metrica*. Padua: S.A.R.G.O.N.

Delebecque, E. 1951. *Euripide et la guerre du Péloponnèse*. Paris: Klincksieck.

Denniston, J. D., ed. 1939. *Euripides Electra*. Oxford: Clarendon Press.

Depew, M., and D. Obbink, eds. 2000. *Matrices of Genre: Authors, Canons, and Society*. Cambridge, Mass.: Harvard University Press.

Derrida, J. 1992a. "Force of Law: The 'Mystical Foundation of Authority.'" Trans. M. Quaintance. In *Deconstruction and the Possibility of Justice*. Ed. D. Cornell, M. Rosenfeld, and D. G. Carlson. London: Routldge, 3–67.

———. 1992b. "The Law of Genre." In *Acts of Literature*. Ed. D. Attridge. New York: Routledge, 221–52.

———. 1997. *Politics of Friendship*. Trans. G. Collins. London: Verso.

Dobrov, G. W. 2001. *Figures of Play: Greek Drama and Metafictional Poetics*. Oxford: Oxford University Press.

Dougherty, C. 1996. "Democratic Contradictions and the Synoptic Illusion of Euripides' *Ion*." In *Dēmokratia: A Conversation on Democracies, Ancient and Modern*. Ed. J. Ober and C. W. Hedrick. Princeton: Princeton University Press, 249–70.

Downing, E. 1990. "*Apate*, *Agon*, and Literary Self-Reflexivity in Euripides' *Helen*." In *Cabinet of the Muses: Essays on Classical and Comparative Literature in Honor of Thomas G. Rosenmeyer*. Ed. M. Griffith and D. J. Mastronarde. Atlanta: Scholars Press, 1–16.

Dubischar, M. 2001. *Die Agonszenen bei Euripides: Untersuchungen zu ausgewählten Dramen*. Stuttgart: J. B. Metzler.

Dué, C. 2006. *The Captive Woman's Lament in Greek Tragedy*. Austin: University of Texas Press.

Dunn, F. M. 1989. "Comic and Tragic License in Euripides' *Orestes*." *Classical Antiquity* 8: 238–51.

———. 1990. "The Battle of the Sexes in Euripides' *Ion*." *Ramus* 19: 130–42.

———. 1996. *Tragedy's End: Closure and Innovation in Euripidean Drama*. New York: Oxford University Press.

———. 2000. "Euripidean Aetiologies." *Classical Bulletin* 76: 3–27.

———. 2007. *Present Shock in Late Fifth-Century Greece*. Ann Arbor: University of Michigan Press.

———. 2012. "Metatheatre and Crisis in Euripides' *Bacchae* and Sophocles' *Oedipus at Colonus*." In *Crisis on Stage: Tragedy and Comedy in Late Fifth-Century Athens*. Eds. A. Markantonatos and B. Zimmermann. Berlin: De Gruyter, 359–76.

Dyson, M., and K. H. Lee. 2000. "Talthybius in Euripides' *Troades*." *Greek, Roman, and Byzantine Studies* 41: 141–73.

Eagleton, T. 1990. *The Ideology of the Aesthetic*. Oxford: Blackwell.

———. 2003. *Sweet Violence: The Idea of the Tragic*. Malden, Mass.: Blackwell.

Easterling, P. E. 1985. "Anachronism in Greek Tragedy." *Journal of Hellenic Studies* 105: 1–10.

———. 1993. "The End of an Era? Tragedy in the Early Fourth Century." In *Tragedy, Comedy and the Polis*. Ed. A. H. Sommerstein, S. Halliwell, J. Henderson, and B. Zimmermann. Bari: Levante, 559–69.

———. 1997a. "Constructing the Heroic." In *Greek Tragedy and the Historian*. Ed. C.B.R. Pelling. Oxford: Oxford University Press, 21–37.

———. 1997b. "From Repertoire to Canon." In *The Cambridge Companion to Greek Tragedy*. Ed. P. E. Easterling. Cambridge: Cambridge University Press, 211–27.

Ebener, D. 1966. "Zum Schluss des *Orestes*." *Eirene* 5: 43–49.

Eder, W. 1995. *Die athenische Demokratie im 4. Jahrhundert v. Chr.: Vollendung oder Verfall einer Verfassungsform?* Stuttgart: Franz Steiner.

Erbse, H. 1975. "Zum *Orestes* des Euripides." *Hermes* 103: 434–59.

———. 1984. *Studien zum Prolog der euripideischen Tragödie*. Berlin: de Gruyter.

Erp Taalman Kip, A. M. van. 1987. "Euripides and Melos." *Mnemosyne* 40: 414–19.

Euben, J. P. 1986. "Political Corruption in Euripides' *Orestes*." In *Greek Tragedy and Political Theory*. Ed. J. P. Euben. Berkeley: University of California Press, 222–51.

Farrington, A. 1991. "Γνῶθι σαυτόν: Social Self-Knowledge in Euripides' *Ion*." *Rheinisches Museum für Philologie* 134: 120–36.

Fitton, J. W. 1961. "The *Suppliant Women* and the *Herakleidai* of Euripides." *Hermes* 89: 430–61.

Fletcher, A. 1964. *Allegory: The Theory of a Symbolic Mode*. Ithaca: Cornell University Press.

Fletcher, J. 2009. "Weaving Women's Tales in Euripides' *Ion*." In *The Play of Texts and Fragments: Essays in Honour of Martin Cropp*. Ed. J.R.C. Cousland and J. R. Hume. Leiden: Brill, 127–39.

———. 2012. "Law and Spectacle in Euripides' *Hecuba*." In *Greek Drama IV: Texts, Contexts, Performance*. Ed. D. Rosenbloom and J. Davidson. Oxford: Oxbow, 225–43.

Foley, H. P. 2001. *Female Acts in Greek Tragedy*. Princeton: Princeton University Press.

Friedman, R. D. 2007. "Old Stories in Euripides' New *Helen*: παλαιότης γὰρ τῷ λόγῳ γ'ἔνεστί τις (*Hel.* 1056)." *Phoenix* 61: 195–211.

Frye, N. 1973. *Anatomy of Criticsm: Four Essays*. Princeton: Princeton University Press.

Fuqua, C. 1976. "Studies in the Use of Myth in Sophocles' *Philoctetes* and the *Orestes* of Euripides." *Traditio* 32: 29–95.

———. 1978. "The World of Myth in Euripides' *Orestes*." *Traditio* 34: 1–28.

Gamble, R. B. 1970. "Euripides' 'Suppliant Women': Decision and Ambivalence." *Hermes* 98: 385–405.

Garner, R. 1988. "Death and Victory in Euripides' *Alcestis*." *Classical Antiquity* 7: 58–71.

Gärtner, T. 2005. "Der mythische Held in saekularisierter Umgebung: zum *Orestes* des Euripides." *Prometheus* 31: 1–28.

Garvie, A. 2001. "Euripides' *Trojan Women*: Relevance and Universality." In *Trojan Women: A Collection of Essays*. Ed. D. Stuttard and T. Shasha. York: AOD Publications, 45–60.

Gellie, G. 1980. "*Hecuba* and Tragedy." *Antichthon* 14: 30–44.

———. 1981. "Tragedy and Euripides' *Electra*." *Bulletin of the Institute of Classical Studies* 28: 1–12.

———. 1984. "Apollo in the *Ion*." *Ramus* 13: 93–101.

Gellrich, M. 1995. "Interpreting Greek Tragedy: History, Theory, and the New Philology." In *History, Tragedy, Theory: Dialogues on Athenian Drama*. Ed. B. E. Goff. Austin: University of Texas Press, 38–58.

Giannopoulou, V. 1999–2000. "Divine Agency and *Tyche* in Euripides' *Ion*: Ambiguity and Shifting Perspectives." In *Euripides and Tragic Theatre in the Late Fifth Century*. Ed. M. Cropp, K. Lee, and D. Sansone. *Illinois Classical Studies* 24–25: 257–71.

Gilmartin, K. 1970. "Talthybius in the *Trojan Women*." *American Journal of Philology* 91: 213–22.

Goff, B. E. 1988. "Euripides' *Ion* 1132–65: The Tent." *Proceedings of the Cambridge Philological Society* 34: 42–54.

———. 1991. "The Sign of the Fall: The Scars of Orestes and Odysseus." *Classical Antiquity* 10: 259–67.

———. 1995a. "Introduction: History, Tragedy, Theory." In *History, Tragedy, Theory: Dialogues on Athenian Drama*. Ed. B. E. Goff. Austin: University of Texas Press, 1–37.

———. 1995b. "Aithra at Eleusis." *Helios* 22: 65–78.

———. 1999–2000. "Try to Make it Real Compared to What? Euripides' *Electra* and the Play of Genres." In *Euripides and Tragic Theatre in the Late Fifth Century*. Ed. M. Cropp, K. Lee, and D. Sansone. *Illinois Classical Studies* 24–25: 93–105.

———. 2009. *Euripides: Trojan Women*. London: Duckworth.

Golden, L. 1970–71. "Euripides' *Alcestis*: Structure and Theme." *Classical Journal* 66: 116–25.

Goldfarb, B. E. 1992. "The Conflict of Obligations in Euripides' *Alcestis*." *Greek, Roman, and Byzantine Studies* 33: 109–26.

Goldhill, S. 1986a. *Reading Greek Tragedy*. Cambridge: Cambridge University Press.

———. 1986b. "Rhetoric and Relevance: Interpolation at Euripides *Electra* 367–400." *Greek, Roman, and Byzantine Studies* 27: 157–71.

———. 1987. "The Great Dionysia and Civic Ideology." *Journal of Hellenic Studies* 107: 58–76.

———. 1996. "Collectivity and Otherness—the Authority of the Tragic Chorus: Response to Gould." In *Tragedy and the Tragic: Greek Theatre and Beyond*. Ed. M. S. Silk. Oxford: Oxford University Press, 244–56.

———. 1997. "The Audience of Athenian Tragedy." In *The Cambridge Companion to Greek Tragedy*. Ed. P. E. Easterling. Cambridge: Cambridge University Press, 54–68.

———. 2000a. "Civic Ideology and the Problem of Difference: The Politics of Aeschylean Tragedy, Once Again." *Journal of Hellenic Studies* 120: 34–56.

———. 2000b. "Greek Drama and Political Theory." In *The Cambridge History of Greek and Roman Political Thought*. Ed. C. Rowe and M. Schofield. Cambridge: Cambridge University Press, 60–88.

———. 2008. "Generalizing About Tragedy." In *Rethinking Tragedy*. Ed. R. Felski. Baltimore: Johns Hopkins, 45–65.

———. 2012. *Sophocles and the Language of Tragedy*. Oxford: Oxford University Press.

Goossens, R. 1932. "Périclès et Thésée: à propos des *Suppliantes* d'Euripide." *Bulletin de l'Association Guillaume Budé* 35: 9–40.

———. 1962. *Euripide et Athènes. Académie Royale de Belgique 55*. Brussels: Palais des Académies.

Gould, J. 1996. "Tragedy and Collective Experience." In *Tragedy and the Tragic: Greek Theatre and Beyond*. Ed. M. S. Silk. Oxford: Oxford University Press, 217–43.

Goward, B. 2004. *Telling Tragedy: Narrative Technique in Aeschylus, Sophocles and Euripides*. London: Duckworth.

Green, P. 1999. "War and Morality in Fifth-Century Athens: The Case of Euripides' *Trojan Women*." *Ancient History Bulletin* 13: 97–110.

Greenberg, N. A. 1962. "Euripides' *Orestes*: An Interpretation." *Harvard Studies in Classical Philology* 66: 157–92.

Grégoire, H., ed. 1950a. *Euripide. Tome III*. Paris: Belles Lettres.

———., ed. 1950b. *Euripide. Tome V*. Paris: Belles Lettres.

Gregory, J. 1991. *Euripides and the Instruction of the Athenians*. Ann Arbor: University of Michigan Press.

———., ed. 1999. *Euripides: Hecuba. Introduction, Text, and Commentary*. Atlanta: Scholars Press.

———. 1999–2000. "Comic Elements in Euripides." In *Euripides and Tragic Theatre in the Late Fifth Century*. Ed. M. Cropp, K. Lee, and D. Sansone. *Illinois Classical Studies* 24–25: 59–74.

———. 2002. "*Hecuba* and the Political Dimension of Greek Tragedy." In *Approaches to Teaching the Dramas of Euripides*. Ed. R. Mitchell-Boyask. New York: Modern Language Association of America, 166–77.

Grethlein, J. 2003. *Asyl und Athen: die Konstruktion kollektiver Identität in der griechischen Tragödie*. Stuttgart: J. B. Metzler.

Griffin, J. 1998. "The Social Function of Attic Tragedy." *Classical Quarterly* 48: 39–61.

Griffith, M. 1995. "Brilliant Dynasts: Power and Politics in the *Oresteia*." *Classical Antiquity* 14: 62–129.

———. 1998. "The King and Eye: The Rule of the Father in Greek Tragedy." *Proceedings of the Cambridge Philological Society* 44: 20–84.

———. 2002. "Slaves of Dionysos: Satyrs, Audience, and the Ends of the *Oresteia*." *Classical Antiquity* 21: 195–258.

———. 2009. "Orestes and the In-laws." In *Bound By the City: Greek Tragedy, Sexual Difference, and the Formation of the Polis*. Ed. D. E. McCoskey and E. Zakin. Albany: SUNY Press, 275–330.

———. 2011. "Extended Families, Marriage, and Inter-City Relations in (Later) Athenian Tragedy." In *Why Athens?: A Reappraisal of Tragic Politics*. Ed. D. M. Carter. Oxford: Oxford University Press, 175–208.

Hall, E. 1993. "Political and Cosmic Turbulence in Euripides' *Orestes*." In *Tragedy, Comedy and the Polis*. Ed. A. H. Sommerstein, S. Halliwell, J. Henderson, and B. Zimmermann. Bari: Levante, 263–85.

———. 1996. "Is There a Polis in Aristotle's *Poetics*?" In *Tragedy and the Tragic: Greek Theatre and Beyond*. Ed. M. S. Silk. Oxford: Oxford University Press, 295–309.

———. 1997. "The Sociology of Athenian Tragedy." In *The Cambridge Companion to Greek Tragedy*. Ed. P. E. Easterling. Cambridge: Cambridge University Press, 93–126.

———. 2006. *The Theatrical Cast of Athens: Interactions between Ancient Greek Drama and Society*. Oxford: Oxford University Press.

———. 2007. "Greek Tragedy 430–380 BC." In *Debating the Athenian Cultural Revolution: Art, Literature, Philosophy, and Politics 430–380 BC*. Ed. R. Osborne. Cambridge: Cambridge University Press, 264–87.

Halliwell, S., ed. 1987. *The Poetics of Aristotle: Translation and Commentary*. Chapel Hill: University of North Carolina Press.

———. 1998. *Aristotle's Poetics*. Chicago: University of Chicago Press.

———. 2002. *The Aesthetics of Mimesis: Ancient Texts and Modern Problems*. Princeton: Princeton University Press.

Halporn, J. W. 1983. "The Skeptical Electra." *Harvard Studies in Classical Philology* 87: 101–18.

Hammond, N.G.L. 1984. "Spectacle and Parody in Euripides' *Electra*." *Greek, Roman, and Byzantine Studies* 25: 373–87.

Hanink, J. 2008. "Literary Politics and the Euripidean *Vita*." *Proceedings of the Cambridge Philological Society* 54: 115–35.

———. 2010. "The Classical Tragedians, From Athenian Idols to Wandering Poets." In *Beyond the Fifth Century: Interactions with Greek Tragedy from the*

Fourth Century B.C.E. to the Middle Ages. Ed. I. Gildenhard and M. Revermann. Berlin: De Gruyter, 39–67.

———. 2014. *Lycurgan Athens and the Making of Classical Tragedy.* Cambridge: Cambridge University Press.

Hartigan, K. 1991. *Ambiguity and Self-Deception: The Apollo and Artemis Plays of Euripides.* Frankfurt: Peter Lang.

Havelock, A. E. 1968. "Watching the *Trojan Women.*" In *Euripides: A Collection of Critical Essays.* Ed. E. Segal. Engelwood Cliffs, N. J.: Prentice-Hall, 115–27.

Heath, M. 1987. *The Poetics of Greek Tragedy.* London: Duckworth.

———. 1989. *Unity in Greek Poetics.* Oxford: Oxford University Press.

———. 2003. "'*Iure Principem Locum Tenet*': Euripides' *Hecuba.*" In *Oxford Readings in Euripides.* Ed. J. Mossman. Oxford: Oxford University Press, 218–60.

———. 2006. "The 'Social Function' of Tragedy: Clarifications and Questions." In *Dionysalexandros: Essays on Aeschylus and His Fellow Tragedians in Honour of Alexander F. Garvie.* Ed. D. Cairns and V. Liapis. Swansea: Classical Press of Wales, 253–81.

Hegel, G.W.F. 2011 [1822–23]. *Lectures on the Philosophy of World History.* Vol. 1. Ed. and trans. R. F. Brown and P. C. Hodgson. Oxford: Clarendon Press.

Herman, G. 1987. *Ritualised Friendship and the Greek City.* Cambridge: Cambridge University Press.

Hesk, J. 2011. "Euripidean *Euboulia* and the Problem of 'Tragic Politics.'" In *Why Athens?: A Reappraisal of Tragic Politics.* Ed. D. M. Carter. Oxford: Oxford University Press, 119–43.

———. 2013. "Leadership and Individuality in the Athenian Funeral Orations." *Bulletin of the Institute of Classical Studies* 56: 49–65.

Hoffer, S. E. 1996. "Violence, Culture, and the Workings of Ideology in Euripides' *Ion.*" *Classical Antiquity* 15: 289–318.

Honig, B. 2013. *Antigone, Interrupted.* Cambridge: Cambridge University Press.

Hose, M. 1990–91. *Studien zum Chor bei Euripides.* Stuttgart: Teubner.

———. 1994. "Der 'unnötig schlechte Charakter': Bemerkungen zu Aristoteles' *Poetik* und Euripides' *Orestes.*" *Poetica* 26: 233–55.

———., ed. 1995. *Drama und Gesellschaft. Studien zur dramatischen Produktion in Athen am Ende des 5. Jahrhunderts.* Stuttgart: M&P Verlag für Wissenschaft und Forschung.

———. 2008. *Euripides: der Dichter der Leidenschaften.* Munich: Beck.

Hourmouziades, N. C. 1965. *Production and Imagination in Euripides: Form and Function of the Scenic Space.* Athens: Greek Society for Humanistic Studies.

Jameson, F. 1972. *The Prison-House of Language: A Critical Account of Structuralism and Russian Formalism.* Princeton: Princeton University Press.

———. 1981. *The Political Unconscious: Narrative as a Socially Symbolic Act.* Ithaca: Cornell University Press.

———. 1988. *The Ideologies of Theory: Essays 1971–1986.* Vol. 1. *Situations of Theory.* Minneapolis: University of Minnesota Press.

Jens, W., ed. 1971. *Die Bauformen der griechischen Tragödie.* Munich: W. Fink.

Johnson, J. F., and D. C. Clapp. 2005. "Athenian Tragedy: An Education in Pity." In *Pity and Power in Ancient Athens.* Ed. R. H. Sternberg. Cambridge: Cambridge University Press, 123–64.

de Jong, I.J.F. 1991. *Narrative in Drama: The Art of the Euripidean Messenger-Speech*. Leiden: E. J. Brill.

Jouan, F. 1997. "Les rites funéraires dans les *Suppliantes* d'Euripide." *Kernos* 10: 215–32.

Kannicht, R., ed. 1969. *Euripides Helena*. Heidelberg: Winter.

Kaufman, R. 2000. "Red Kant, or the Persistence of the Third *Critique* in Adorno and Jameson." *Critical Inquiry* 26: 682–724.

———. 2004. "Adorno's Social Lyric, and Literary Criticism Today: Poetics, Aesthetics, Modernity." In *The Cambridge Companion to Adorno*. Ed. T. Huhn. Cambridge: Cambridge University Press, 354–75.

Kavoulaki, A. 2008. "The Last Word: Ritual, Power and Performance in Euripides' *Hiketides*." In *Performance, Iconography, Reception: Studies in Honour of Oliver Taplin*. Ed. M. Revermann and P. Wilson. Oxford: Oxford University Press, 291–317.

Kermode, F. 1967. *The Sense of an Ending: Studies in the Theory of Fiction*. New York: Oxford University Press.

King, K. C. 1980. "The Force of Tradition: The Achilles Ode in Euripides' *Electra*." *Transactions of the American Philological Association* 110: 195–212.

———. 1985. "The Politics of Imitation: Euripides' *Hekabe* and the Homeric Achilles." *Arethusa* 18: 47–66.

Kirkwood, G. M. 1947. "Hecuba and Nomos." *Transactions of the American Philological Association* 78: 61–68.

Kitto, H.D.F. 1973 [1939]. *Greek Tragedy*. New York: Methuen.

Knox, B. 1979. *Word and Action: Essays on the Ancient Theater*. Baltimore: Johns Hopkins University Press.

Komorowska, J. 2000. "A Reenactment of Aulis? Hermione within the Frame of the *Orestes*." *Eos* 87: 207–14.

Konstan, D. 2001. *Pity Transformed*. London: Duckworth.

———. 2006. *The Emotions of the Ancient Greeks: Studies in Aristotle and Classical Literature*. Toronto: University of Toronto Press.

Kovacs, D. 1987. *The Heroic Muse: Studies in the Hippolytus and Hecuba of Euripides*. Baltimore: Johns Hopkins University Press.

Krummen, E. 1993. "Athens and Attica: Polis and Countryside in Greek Tragedy." In *Tragedy, Comedy and the Polis*. Ed. A. H. Sommerstein, S. Halliwell, J. Henderson, and B. Zimmermann. Bari: Levante, 191–217.

Kubo, M. 1967. "The Norm of Myth: Euripides' *Electra*." *Harvard Studies in Classical Philology* 71: 15–31.

Kuch, H. 1978a. "Zur Euripides-Rezeption im Hellenismus." *Klio* 60: 191–202.

———. 1978b. *Kriegsgefangenschaft und Sklaverei bei Euripides*. Berlin: Akademie-Verlag.

———, ed. 1983a. *Die griechische Tragödie in ihrer gesellschaftlichen Funktion*. Berlin: Akademie-Verlag.

———. 1983b. "Gesellschaftliche Voraussetzungen und Sujet der griechischen Tragödie." In *Die griechische Tragödie in ihrer gesellschaftlichen Funktion*. Ed. H. Kuch. Berlin: Akademie-Verlag, 11–39.

———. 1993. "Continuity and Change in Greek Tragedy under Post-Classical

Conditions." In *Tragedy, Comedy and the Polis*. Ed. A. H. Sommerstein, S. Halliwell, J. Henderson, and B. Zimmermann. Bari: Levante, 545–57.

———. 1998. "Euripides und Melos." *Mnemosyne* 51: 147–53.

———. 2005. "Euripides und das Heroische: Reflexionen zu den *Hiketiden*." *Acta Ant. Hung.* 45: 1–25.

Kucharski, J. 2004. "Orestes' Lock: The Motif of Tomb Rituals in the *Oresteia* and the Two *Electra* Plays." *Eos* 91: 9–33.

Kullmann, W. 1967. "Zum Sinngehalt der euripideischen *Alkestis*." *Antike und Abendland* 13: 127–49.

Kurke, L. 1999. *Coins, Bodies, Games, and Gold: The Politics of Meaning in Archaic Greece*. Princeton: Princeton University Press.

Lacan, J. 1992. *The Ethics of Psychoanalysis: The Seminar of Jacques Lacan, Book VII*. Ed. J.-A. Miller. Trans. D. Porter. New York: W. W. Norton.

Lada, I. 1996. "'Weeping for Hecuba': Is it a 'Brechtian' Act?" *Arethusa* 29: 87–124.

Lanza, D. 1961. "Unità e significato dell' *Oreste* euripideo." *Dionisio* 35: 58–72.

Lape, S. 2010. *Race and Citizen Identity in the Classical Athenian Democracy*. Cambridge: Cambridge University Press.

Larue, J. 1963. "Creusa's Monody: *Ion* 859–922." *Transactions of the American Philological Association* 94: 126–36.

Lee, K. H., ed. 1976. *Euripides: Troades*. London: St. Martin's Press.

———., ed. 1997. *Euripides: Ion*. Warminster: Aris & Phillips.

Leonard, M. 2005. *Athens in Paris: Ancient Greece and the Political in Postwar French Thought*. Oxford: Oxford University Press.

———. 2012. "Tragedy and the Seductions of Philosophy." *Cambridge Classical Journal* 58: 145–64.

———. in press, 2015. *Tragic Modernities*. Cambridge, Mass.: Harvard University Press.

Lesky, A. 1925. "Alkestis, der Mythos und das Drama." *Sitzungsberichte der Österreichischen Akademie der Wissenschaft in Wien* 203.2: 1–86.

Lloyd, M. 1984. "The Helen Scene in Euripides' *Troades*." *Classical Quarterly* 34: 303–13.

———. 1985. "Euripides' *Alcestis*." *Greece and Rome* 32: 119–31.

———. 1986a. "Realism and Character in Euripides' *Electra*." *Phoenix* 40: 1–19.

———. 1986b. "Divine and Human Action in Euripides' *Ion*." *Antike und Abendland* 31: 33–45.

———. 1992. *The Agon in Euripides*. Oxford: Oxford University Press.

Longo, O. 1975. "Proposte di lettura per l'*Oreste* di Euripide." *Maia* 27: 265–87.

———. 1990. "The Theater of the *Polis*." Trans. J. J. Winkler. In *Nothing to Do with Dionysos? Athenian Drama in Its Social Context*. Ed. J. J. Winkler and F. I. Zeitlin. Princeton: Princeton University Press, 12–19.

Loraux, N. 1986. *The Invention of Athens: The Funeral Oration in the Classical City*. Trans. A. Sheridan. Cambridge, Mass.: Harvard University Press.

———. 1993. *The Children of Athena: Athenian Ideas about Citizenship and the Division Between the Sexes*. Trans. C. Levine. Princeton: Princeton University Press.

——. 1998. *Mothers in Mourning: With the Essay, Of Amnesty and Its Opposite.* Trans. C. Pache. Ithaca: Cornell University Press.

——. 2002a. *The Mourning Voice: An Essay on Greek Tragedy.* Trans. E. T. Rawlings. Ithaca: Cornell University Press.

——. 2002b. *The Divided City: On Memory and Forgetting in Ancient Athens.* Trans. C. Pache with J. Fort. New York: Zone Books.

Lukács, G. 1977 [1938]. "Realism in the Balance." Trans. R. Livingstone. In *Aesthetics and Politics.* By E. Bloch, T. W. Adorno, W. Benjamin, B. Brecht, and G. Lukács. London: Verso, 28–59.

Luschnig, C.A.E. 1995. *The Gorgon's Severed Head: Studies in Alcestis, Electra, and Phoenissae.* Leiden: Brill.

Marshall, C. W. 2000. "*Alcestis* and the Problem of Prosatyric Drama." *Classical Journal* 95: 229–38.

Marx, K., and F. Engels. 1976 [1845–46]. "The German Ideology." Trans. W. Lough. In *Karl Marx and Frederick Engels. Collected Works.* Vol. 5. New York: International Publishers, 19–539.

Marx, K. 1979 [1852]."The Eighteenth Brumaire of Louis Bonaparte." In *Karl Marx and Frederick Engels. Collected Works.* Vol. 2. New York: International Publishers, 99–197.

Mastronarde, D. J. 1975. "Iconography and Imagery in Euripides' *Ion*." *California Studies in Classical Antiquity* 8: 163–76.

——. 1986. "The Optimistic Rationalist in Euripides: Theseus, Jocasta, Tiresias." In *Greek Tragedy and Its Legacy: Essays Presented to Desmond Conacher.* Ed. M. Cropp, E. Fantham, and S. Scully. Calgary: University of Calgary Press, 201–11.

——. 1990. "Actors on High: The Skene Roof, the Crane, and the Gods in Attic Drama." *Classical Antiquity* 9: 247–94.

——. 1999. "Knowledge and Authority in the Choral Voice of Euripidean Tragedy." *Syllecta Classica* 10: 87–104.

——. 1999–2000. "Euripidean Tragedy and Genre: The Terminology and Its Problems." In *Euripides and Tragic Theatre in the Late Fifth Century.* Ed. M. Cropp, K. Lee, and D. Sansone. *Illinois Classical Studies* 24–25: 23–39.

——. 2010. *The Art of Euripides: Dramatic Technique and Social Context.* Cambridge: Cambridge University Press.

Matthiessen, K., ed. 2010. *Euripides Hekabe: Edition und Kommentar.* Berlin: De Gruyter.

Meier, C. 1993. *The Political Art of Greek Tragedy.* Trans. A. Webber. Baltimore: Johns Hopkins University Press.

Meltzer, G. S. 1994. "Where is the Glory of Troy? *Kleos* in Euripides' *Helen.*" *Classical Antiquity* 13: 234–55.

——. 2006. *Euripides and the Poetics of Nostalgia.* Cambridge: Cambridge University Press.

Mendelsohn, D. A. 2002. *Gender and the City in Euripides' Political Plays.* Oxford: Oxford University Press.

Meridor, R. 1978. "Hecuba's Revenge: Some Observations on Euripides' *Hecuba.*" *American Journal of Philology* 99: 28–35.

———. 1984. "Plot and Myth in Euripides' *Heracles* and *Troades.*" *Phoenix* 38: 205–15.

———. 2000. "Creative Rhetoric in Euripides' *Troades*: Some Notes on Hecuba's Speech." *Classical Quarterly* 50: 16–29.

Michelini, A. N. 1987. *Euripides and the Tragic Tradition*. Madison: University of Wisconsin Press.

———. 1991. "The Maze of *Logos*: Euripides, *Suppliants*, 163–249." *Ramus* 20: 16–37.

———. 1994. "Political Themes in Euripides' *Suppliants.*" *American Journal of Philology* 155: 219–52.

———. 1997. "Euripides: Conformist, Deviant, Neo-Conservative?" *Arion* 4: 208–22.

———. 1999–2000. "The Expansion of Myth in Late Euripides: *Iphigeneia at Aulis.*" In *Euripides and Tragic Theatre in the Late Fifth Century*. Ed. M. Cropp, K. Lee, and D. Sansone. *Illinois Classical Studies*, 24–25: 41–57.

Miller, W. I. 2006. *Eye for an Eye*. Cambridge: Cambridge University Press.

Mills, S. 1997. *Theseus, Tragedy, and the Athenian Empire*. Oxford: Clarendon Press.

Mitchell-Boyask, R. 1993. "Sacrifice and Revenge in Euripides' *Hecuba.*" *Ramus* 22: 116–34.

Morwood, J., ed. 2007. *Euripides: Suppliant Women*. Oxford: Aris & Phillips.

Morwood, J.H.W. 1981. "The Pattern of Euripides' *Electra.*" *American Journal of Philology* 102: 362–70.

Mossman, J. 1995. *Wild Justice: A Study of Euripides' Hecuba*. Oxford: Clarendon Press.

Most, G. W. 2000. "Generating Genres: The Idea of the Tragic." In *Matrices of Genre: Authors, Canons, and Society*. Ed. M. Depew and D. Obbink. Cambridge, Mass.: Harvard University Press, 15–35.

Müller, G. 1975. "Beschreibung von Kunstwerken im *Ion* des Euripides." *Hermes* 103: 25–44.

Mulryne, J. R. 1977. "Poetic Structures in the *Electra* of Euripides." *Liverpool Classical Monthly* 2: 31–38, 41–50.

Munteanu, D. L. 2012. *Tragic Pathos: Pity and Fear in Greek Philosophy and Tragedy*. Cambridge: Cambridge University Press.

Murnaghan, S. 2011. "*Choroi Achoroi:* The Athenian Politics of Tragic Choral Identity." In *Why Athens?: A Reappraisal of Tragic Politics*. Ed. D. M. Carter. Oxford: Oxford University Press, 245–67.

Neitzel, H. 1988. "Apollons Orakelspruch im *Ion* des Euripides." *Hermes* 116: 272–79.

Ngai, S. 2004. *Ugly Feelings*. Cambridge, Mass.: Harvard University Press.

Nielsen, R. M. 1976. "Alcestis: A Paradox in Dying." *Ramus* 5: 92–102.

Nisetich, F. J. 1986. "The Silencing of Pylades (*Orestes* 1591–92)." *American Journal of Philology* 107: 46–54.

Nussbaum, M. C. 1986. *The Fragility of Goodness: Luck and Ethics in Greek Tragedy and Philosophy*. Cambridge: Cambridge University Press.

———. 2001. *Upheavals of Thought: The Intelligence of Emotions*. Cambridge: Cambridge University Press.

O'Brien, M. J. 1964. "Orestes and the Gorgon: Euripides' *Electra*." *American Journal of Philology* 85: 13–39.

O'Higgins, D. 1993. "Above Rubies: Admetus' Perfect Wife." *Arethusa* 26: 77–97.

O'Neill, E. G. 1941."The Prologue of the *Troades* of Euripides." *Transactions of the American Philological Association* 72: 288–320.

O'Sullivan, P. 2008. "Aeschylus, Euripides, and Tragic Painting: Two Scenes from *Agamemnon* and *Hecuba*." *American Journal of Philology* 129: 173–98.

Ober, J., and B. Strauss. 1990. "Drama, Political Rhetoric, and the Discourse of Athenian Democracy." In *Nothing to Do with Dionysos? Athenian Drama in Its Social Context*. Ed. J. J. Winkler and F. I. Zeitlin. Princeton: Princeton University Press, 237–70.

Ormand, K. 2009. "Electra in Exile." In *Bound By the City: Greek Tragedy, Sexual Difference, and the Formation of the Polis*. Ed. D. E. McCoskey and E. Zakin. Albany: SUNY Press, 247–73.

Osborne, R., ed. 2007. *Debating the Athenian Cultural Revolution: Art, Literature, Philosophy, and Politics, 430–380 BC*. Cambridge: Cambridge University Press.

Ostwald, M. 1986. *From Popular Sovereignty to the Sovereignty of Law: Law, Society, and Politics in Fifth-Century Athens*. Berkeley: University of California Press.

Owen, A. S., ed. 1939. *Euripides: Ion*. Oxford: Clarendon Press.

Parker, L.P.E., ed. 2007. *Euripides: Alcestis*. Oxford: Oxford University Press.

Parry, H. 1969. "Euripides' *Orestes*: The Quest for Salvation." *Transactions of the American Philological Association* 100: 337–53.

Pedilla, M. 2000. "Gifts of Humiliation: *Charis* and Tragic Experience in *Alcestis*." *American Journal of Philology* 121: 179–211.

Pedrick, V. 2007. *Euripides, Freud, and the Romance of Belonging*. Baltimore: Johns Hopkins University Press.

Pelling, C.B.R., ed. 1997a. *Greek Tragedy and the Historian*. Oxford: Oxford University Press.

———. 1997b. "Conclusion." In *Greek Tragedy and the Historian*. Ed. C.B.R. Pelling. Oxford: Oxford University Press, 213–35.

———. 2000. *Literary Texts and the Greek Historian*. London: Routledge.

Peponi, A.-E. 2012. *Frontiers of Pleasure: Models of Aesthetic Response in Archaic and Classical Greek Thought*. New York: Oxford University Press.

Petrides, A. K. 2010. "New Performance." In *New Perspectives on Postclassical Comedy*. Ed. A. K. Petrides and S. Papaioannou. Newcastle: Cambridge Scholars, 79–124.

Pfister, M. 1988. *The Theory and Analysis of Drama*. Trans. J. Halliday. Cambridge: Cambridge University Press.

Podlecki, A. 1975–76. "A Pericles *Prosōpon* in Attic Tragedy?" *Euphrosyne* 7: 22–27.

Poole, A. 1976. "Total Disaster: Euripides' *The Trojan Women*." *Arion* 3: 257–87.

Porter, J. I. 2010. *The Origins of Aesthetic Thought in Ancient Greece: Matter, Sensation, and Experience*. Cambridge: Cambridge University Press.

Porter, J. R. 1994. *Studies in Euripides' Orestes*. Leiden: Brill.

Prag, A.J.N.W. 1985. *The Oresteia: Iconographic and Narrative Tradition*. Chicago: Bolchazy-Carducci.

Pucci, P. 1967. "Euripides Heautontimoroumenos." *Transactions of the American Philological Association* 98: 365–71.

———. 1977. "Euripides: The Monument and the Sacrifice." *Arethusa* 10: 165–95.

———. 1980. *The Violence of Pity in Euripides' Medea*. Ithaca: Cornell University Press.

———. 1992. *Oedipus and the Fabrication of the Father: Oedipus Tyrannus in Modern Criticism and Philosophy*. Baltimore: Johns Hopkins University Press.

———. 1997. "The *Helen* and Euripides' 'Comic' Art." *Colby Quarterly* 33: 42–75.

Rabinowitz, N. S. 1993. *Anxiety Veiled: Euripides and the Traffic in Women*. Ithaca: Cornell University Press.

Raeburn, D. 2000. "The Significance of Stage Properties in Euripides' *Electra*." *Greece and Rome* 47: 149–68.

Rasmussen, M. D., ed. 2002. *Renaissance Literature and Its Formal Engagements*. New York: Palgrave.

Rawson, E. 1972. "Aspects of Euripides' *Orestes*." *Arethusa* 5: 155–67.

Reckford, K. J. 1985. "Concepts of Demoralization in the *Hecuba*." In *Directions in Euripidean Criticism*. Ed. P. Burian. Durham: Duke University Press, 112–28.

———. 1991. "Pity and Terror in Euripides' *Hecuba*." *Arion* 1: 24–43.

Rehm, R. 1988. "The Staging of Suppliant Plays." *Greek, Roman, and Byzantine Studies* 29: 263–307.

———. 1994. *Marriage to Death: The Conflation of Wedding and Funeral Rituals in Greek Tragedy*. Princeton: Princeton University Press.

Reinhardt, K. 2003 [1960]. "The Intellectual Crisis in Euripides." Trans. J. Mossman and J. M. Mossman. In *Oxford Readings in Euripides*. Ed. J. Mossman. Oxford: Oxford University Press, 16–46.

Revermann, M. 1999–2000. "Euripides, Tragedy and Macedon: Some Conditions of Reception." In *Euripides and Tragic Theatre in the Late Fifth Century*. Ed. M. Cropp, K. Lee, and D. Sansone. *Illinois Classical Studies* 24–25: 451–67.

———. 2006. "The Competence of Theatre Audiences in Fifth- and Fourth-Century Athens." *Journal of Hellenic Studies* 126: 99–124.

Rhodes, J. P. 2003. "Nothing to Do with Democracy: Athenian Drama and the Polis." *Journal of Hellenic Studies* 123: 104–19.

Riemer, P. 1989. *Die Alkestis des Euripides: Untersuchungen zur tragischen Form*. Frankfurt am Main: Athenäum.

Rivier, A. 1972. "En marge d'*Alceste* et de quelques interprétations récentes." *Museum Helveticum* 29: 124–40.

———. 1975. *Essai sur le tragique d'Euripide*. Paris: Boccard.

Roberts, D. H. 1987. "Parting Words: Final Lines in Sophocles and Euripides." *Classical Quarterly* 37: 51–64.

Roisman, J. 1997. "Contemporary Allusions in Euripides' *Trojan Women*." *Studi Italiani di filologia classica* 15: 38–47.

Romilly, J. de. 1972. "L'assemblée du peuple dans l'*Oreste* d'Euripide." In *Studi classici in onore di Quintino Cataudella.* Vol. 1. Catania: Università di Catania, 237–51.

———. 1980. *L'évolution du pathètique d'Eschyle à Euripide.* Paris: Presses Universitaires de France.

———. 1986. *La modernité d'Euripide.* Paris: Presses Universitaires de France.

Rooney, E. 2000. "Form and Contentment." *Modern Language Quarterly* 61: 17–40.

Rose, P. W. 1992. *Sons of the Gods, Children of Earth: Ideology and Literary Form in Ancient Greece.* Ithaca: Cornell University Press.

Roselli, D. K. 2005. "Vegetable-Hawking Mom and Fortunate Son: Euripides, Tragic Style, and Reception." *Phoenix* 59: 1–49.

———. 2007. "Gender, Class and Ideology: The Social Function of the Virgin Sacrifice in Euripides' *Children of Heracles.*" *Classical Antiquity* 26: 81–169.

———. 2011. *Theater of the People: Spectators and Society in Ancient Athens.* Austin: University of Texas Press.

Rosenbloom, D. 1993. "Shouting 'Fire' in a Crowded Theater: Phrynichos' *Capture of Miletos* and the Politics of Fear in Early Attic Tragedy." *Philologus* 137: 159–96.

———. 2006. "Empire and Its Discontents: *Trojan Women, Birds,* and the Symbolic Economy of Athenian Imperialism." In *Greek Drama III: Essays in Honour of Kevin Lee.* Ed. J. Davidson, F. Muecke, and P. Wilson. London: Institute of Classical Studies, 245–71.

———. 2012. "Scripting Revolution: Democracy and Its Discontents in Late Fifth-Century Drama." In *Crisis on Stage: Tragedy and Comedy in Late Fifth-Century Athens.* Ed. A. Markantonatos and B. Zimmermann. Berlin: De Gruyter, 405–41.

Rosivach, V. J. 1975. "The First Stasimon of the *Hecuba*, 444ff." *American Journal of Philology* 96: 349–62.

———. 1977. "Earthborns and Olympians: The Parodos of the *Ion.*" *Classical Quarterly* 27: 284–94.

———. 1978. "The 'Golden Lamb' Ode in Euripides' *Electra.*" *Classical Philology* 73: 189–99.

Rösler, W. 1980. *Polis und Tragödie: Functionsgeschichtliche Betrachtungen zu einer antiken Literaturgattung.* Konstanz: Universitätsverlag Konstanz.

Rousseau, J.-J. 1960 [1758]. *Politics and the Arts: Letter to M. D'Alembert on the Theater.* Trans. A. Bloom. Ithaca: Cornell University Press.

Roy, J. 1996. "The Countryside in Classical Greek Drama, and Isolated Farms in Dramatic Landscapes." In *Human Landscapes in Classical Antiquity: Environment and Culture.* Ed. G. Shipley and J. Salmon. New York: Routledge, 98–118.

Rutherford, R. B. 2012. *Greek Tragic Style: Form, Language, and Interpretation.* Cambridge: Cambridge University Press.

Saïd, S. 1998. "Tragedy and Politics." In *Democracy, Empire, and the Arts in Fifth-Century Athens.* Ed. D. Boedeker and K. Raaflaub. Cambridge, Mass.: Harvard University Press, 275–95.

———. 2003. "Le peuple dans les tragédies d'Euripide." In *Fondements et crises du pouvoir*. Ed. S. Franchet d'Espèrey, V. Fromentin, S. Gotteland, and J.-M. Roddaz. Bordeaux: Ausonius, 189–200.

Saxonhouse, A. 1986. "Myths and the Origins of Cities: Reflections on the Autochthony Theme in Euripides' *Ion*." In *Greek Tragedy and Political Theory*. Ed. J. P. Euben. Berkeley: University of California Press, 252–73.

Scarry, E. 1999. *On Beauty and Being Just*. Princeton: Princeton University Press.

Schein, S. 1975. "Mythical Illusion and Historical Reality in Euripides' *Orestes*." *Wiener Studien* 9: 49–66.

———. 1988. "Φιλία in Euripides' *Alcestis*." *Mètis* 3: 179–206.

Schmidt, H. W. 1971. "Die Struktur des Eingangs." In *Die Bauformen der griechischen Tragödie*. Ed. W. Jens. Munich: W. Fink, 1–46.

Schottlaender, R. 1982. "Fortschrittsverküngung oder Adelsrhetorik? Zu einer euripideischen Maxime." *Hermes* 110: 490–94.

Schwinge, E.-R. 1968. *Die Verwendung der Stichomythie in den Dramen des Euripides*. Heidelberg: C. Winter.

Scodel, R. 1979. "᾽Αδμήτου Λόγος and the *Alcestis*." *Harvard Studies in Classical Philology* 83: 51–62.

———. 1980. *The Trojan Trilogy of Euripides*. Hypomnemata 60. Göttingen: Vandenhoeck and Ruprecht.

———. 1996. "Δόμων Ἄγαλμα: Virgin Sacrifice and Aesthetic Object." *Transactions of the American Philological Association* 126: 111–28.

Scullion, S. 1999–2000. "Tradition and Invention in Euripidean Aetiology." In *Euripides and Tragic Theatre in the Late Fifth Century*. Ed. M. Cropp, K. Lee, and D. Sansone. *Illinois Classical Studies* 24–25: 217–33.

Seaford, R. 2009. "Aitiologies of Cult in Euripides: A Response to Scott Scullion." In *The Play of Texts and Fragments: Essays in Honour of Martin Cropp*. Ed. J.R.C. Cousland and J. R. Hume. Leiden: Brill, 221–34.

Segal, C. 1971. "The Two Worlds of Euripides' *Helen*." *Transactions of the American Philological Association* 102: 553–614.

———. 1982. *Dionysiac Poetics and Euripides' Bacchae*. Princeton: Princeton University Press.

———. 1992. "Tragic Beginnings: Narration, Voice, and Authority in the Prologues of Greek Drama." *Yale Classical Studies* 29: 85–112.

———. 1993. *Euripides and the Poetics of Sorrow: Art, Gender, and Commemoration in Alcestis, Hippolytus, and Hecuba*. Durham: Duke University Press.

———. 1996. "Catharsis, Audience, and Closure in Greek Tragedy." In *Tragedy and the Tragic: Greek Theatre and Beyond*. Ed. M. S. Silk. Oxford: Oxford University Press, 149–72.

Seidensticker, B. 1971. "Die Stichomythie." In *Die Bauformen der griechischen Tragödie*. Ed. W. Jens. Munich: W. Fink, 183–220.

———. 1982. *Palintonos Harmonia: Studien zu komischen Elementen in der griechischen Tragödie*. Göttingen: Vandenhoeck and Ruprecht.

Shaw, M. H. 1982. "The Ἦθος of Theseus in the *Suppliant Women*." *Hermes* 110: 3–19.

Shklovsky, V. 1965a [1917]. "Art as Technique." In *Russian Formalist Criticism: Four Essays*. Ed. and trans. L. T. Lemon and M. J. Reis. Lincoln: University of Nebraska Press, 3–24.

——. 1965b [1921]. "Sterne's Tristram Shandy: Stylistic Commentary." In *Russian Formalist Criticism: Four Essays*. Ed. and trans. L. T. Lemon and M. J. Reis. Lincoln: University of Nebraska Press, 25–57.

Sidwell, K. 2001. "Melos and the *Trojan Women*." In *Trojan Women: A Collection of Essays*. Ed. D. Stuttard and T. Shasha. York: AOD Publications, 30–44.

Smith, B. H. 1968. *Poetic Closure: A Study of How Poems End*. Chicago: University of Chicago Press.

Smith, W. D. 1960."The Ironic Structure in *Alcestis*." *Phoenix* 14: 127–45.

——. 1967. "Expressive Form in Euripides' *Suppliants*." *Harvard Studies in Classical Philology* 71: 151–70.

Solmsen, F. 1934. "Euripides *Ion* im Vergleich mit anderen Tragödien." *Hermes* 69: 390–419.

——. 1982. "Electra and Orestes: Three Recognitions in Greek Tragedy." In *Kleine Schriften*. Vol. 3. New York: Georg Olms, 32–63.

Sommerstein, A. H. 1997. "The Theatre Audience, the *Demos*, and the *Suppliants* of Aeschylus." In *Greek Tragedy and the Historian*. Ed. C.B.R. Pelling. Oxford: Oxford University Press, 62–79.

Sourvinou-Inwood, C. 2003. *Tragedy and Athenian Religion*. Lanham, Md.: Lexington Books.

Spira, A. 1960. *Untersuchungen zum Deus ex Machina bei Sophokles und Euripides*. Kallmunz: Lassleben.

Spivak, G. C. 1994. "Can the Subaltern Speak?" In *Colonial Discourse and Post-Colonial Theory*. Ed. P. Williams and L. Chrisman. New York: Columbia University Press, 66–123.

Stanford, W. B. 1983. *Greek Tragedy and the Emotions: An Introductory Study*. London: Routledge & Kegan Paul.

Stanton, G. R. 1990. "Φιλία and Ξενία in Euripides' *Alkestis*." *Hermes* 118: 42–54.

Steidle, W. 1968. *Studien zum antiken Drama. Unter besonderer Berücksichtigung des Bühnenspiels*. Munich: W. Fink.

Steiner, D. 2001. *Images in Mind: Statues in Archaic and Classical Greek Literature and Thought*. Princeton: Princeton University Press.

Sternberg, R. H. 2006. *Tragedy Offstage: Suffering and Sympathy in Ancient Athens*. Austin: University of Texas Press.

Strohm, H. 1957. *Euripides. Interpretationen zur dramatischen Form*. Munich: Beck.

Sutton, D. F. 1980. *The Greek Satyr Play*. Meisenheim am Glan: Hain.

Swift, L., ed. 2008. *Euripides: Ion*. London: Duckworth.

——. 2010. *The Hidden Chorus: Echoes of Genre in Tragic Lyric*. Oxford: Oxford University Press.

Taplin, O. 1978. *Greek Tragedy in Action*. London: Methuen.

——. 1983. "Emotion and Meaning in Greek Tragedy." In *Oxford Readings in Greek Tragedy*. Ed. E. Segal. Oxford: Oxford University Press, 1–12.

——. 2007. *Pots and Plays: Interactions between Tragedy and Greek Vase-Painting of the Fourth Century B.C.* Los Angeles: J. Paul Getty Museum.

Tarkow, T. 1981. "The Scar of Orestes: Observations on a Euripidean Innovation." *Rheinisches Museum für Philologie* 124: 143–53.

Thalmann, W. G. 1993. "Euripides and Aeschylus: The Case of the *Hekabe*." *Classical Antiquity* 12: 126–59.

Thévenet, L. 2009. *Le personnage du mythe au théâtre: la question de l'identité dans la tragédie grecque*. Paris: Belles Lettres.

Thornburn, J. E. 2000. "Euripides' *Ion*: The Gold and the Darkness." *Classical Bulletin* 76: 39–49.

Thury, E. M. 1985. "Euripides' *Electra*: An Analysis Through Character Development." *Rheinisches Museum für Philologie* 128: 5–22.

Toher, M. 2001. "Euripides' *Supplices* and the Social Function of Funeral Ritual." *Hermes* 129: 332–43.

Torrance, I. 2011. "In the Footprints of Aeschylus: Recognition, Allusion, and Metapoetics in Euripides." *American Journal of Philology* 132: 177–204.

———. 2013. *Metapoetry in Euripides*. Oxford: Oxford University Press.

Travis, R. 1999. *Allegory and the Tragic Chorus in Sophocles' Oedipus at Colonus*. Lanham, Md.: Rowman & Littlefield.

Troiano, E. M. 1985. "The *Ion*: The Relationship of Character and Genre." *Classical Bulletin* 61: 45–52.

Tzanetou, A. 2011. "Supplication and Empire in Athenian Tragedy." In *Why Athens?: A Reappraisal of Tragic Politics*. Ed. D. M. Carter. Oxford: Oxford University Press, 305–24.

———. 2012. *City of Suppliants: Tragedy and the Athenian Empire*. Austin: University of Texas Press.

Vellacott, P. 1975. *Ironic Drama: A Study of Euripides' Method and Meaning*. Cambridge: Cambridge University Press.

Vernant, J.-P.1988a. "Tensions and Ambiguities in Greek Tragedy." Trans. J. Lloyd. In *Myth and Tragedy in Ancient Greece*. Ed. J.-P. Vernant and P. Vidal-Naquet. New York: Zone Books, 29–48.

———. 1988b. "The Historical Moment of Tragedy in Greece." Trans. J. Lloyd. In *Myth and Tragedy in Ancient Greece*. Ed. J.-P. Vernant and P. Vidal-Naquet. New York: Zone Books, 23–28.

Vinh, G. 2011. "Athens in Euripides' *Suppliants*: Ritual, Politics, and Theatre." In *Why Athens?: A Reappraisal of Tragic Politics*. Ed. D. M. Carter. Oxford: Oxford University Press, 325–44.

Visvardi, E. 2011. "Pity and Panhellenic Politics: Choral Emotion in Euripides' *Hecuba* and *Trojan Women*." In *Why Athens?: A Reappraisal of Tragic Politics*. Ed. D. M. Carter. Oxford: Oxford University Press, 269–91.

Von Fritz, K. 1956. "Euripides' *Alkestis* und ihre modernen Nachahmer und Kritiker." *Antike und Abendland* 5: 27–70.

Wallace, R. W. 2004. "Damon of Oa: A Music Theorist Ostracized?" In *Music and the Muses: The Culture of Mousike in the Classical Athenian City*. Ed. P. Murray and P. Wilson. Oxford: Oxford University Press, 249–67.

Walsh, G. B. 1977. "The First Stasimon of Euripides' *Electra*." *Yale Classical Studies* 25: 277–89.

———. 1978. "The Rhetoric of Birthright and Race in Euripides' *Ion*." *Hermes* 106: 301–15.

Wardy, R. 1996. *The Birth of Rhetoric: Gorgias, Plato, and Their Successors*. New York: Routledge.

Wassermann, F. M. 1940. "Divine Violence and Providence in Euripides' *Ion*." *Transactions of the American Philological Association* 71: 587–604.

Webster, T.B.L. 1954. "Fourth Century Tragedy and the *Poetics*." *Hermes* 82: 294–308.

West, M. L. 1982. *Greek Metre*. Oxford: Clarendon Press.

———., ed. 1987. *Euripides: Orestes*. Warminster: Aris & Phillips.

White, H. V. 1973. *Metahistory: The Historical Imagination in Nineteenth-Century Europe*. Baltimore: Johns Hopkins University Press.

———. 1978. *Tropics of Discourse: Essays in Cultural Criticism*. Baltimore: Johns Hopkins University Press.

Whitman, C. H. 1974. *Euripides and the Full Circle of Myth*. Cambridge, Mass.: Harvard University Press.

Willetts, R. F. 1973. "Action and Character in the *Ion* of Euripides." *Journal of Hellenic Studies* 93: 201–9.

Williams, R. 1966. *Modern Tragedy*. London: Chatto and Windus.

———. 1977. *Marxism and Literature*. Oxford: Oxford University Press.

Willink, C. W., ed. 1986. *Euripides: Orestes*. Oxford: Clarendon Press.

Wilson, P. 1996. "Tragic Rhetoric: The Use of Tragedy and the Tragic in the Fourth Century." In *Tragedy and the Tragic: Greek Theatre and Beyond*. Ed. M. S. Silk. Oxford: Oxford University Press, 310–31.

———. 2000. *The Athenian Institution of the Khoregia: The Chorus, the City, and the Stage*. Cambridge: Cambridge University Press.

———. 2011. "The Glue of Democracy? Tragedy, Structure, and Finance." In *Why Athens?: A Reappraisal of Tragic Politics*. Ed. D. M. Carter. Oxford: Oxford University Press, 19–43.

Wilson, P., and O. Taplin. 1993. "The 'Aetiology' of Tragedy in the *Oresteia*." *Proceedings of the Cambridge Philological Society* 39: 169–80.

Winkler, J. J., and F. I. Zeitlin, eds. 1990. *Nothing to Do with Dionysos? Athenian Drama in Its Social Context*. Princeton: Princeton University Press.

Winkler, J. J. 1990. "The Ephebes' Song: *Tragōidia* and *Polis*." In *Nothing to Do with Dionysos? Athenian Drama in Its Social Context*. Ed. J. J. Winkler and F. I. Zeitlin. Princeton: Princeton University Press, 20–62.

Winnington-Ingram, R. P. 1969. "Euripides: *Poiētēs Sophos*." *Arethusa* 2: 127–42.

Wohl, V. 1998. *Intimate Commerce: Exchange, Gender, and Subjectivity in Greek Tragedy*. Austin: University of Texas Press.

———. 2010. *Law's Cosmos: Juridical Discourse in Athenian Forensic Oratory*. Cambridge: Cambridge University Press.

———. 2011. "The Politics of Enmity in Euripides' *Orestes*." In *Greek Drama IV: Texts, Contexts, Performance*. Ed. D. Rosenbloom and J. Davidson. Oxford: Oxbow, 244–69.

———. 2014. "Play of the Improbable: Euripides' Unlikely *Helen*." In *Probabilities, Hypotheticals, and Counterfactuals in Ancient Greek Thought*. Ed. V. Wohl. Cambridge: Cambridge University Press, 142–59.

Wolff, C. 1965. "The Design and Myth in Euripides' *Ion*." *Harvard Studies in Classical Philology* 69: 169–94.

———. 1968. "*Orestes*." In *Euripides: A Collection of Critical Essays*. Ed. E. Segal. Engelwood Cliffs, N.J.: Prentice-Hall, 132–49.

Wolfson, S., and M. Brown, eds. 2000. *Reading for Form. Modern Language Quarterly* 61.1.

Wolin, S. S. 1994. "Norm and Form: The Constitutionalizing of Democracy." In *Athenian Political Thought and the Reconstruction of American Democracy*. Ed. J. P. Euben, J. R. Wallach, and J. Ober. Ithaca: Cornell University Press, 29–58.

Woodruff, P. 2008. *The Necessity of Theater: The Art of Watching and Being Watched*. Oxford: Oxford University Press.

Wright, M. 2005. *Euripides' Escape-Tragedies: A Study of Helen, Andromeda, and Iphigenia among the Taurians*. Oxford: Oxford University Press.

———. 2006. "*Orestes*, a Euripidean Sequel." *Classical Quarterly* 56: 33–47.

———. 2008. *Euripides: Orestes*. London: Duckworth.

Xanthakis-Karamanos, G. 1980. *Studies in Fourth-Century Tragedy*. Athens: Athens Academy.

Zacharia, K. 2003. *Converging Truths: Euripides' Ion and the Athenian Quest for Self-Definition*. Leiden: Brill.

Zeitlin, F. I. 1970. "The Argive Festival of Hera and Euripides' *Electra*." *Transactions of the American Philological Association* 101: 645–69.

———. 1980. "The Closet of Masks: Role-Playing and Myth-Making in the *Orestes* of Euripides." *Ramus* 9: 51–77.

———. 1990a. "Playing the Other: Theater, Theatricality, and the Feminine in Greek Drama." In *Nothing to Do with Dionysos? Athenian Drama in Its Social Context*. Ed. J. J. Winkler and F. I. Zeitlin. Princeton: Princeton University Press, 63–96.

———. 1990b. "Thebes: Theater of Self and Society in Athenian Drama." In *Nothing to Do with Dionysos? Athenian Drama in Its Social Context*. Ed. J. J. Winkler and F. I. Zeitlin. Princeton: Princeton University Press, 130–67.

———. 1994. "The Artful Eye: Vision, Ecphrasis and Spectacle in Euripidean Theatre." In *Art and Text in Ancient Greek Culture*. Ed. S. Goldhill and R. Osborne. Cambridge: Cambridge University Press, 138–96.

———. 1995. "Art, Memory, and *Kleos* in Euripides' *Iphigeneia in Aulis*." In *History, Tragedy, Theory: Dialogues on Athenian Drama*. Ed. B. E. Goff. Austin: University of Texas Press, 174–201.

———. 1996a. "Mysteries of Identity and Designs of the Self in Euripides' *Ion*." In *Playing the Other: Gender and Society in Classical Greek Literature*. Ed. F. I. Zeitlin. Chicago: University of Chicago Press, 285–338.

———. 1996b. "The Body's Revenge: Dionysos and Tragic Action in Euripides' *Hekabe*." In *Playing the Other: Gender and Society in Classical Greek Literature*. Ed. F. I. Zeitlin. Chicago: University of Chicago Press, 172–216.

———. 2012. "A Study in Form: Recognition Scenes in the Three Electra Plays." *Lexis* 30: 361–78.

Žižek, S. 1989. *The Sublime Object of Ideology*. London: Verso.

Zuntz, G. 1955. *The Political Plays of Euripides*. Manchester: Manchester University Press.

———. 1958. "Contemporary Politics in the Plays of Euripides." In *Acta Congressus Madvigiani*. Vol. 1. Copenhagen: Munksgaard, 155–62.

INDEX

Numbers in italics refer to line numbers in extended discussions of text

Adorno, Theodor, 4–5, 18, 88, 134, 138, 159n5, 165n14

Aeschines, 106

Aeschylus: *Agamemnon*, 52, 53, 79; *Choephoroi*, 66, 68, 73, 81, 82, 83, 125; *Eumenides*, 83, 123; *Oresteia*, 2, 5, 67, 84, 121, 122, 154n31; *Suppliants*, 160n13

aesthetics: ancient theorization of, 6–7; and ethics, 39–62; Euripidean, 1–3, 5, 21, 41–42, 62, 110–11, 134–35, 139. *See also* beauty; ugliness

affect, xi–xii, 22, 106–9, 112, 135–37. *See also* structures of feeling

agency, collective, 93, 162n23

agōn, 45, 93, 97–98, 134, 149n28, 152n12, 158n30

aitia, 115, 147n35, 163n36, 164n6

Alcestis. *See* Euripides: *Alcestis*

alienation-effect, 62, 145n22

allegory, 91–92, 105, 107–9, 159n2; and historicism, 91–92, 98, 110, 159n3; limits of, 94–98, 99, 100

amnesty, Athenian, 129–30

anachronism, 90–92, 94, 101, 105

anagnōrisis, 28–32, 64–65, 134, 149n21; Aristotle's definition of, 157n22; artificiality of, 72–76, 81; in Thucydides, 117. *See also* recognition; recognition scenes

anankē, 15, 20, 21, 22, 26, 82–83. *See also* necessity

Andocides, 164n11

anti-politics, 89, 98–100, 103, 105, 108

antilabe, 43

Apollo: in *Alcestis*, 10, 12–16; in *Electra*, 81–85; in *Ion*, 23, 24, 26–27, 34–36; in *Orestes*, 21, 123, 128–30

apophasis, 125, 127, 128, 129

Argos (historical), 92, 108

aristocracy. *See* elite

Aristophanes: on the democratic nature of Euripides' tragedy, 21, 37, 63–64; on Euripides' innovation, 5–6; on Euripides' intellectualism, 135; on Euripides' monodies, 64, 102

Aristotle, 140; on *anagnōrisis*, 134, 157n22; on Euripides, 9, 63, 122, 135; on *muthos*, ix–x, 7, 134, 137; on pity, 40–41, 44; on *psukhagōgia*, 7, 145n19; on reversals, 9, 167n35; on tragic protagonists, 65, 66; on tragic unity, 19–20, 134–35

Arrowsmith, William, 111, 119–20, 163n2

artifice, dramatic, 73–76, 128–29

assembly, 53, 94–95, 122, 123

Athena: in *Ion*, 27, 31, 32, 33, 36–37; in *Suppliants*, 108; in *Trojan Women*, 46

Athenian empire, 21–22, 24, 28, 32, 47, 93, 116–17

Athens, 3–4, 110–12, 139–41; contingent histories of, 25–26, 36; "death" of, 140; "encomium" of, 89; as represented in tragedy, 31, 47, 92, 93–98

audience: as democratic citizens, xii–xiii, 3, 15, 105–9, 136–37; division of, 120, 126–28; as human beings, xii–xiii, 99, 105–9, 136–37; implication in dramatic action of, 32–36, 47–49, 53–55; internal,